Slaying the Dragons

"*The dragons of the title are the myths, half-truths, and downright untruths that have become fixed in secular thinking and have thus distorted strongly the science–religion debate. The author attacks these dragons with the passion of a latter-day St George and, in a book that is forthright, clear, readable, convincing and sometimes humorous, he sets the record straight. I recommend this book to anyone interested in the relationship between science and religion.*"

John Bryant, Professor Emeritus of Biological Sciences at the University of Exeter

"*An informed examination of the claim that there is a 'war' between science and religion. Historian of science Allan Chapman shows how this claim is mostly founded on myths and legends. A very enjoyable and instructive read.*"

Keith Ward, Fellow of the British Academy and Professional Research Fellow at Heythrop College, London.

"*In magisterial style, and from an encyclopaedic knowledge of his subject matter, Allan Chapman systematically exposes the multiple myths and flagrant falsehoods propagated by the so-called 'New Atheists'. Chapman convincingly demonstrates how, far from displaying conflict between science and religion, the historical record is shot through with a profound harmony between these two paths to truth, and how Western Christendom provided the fertile soil in which modern science as we know it took root.*"

The Revd Dr Rodney D. Holder, Course Director, The Faraday Institute, St Edmund's College, Cambridge

"*This is a fascinating, timely, and highly accessible study of a vital subject. In a world where the great majority of people are believers no-one can doubt the importance of the subject. And after reading this book, no-one can doubt that the supposed clash of science and religion has been greatly distorted.* Slaying the Dragons *will enable intelligent people to enter the debate afresh with renewed interest and open minds.*"

John Pritchard, Bishop of Oxford

"*A brilliantly concise history of the relationship between religion and science, and a passionate defence of Christianity. In* Slaying the Dragons, *Allan Chapman offers a robust and highly readable response to the 'not-so-New' Atheism.*"

Edmund Newell, Principal of Cumberland Lodge and former Chancellor of St Paul's Cathedral

Slaying the Dragons

Destroying Myths in the History of Science and Faith

Allan Chapman

LION

Published by Lion Books
an imprint of
Lion Hudson plc
Wilkinson House, Jordan Hill Road,
Oxford OX2 8DR, England
www.lionhudson.com/lion

ISBN 978 0 7459 5583 4
e-ISBN 978 0 7459 5723 4

First edition 2013

Acknowledgments
Scripture quotations taken from the Authorized Version

A catalogue record for this book is available from the
British Library

Printed and bound in Great Britain, January 2013, LH26

*For Rachel
Wife, Scholar, and
Best Friend*

Acknowledgments

This book has grown out of many years of lecturing, to audiences of all kinds, on the historical relationship of science with Christianity, and the many questions and comments thrown at me in discussion, including "Is there anything I can read on this?" To all those who have listened, questioned, and commented, my thanks are due. I am also deeply indebted to Paul Clifford and Alison Hull of Lion Hudson for their invaluable guidance and perceptive comments, which have led me to make a great many additions and improvements to my original manuscript, resulting, I hope, in a much better book. But my biggest debt of all is to my wife Rachel, who has been ready with her typing and editorial skills, advice, criticism, and scholarship at every stage of the process, and whose patience has been truly monumental. It is to her that this book is dedicated.

Contents

1

Myths, Monotheism, and the Origins of Western Science

For much of the twentieth century, and especially since the 1960s, the Judeo-Christian faith, and Christianity in particular, have been under increasing assault. This assault has come from several directions: from particular interpretations of scientific progress; from certain styles of radical politics, often based on social science presuppositions; from fashionable philosophers and social pundits; and, by the late 1990s, from the media. And one of the great ironies is that while Great Britain has an established church, the Christian faith has become a thing of ridicule and mockery in many circles. National Health Service Trusts have suspended nurses who would not remove crucifixes hanging around their necks, and bed-and-breakfast hotel proprietors and experienced foster parents are threatened with prosecution because they will not countenance certain practices condemned in parts of the Scriptures or permit them to be performed on their private premises (yet a blind eye is not infrequently turned to the customs and practices of non-Christian religions). Indeed, several law-abiding Christians have mentioned to me that if they should utter the word "Jesus" or "Christ" in any context other than that of a joke or a blasphemous expletive, they feel that they would be exposing themselves to accusations of being fundamentalist, narrow-minded, out-of-date, or stupid.

For do not the fashionable "New Atheists" – Richard Dawkins, Sam Harris, Daniel Dennett, the late Christopher Hitchens, et al. –

(so styled by present-day journalists to differentiate them from the Old Guard of atheists, such as Bertrand Russell and Aldous Huxley) constantly remind us that Christianity is a thing of the Dark Ages; that "science" and "reason" have swept its superstitions away, and that sociology, psychology, neurology, and most of all evolution, have delivered us from such bondage? And as our secular political leaders and promoters of "multiculturalism" constantly tell us, do we not now live in a free, open, equal, rational, and transparent global village society? A society so tolerant that every creed and belief must be respected and lovingly nourished as an expression of our natural goodness – unless, of course, that creed comes from the Holy Bible!

This monumental double-think – a double-think of Orwellian proportions – constitutes one of the biggest myths of the age in which we live: a myth that derives its style of thinking from perversions of scientific thinking, in which the absolutism of Newtonian mechanics is combined with the dogmatic determinism of neo-Marxism, and the directionless moral vacuity of postmodernism.

Indeed, these myths, which form so much of the social geography of the late twentieth and early twenty-first centuries, have become so pervasive across much of Western society that many people regard them as natural and unquestioned aspects of modern thought. I remember in my youth, in the late 1960s, being peddled stories of how the free modern world only came into being when brave souls such as Copernicus, Galileo, and the philosophers of the "Enlightenment" had the courage to "stand up" to the church – and often paid dire penalties. Of how poor Charles Darwin had been vilified for daring to present the scientific fact that we all came from monkeys. But as a natural sceptic as far as intellectual fashions go, who has always had a fascination with the nature of myth-making, I became increasingly inclined to treat these socio-myths with caution. As I shall show more fully in Chapter 11, I have always felt that anti-religious scepticism, as a universally lauded instrument of analysis, must itself be regarded sceptically.

But it was when I became an academic science historian that the mythic status of science's secular, liberal, and liberated roots became glaringly obvious. This first became obvious in my reading. Then, as I began to teach, deliver public lectures all over Great Britain and America, and broadcast, the *avalanche* of mythology really hit me. For there is nothing like questions from the floor following a large lecture or a public discussion, where the world and his wife are free to put you on the rack and throw their mental brickbats at you, to reveal the sheer magnitude of the mythology that passes for "the conflict between science and religion". Comments such as "How can an intelligent person believe all that stuff about God and miracles?", or "As everyone knows, until the Enlightenment the church held science back", come to me with monotonous regularity.

And this is what has led me to write this book, for reading apart, pretty well every chapter or sub-chapter between these covers is based on matters that have been raised with me by tutorial students, members of the public following lectures, in private communication, or by people who have engaged me in conversation on train or bus journeys. For the subject of religion and its relationship with science is a topic of growing fascination, to Christians, to secularists, and to puzzled folk who don't know what to think, who stand in awe of the power of science, but who find atheism cold and dead. Without doubt, the passionate, and often virulent, writings of New Atheists, extending from Richard Dawkins back to Bertrand Russell, have been instrumental in fomenting this interest. And while perhaps not read so widely, or evangelized so forcefully, as those of the "New Atheists", the claims and statements of numerous Christian fundamentalists (that is, strict biblical literalists, especially in their interpretation of Genesis and their rejection of evolution) during the latter half of the twentieth century have also added fuel to the flames of *religious* assault on the one hand and defence on the other, resulting in bafflement for large numbers of people.

But as I became more interested in the science and religion scrum – for it rarely rises to the orderliness of a "debate" – in the late 1980s, one thing came to grate on my historian's sense of fact and context time and time again, namely, the proliferation of myths, confabulations, and downright untruths that flew with ever increasing intensity, especially from the New Atheists, against Christian believers. This urban folk mythology or fairy-tale culture of atheism and secularism is the stuff about which this book is written: it is the monstrous regiment of dragons that have to be slain if ever we are going to see science and Christianity in context. Myths as groundless as the one which vehemently affirms that science could only progress once the gargantuan power of "the church" had been successfully challenged and overthrown; and its partner in secularist mumbo-jumbo which asserts that all true scientists must be atheists, for surely a rational scientist cannot believe in God – an assertion still clung to in the teeth of the stark fact that high-profile Nobel Prize Laureates, Fellows of the Royal Society, British scientific knights and dames, and many scientific professors sincerely practise the Christian faith. Indeed, it is such men and women, of differing degrees of eminence, yet all possessing high-powered scientific qualifications, who constitute the membership of such bodies as Christians in Science and the Society of Ordained Scientists (I have had the honour to lecture to both), or are active in the ordained or lay ministry of the Anglican, Methodist, Roman Catholic, or free churches. Jesuits, Anglicans, Presbyterians, Baptists, Pentecostals, Charismatics, Quakers, you name it: you can find highly qualified scientists in their ranks or even in their pulpits. So one pair of myths bites the hard rock of demonstrable evidence early in the story!

Yet I can hear people saying, why are you only talking about Christianity and science? What about other religions? Two factors have to be considered in answering this question. First, the New Atheists are generally careful about which religions they target for the outpouring of their bile. Yes, there is endless ranting against American-based fundamentalist groups, and a constant harping on about the "Monkey Trial" at Dayton, Tennessee, in 1926, with the "by association" flow of ideas intending to imply that Christianity equals anti-evolution, equals biblical fundamentalism, equals anti-science, equals the "Dark Ages". Yet, at least in *legally* "multicultural" Great Britain, they are often surprisingly reticent about other religions: scarcely a squeak against Judaism (as opposed to criticisms of the

State of Israel), from which Christianity springs, and only rather circuitous generalities against Islam (although, in fairness, Sam Harris and others in America and Michel Ornay in France are more blunt in their opinions of non-Christian faiths). I wonder why this should be so? Could it be analogous to the courage displayed by a well-fed household pussycat relishing play with a cornered mouse, as opposed to the blind terror experienced by the same pampered pussycat when faced with a hungry wolf? Hit one faith, and it obediently apologizes and dutifully goes down; hit another, and it bites back!

But in talking about science as it grew up within the territories of Christian Europe, we have to look plainly and impartially at where that approach to understanding the natural world which we now call "science" actually comes from. For its roots are four-square in the Greco-Roman, Judeo-Christian cultural tradition. I have long argued, live, in print, and on television, that science as we know it stems from monotheism. ✓

The Egyptian, Babylonian, Indian, Polynesian, Chinese, and Meso-American cultures all built up complex and sophisticated systems for making sense of the natural world as they understood it within the context of their environments. All of them developed sophisticated systems of counting, classifying, and recording natural phenomena and celestial–terrestrial correlations, either for calendrical purposes or to arm themselves against future storms, famines, plagues, or political overthrow. Yet all of these cultures were polytheistic, seeing the sky, planets, wind, water, agricultural fruitfulness, or earthquake as the province of the individual members of a pantheon of spirit beings who between them made life good or bad for humanity. Understanding the natural world to an Egyptian or a Chaldaean in 2000 BC, therefore, lay in negotiating one's way through the erratic behaviour patterns of a large dysfunctional family of spirits who would get you if you put a foot wrong. If, for example, you failed to offer the right sacrifices, or perform the correct rituals, at the ordained time. However much you might record the risings and settings of the stars, or list eclipses, comets, or falling stars, and however much you described the habits of plants, animals, birds, or diseases, this is not what later ages would consider *scientia*, or organized knowledge. It was, rather, record-keeping for liturgical purposes, or perhaps practical purposes, such as land measurement, administrative efficiency, or commercial reckoning. "Nature" was not conceived of as having an independent existence, but was, rather, an expression of many fickle deities in action, and could suddenly change at the failure of a sacrifice or the omission of a ritual.

Of course things were not much better in Homeric Greece around 1000 BC, where mere humans could easily become the victims of that pack of eternally misbehaving self-indulgent divine brats who lived on Mount Olympus. Profound changes took place in Greece, however, between the days of Thales and Pythagoras, from around 600 BC, to the death of Aristotle in 322 BC. Perhaps this came about through the complex geography of Greece, with its many scattered mountain, island, and valley city-state communities, which made it far less centralized and easily controlled than were the great river flood-plain empires of the Nile, Euphrates, or Indus, where government tax collectors or squads of soldiers could easily enforce the will of the officialdom along an arterial waterway. Certainly, trade organized by independent merchants (as opposed to by the king) across the Mediterranean and the Black Seas generated much more purely private wealth than one found in Egypt or Babylon. Such travel in pursuit of profit taught you about all sorts of things that a river- or desert-dweller would never encounter, such as winds, sea and ocean currents, odd meteorological phenomena, and all manner of strange living creatures. Oceanic travel also taught you that the land disappeared once you got a few miles out to sea, and mysteriously reappeared as you approached your destination, suggesting that you might be sailing around a curve or sphere. Different stars could be seen if you were trading off the south of what would later be called France than if you were off Egypt, while a solar eclipse seen at 9 a.m. in Spain would be seen at noon in Greece, adding to the idea of a round earth, a round sky, and, perhaps, different time zones, in contrast to the flat earth and sky cosmology of Egypt or Mesopotamia.

The geographical isolation of the regions of Greece probably led to a greater cultural individualism. It is not for nothing that the Greeks

14

invented "civic society" and "public consciousness" in the city-state, of which there were well over 158 in Greece by the time of Aristotle.

I would argue that it was from this dynamic cauldron of circumstances that the leisure, thinking space, and resources emerged out of which the arts and sciences were born in Greece. Geometry, after Thales and Pythagoras, opened up a dazzling world of eternal and apparently unfalsifiable truths – such as the properties of triangles, circles, and prime numbers, and the elegant curves that resulted when you cut a cone into angled slices, to produce the ellipse, parabola, and hyperbola. Likewise, there was the analysis of the perfect, harmonious proportions in a musical sequence, first studied by Pythagoras, along with the intellectual certainty and elegance of conceptual mathematics (as opposed to mere counting). And then, one encounters that whole raft of philosophical ideas that led to people discussing and analysing the abstract yet immediately recognizable concepts of truth, beauty, justice, reason, and deductive logical propositions. And rather like in our Western civilization today, deriving as it does from that ancient ancestry, much of this was a product of free "market forces": people with commercially derived cash in their pockets wanting to educate their sons (thereby encouraging teachers like Socrates, Plato, and Aristotle), patronize painters and architects, improve the amenities of their city, or laugh at a comedy by Aristophanes.

But what, you might ask, has this interpretation of classical history to do with science, religion, and mythology today? Everything, I would respectfully argue, for out of Greece came the social practice of well-funded creative leisure, a necessary preliminary to having the mental space and the freedom to ask questions, challenge orthodoxies, think your own thoughts, and do your own thing – at least, if you were free, a man, and a comfortably off voting citizen of a city-state. And yes, that might have been narrow by modern-day standards of freedom, but it was a lot better than spending your life quarrying granite for Pharaoh or digging irrigation ditches for the priests of Babylon.

And very significantly for future religious thinking, some Greek philosophers, such as Heraclitus and Anaxagoras, were asking by the fifth century BC whether there might be a higher power beyond the gods of Olympus. It was not personalized, but rather some kind of organizing power or principle of order, which might have something to do with why mathematics, logic, and reason made sense. A grand philosophical principle, in fact. Analogous, perhaps, to the *Forms*, or ideal defining principles which lay behind things, and not only made them make sense, but also enabled the human intellect to identify and even work with them. For a Form, as it came to be spoken of by Socrates and Plato, was that eternal principle which all similar, yet diverse, things share. Each individual cat, for example, differs in a myriad of ways from every other cat, yet they all share a defining characteristic that unites them. This, one might say, is the Form of the cat, or what one might recognize as *cattishness*, instantly differentiating it from a small dog – which possesses *doggishness*. Now these Forms are hard to pin down in abstract, yet when you see one embodied, you somehow recognize it in a flash.

Could it be that all these ideal Forms were part of a great preexisting *Logos*, or foundational intellectual principle? And might this principle be eternal and unchanging? If this were the case, then one might suggest that certain Greek philosophers mixed their philosophical geometry, mathematics, and logic with their theology, for in this Logos was something resembling monotheism. Perhaps one great, eternal, transcendent, divine rational principle unified not only the whole realm of mind, but went on to connect our human intellects with the Logos itself, thereby enabling human beings to understand and reason their way through the visible and invisible creation.

By the time of Plato and Aristotle, in the fourth century BC, Greeks were even discussing creation itself. Did the cosmos come about, as Plato proposed in his *Timaeus* narrative, by a divine craftsman imposing order on rough materials in the same way as a potter imposes the Form of a pot upon every vessel he makes on the wheel? Or did it come about, as Aristotle proposes in his *Physics*, by an Unmoved Mover setting creation in motion? Indeed, it was not for nothing that early Christian theologians would equate this creative Unmoved Mover or Logos with God in Christ Jesus, as did the writer of St John's Gospel.

But this radical and world-changing insight only emerged when these fifth-century-BC Greek ideas took a new direction as they came to be combined with the vastly more ancient ideas of the Jews. For in the Judeo-Christian tradition, as it would develop, this Greek *Logos* first revealed himself as "I AM", or "JEHOVA", to Abraham in Mesopotamia around 2000 BC as a very personal creator of all things. Indeed, he was not a *concept* like the Logos, but an eternal, divine, living being who formed the very image of mankind from himself, who gave us our intelligence, and for whom we, and especially those descendants of Abraham who would become the Jews, were the supreme, albeit disobedient, fruits of creation.

Here was something emerging in human experience that left the offering of sacrifices to the Egyptian or Mesopotamian nature spirits way behind when it came to a new, higher kind of theological understanding. And nowhere more so than when that supreme being identified himself so closely with the human race that he had created that he took human flesh in the form of Jesus the saviour.

So here we have that dynamic of creator, giver of life and reason, lifting humanity from the cowering slave caste of the ancient Egyptian and Mesopotamian religions, and affirming us as beings with a value and a divine destiny in our own right. Irrespective of whatever religious beliefs the reader may hold, it is hard to deny two aspects of what I have outlined above. Firstly, it possesses a grandeur and a visionary scope pertaining to the human condition that is unique in the annals of human thought, in its combination of creation, logic, reason, humanity, divinity, love, redemption, and purpose. And secondly, it unleashed a creative dynamic into the world, the tidal force of which still carries us along today. For whether you are a Jew, a Christian, a philosopher, or a passionate atheist, it is this essential dynamic that still provides the ground plan which you will embrace lovingly, or feel you must reject. But it refuses to be ignored.

This, I would suggest, is the origin of monotheism, and without it we would not have that unified concept of nature and its accessibility to human intelligence without which modern science is impossible. For irrespective of where a person may stand today on the creedal scale, it is monotheism that is the father and mother of the concept of a natural world that makes (or appears to make) logical sense.

Yet, these essential intellectual components of monotheism derived from rabbinic Judaism on the one hand and pagan Greek philosophy on the other. Why should it have been in European – and later American – *Christendom* that science assumed the dominant cultural role it holds today? There is nothing especially scientific in the teachings of Abraham, Moses, Jesus, St Paul, or any other of the Christian apostles. But what I would argue is that science entered early Christian and medieval Europe by a process of cultural osmosis. For one of the formative and enduring features of Christianity, from the AD 30s and 40s onwards, was its social and cultural flexibility. One did not have to belong to any given racial or cultural group, wear any approved style of clothing, cut one's beard in a prescribed way, speak a special holy language, or follow essential rituals to be a Christian. Women in particular, amazingly, considering their limited social role in antiquity, were drawn to Christianity in large numbers, as the Gospels and the Acts of the Apostles make clear, where they are shown as openly expressing their views. They were even the original witnesses of the resurrection, while St Paul's first European convert was Lydia of Thyatira, a Greek merchant woman.

In fact Christianity moved into the pre-existing social, legal and administrative structures of Greco-Roman paganism, as Greek civic virtue became infused with Judeo-Christian charity. Roman legal objectivity absorbed key aspects of the teachings of the Sermon on the Mount and the Beatitudes to create a concept of social justice; even the modes of dress of late Roman officials became the vestments of Christian priests; while words like "bishop" and "diocese" derived from classical administrative sources. Christianity, instead of overthrowing the genius of Greece and Rome, simply absorbed its best practical components, and allied them with the teachings of Jesus. The law codes of Christendom, moreover, came to develop non-theological components. The circuit judge system set up by King Henry II in the twelfth century, for instance, might have carried resonances of the assistant judges of Israel appointed by Moses in Exodus, or the judgment towns visited by the prophet Samuel in 1 Samuel, but in practice it administered a new, practical English "Common Law", and the judges often sat with that innovation of the age, a twelve-man *lay* jury.

This is how medieval students in Oxford, Paris, Bologna, or Salamanca came to study the pagan philosophies of Plato and Aristotle, the classical Latin poetry of Virgil, and the humane ethics of Cicero along with the Gospels. And very important for the rise of a *civil* society in which there was an acknowledged *saeculum* or non-theological exclusivity, the law students at the medieval Inns of Court in London, then as today, learned a pragmatic, case-based evolving *civil* law that was not especially theological in its foundation. For medieval Christendom was open to non-Christian ideas, provided that they could be reconciled in their broader principles with Christianity.

Exactly the same thing happened with science. The astronomy of Ptolemy, the physics of Aristotle, and the medicine of Hippocrates became part of the curriculum in Europe's great new universities by 1250. Indeed, it was generally accepted that many honest pagans had glimpsed key truths of God's creation, and who could blame the wise Socrates and Aristotle if they happened to have been born 400 years before Jesus, for their wisdom and honest contributions to learning were beyond question. This is how ancient science came to slide effortlessly into the Christian world, for it was useful for making calendars, treating diseases, and explaining the physical nature of things from the facts then available.

But, you might ask, when talking about science and Christendom, what happened in monotheistic Islam? It is an evident fact of history that, after its initial military conquests in the century after AD 622, Muslim scholars in Baghdad, Cairo, and southern Spain encountered the scientific and medical writings of the Greeks, which they translated into Arabic. And amidst a galaxy of figures such as Ibn Jabir in chemistry, Ibn Sina (Avicenna) in medicine, Ibn Tusi in astronomy, and Al-Haythem (Alhazen) in optics, Arabic science took the Greek scientific tradition further, research-wise, than anyone in Europe over the centuries AD 800–1200. But then, due to a variety of factors embedded within Islamic culture, it stalled and came to a standstill, especially after their last great scientist, the astronomer Ulugh Beigh of Samarkand, was murdered, it was said, by one of his own sons in 1449.

There has been much discussion among scholars as to why Islamic science declined as an intellectual and technical force, and why Christian Europe after 1200 developed a momentum which absorbed – with full acknowledgment – the achievements of the great Muslim scholars and scientists, and accelerated in an unbroken line of development down to the present day. For Islam, just like Judaism and Christianity, is a monotheistic faith, seeing the God of Abraham as the original and only creative force behind the universe. So why did the Islamic monotheistic tradition stall scientifically, while the Judeo-Christian tradition flourished? I think much has to do with a broader receptivity to classical Greco-Roman culture.

As was shown above, Christianity grew directly out of a combination of Judaism and wider Greco-Roman culture. Jesus the man was incarnated as a Jewish rabbi who preached in vernacular Aramaic and could read Hebrew, yet whose teachings, not to mention the commentaries of his disciples, were committed to posterity in Greek and, somewhat later, in Latin. The Jesus of the Gospels, moreover, respected Caesar, the Roman state and its officials; and his disciples even held an election to decide whether Barnabas or Matthias should be co-opted into the Twelve after Judas's treachery; while St Paul, a Jewish native of the Hellenized "university town" of Tarsus in Cilicia (now Turkey), argued like a Socratic philosopher in his letters and was deeply proud of being a hereditary Roman citizen. Islam, on the other hand, came about in a very different way. The Prophet Mohammed's roots lay in the essentially tribal society of the seventh-century-AD Arabian peninsula, east of the Red Sea. Tribal custom and not Greco-Roman "civic virtue" moulded its social and cultural practices, and Islam's lack of a theology of free grace and atonement gave emphasis to an internal legalism that could all too easily generate centuries long sectarian disputes, such as those between the Shi'ites and the Sunnis. And while I fully admit that Christendom has had its own spasms of internal violent reprisal, most recently witnessed in the Troubles in Northern Ireland, I would suggest that Christendom's classically derived *constitutional*, negotiated, approach to politics has always provided mechanisms for containment and reconciliation. This has been seen most notably in the active cooperation between the Roman Catholic and Protestant mainstreams, often on an overtly religious level, although splinter groups can remain active until changes in public attitudes eventually render them obsolete.

Islam took from Greco-Roman culture what it found useful in the territories it conquered. These included Greek astronomy, optics, medicine, chemistry, and technology, each of which it amplified and expanded, producing major treatises, often based upon freshly accumulated and carefully classified observational data. Chemistry came to owe an enormous debt to Arabic researchers, as would astronomical, medical, and botanical nomenclature. Indeed, well over a dozen major Arabic works made their way into Europe, where they were translated into Latin, influencing figures like Bishop Robert Grosseteste and Friar Roger Bacon of Oxford, and began to be widely studied in detail in the post-1100 European universities. (On the other hand, I am not aware of the foundational works of European science, such as those of Copernicus, Kepler, Galileo, Vesalius, or Harvey, being translated into Arabic until recent times.) And among other things, that astronomical computing instrument known as the astrolabe, upon which the poet Geoffrey Chaucer wrote the first technical "workshop manual" in the English language around 1381, was a sophisticated Arabic development of a device first outlined by Ptolemy in the second century AD.   ?

Yet while Greek ideas were profoundly formative upon Arabic concepts of the natural world, Islam did not absorb other key ideas of Greek and Roman culture which would become formative to Christian Europe. Greek democratic political ideals, "civic virtue", and legal monogamy (divorce and mistresses notwithstanding) never became an integral part of Islam as they did of Christendom. Nor did the descent of kingship through holy anointing, which began with Samuel, Saul, and David in 1 Samuel in the Old Testament and

21

entered early Christian kingship practices as the act of coronation, and is still enshrined in the person of HM Queen Elizabeth II.

It is for these reasons, I would argue, that modern science is a child of Judeo-Christian, Greco-Roman parentage, and why I speak of *Western* science as becoming the dominant style of thinking about the natural world and humanity's inquisitive relationship with it. Indeed, it is not just about the science and technology, but about the social, intellectual, and cultural assumptions and practices in which modern science is embedded. The very institutions within which science has grown up over the last 900 years, moreover, testify to this inheritance: universities with enduring corporate structures borrowed from Greek and Roman linguistic and civic practice; learned societies – such as the Royal Society of London after 1660 – which were self-electing, self-governing bodies modelled on the "collegiate", "civic virtue" style Oxford and Cambridge colleges; and rich, free-trading merchant-driven cities such as London, Florence, Venice, Nuremberg, Amsterdam, Antwerp, and Hamburg.

As will be shown in more detail in the following chapters, historical Christianity has never been rigidly literalistic in its interpretation of the physical world of Scripture, and it is that very flexibility that has made the faith so versatile and adaptive in its social expression over 2,000 years. A faith that made its first utterance among Aramaic-speaking fishermen and farmers around Galilee (occupying a land surface area no bigger than modern Birmingham), quickly went on to enchant Greek-writing scholars, led to the conversion of the Roman Empire, encompassed people between Mesopotamia, Spain, Britannia, and Ethiopia by AD 600, would inspire the new Latin-speaking universities of Europe by 1200, would engraft onto itself the science, philosophy, legal and social practices of the high classical Mediterranean, would explore possible connections between the teachings of Jesus and the writings of Plato and Virgil, and whose Scriptures would be translated into the vernacular languages of Europe by 1550. Christianity would then go on to inspire the natural theology of the Royal Society Fellows, be the driving force behind the abolition of slavery, supply the moral and spiritual tools that constitute the best and noblest aspects of what we now call "human rights" – and become the prime target for some of the bitterest abuse that many twenty-first-century sceptics feel compelled to heap upon religious belief (and I have heard a good deal of that at first hand!).

Indeed, considering the magnitude of Christianity's moulding influence upon Western civilization, and its provision of that rich soil in which post-classical science could flourish and grow, it is hardly surprising that, in this imperfect world, it has detractors. I might suggest the British National Health Service as an analogy. For just like Christianity, the NHS, in its noble aspiration of cradle-to-grave care for all, wastes large sums of money, makes mistakes, and inevitably gets attacked, sued, and criticized across the board. On the other hand, it continues to transform, extend, and fundamentally improve the lives of millions of people, as it has done since its foundation in 1948. And most of all, it has done so most dramatically for the poor, the vulnerable, and those incapable of purchasing their own health care – rather like Christianity, in fact!

Nor is it surprising that, within a post-classical and modern West with its ancient traditions of respect for argument, debate, and – in varying degrees – toleration, myths have abounded. Yet why myths about Christianity abound so richly and often with so little apparent opposition in our own time will constitute the subject of the present book. So read on.

2

The Origins of Unbelief
Part 1: Ancients
and Early Moderns

Psalm 14 in the Bible begins with the remarkable statement "The fool hath said in his heart 'There is no God'." While this designation might cover those whom we today would call honest doubters, the fact remains that even in the days of King David around 1000 BC, or of his Jewish poetic successors, there were atheists of a sort.

The Popular Myth that Atheism is New

Yet one of the twentieth century's foremost contributions to urban mythology is the notion that atheism and secularism are somehow new and radical, and only became possible once courageous "moderns" dared to challenge the totalitarian church. On the other hand, and as we shall see in this chapter, ideas about the powers or even the existence of God or "the gods" possessed an ambivalence or multi-layeredness which is not easy to reconcile with the strident ideological assertions of New Atheists such as Daniel Dennett, Richard Dawkins, and the late Christopher Hitchens, for whom God is a "Delusion", "Is Not Great", or is a symptom of cultural infantilism. For these thinkers – mistakenly – see science, and especially recent discoveries in neuroscience and genetics, as revealing new certainties that transcend the philosophical quibbles of earlier unbelief; indeed, they turn the experimental method itself into an absolutist God before which everything else must stand or fall, while remaining oblivious to the yawning philosophical and interpretative chasm which runs through their grand and godless schemes (in an earlier cultural incarnation this was called "positivism", as we shall see in Chapter 3).

In Old Testament times in 1000 BC, however, very little was known about the extent or workings of the natural world. As we saw in the last chapter, the whole of Old Testament history was acted out in an area of rivers, fields, and deserts between the Nile and the Tigris that covered a land surface smaller than that of modern-day France and Germany combined. And what better way had the people of those times to explain the facts of their physical lives than through the doings of their perceived gods and spirits? Yet as Psalm 14 (and Psalm 53) tells us, it seems that even people living in that small and vulnerable world could somehow doubt the existence or efficacy of the spiritual realm.

As we shall see, the arguments of atheism, far from developing daring and radical powers, have remained astonishingly repetitious. Indeed, the only "newish" argument that I have encountered that would not have been familiar to the brothers John and Charles Wesley when they were undergraduates at Christ Church, Oxford, in the 1720s, is evolution by natural selection, which came in with Charles Darwin in 1859. Yet even the Wesley brothers – very highly educated young gentlemen with a well-documented interest in the science and medicine of their day – would have been aware of the work of comparative anatomists. For had not Galen in AD 150, Andreas Vesalius in 1543, Dr William Harvey in 1628, Christ Church's very own Dr Thomas Willis in the 1660s, and many others besides drawn attention to the astonishing parallels between human and animal anatomy? And did not the cardiovascular, nervous, muscular, and skeletal systems of men, monkeys, dogs, and pigs share a great many structural and functional features? This may not have been *evolution*, but it certainly had much to do with the perceived connectedness of living things, and was fully familiar to men of learning long before John Wesley preached his first sermon.

So perhaps we might smile benignly at the New Atheists and their fanatical secularist friends for beating the evolutionary drum with such vigour, for it is the only remotely new trick they have up their sleeves – albeit a trick that is now over 150 years old! And as we shall see below, even the idea that our "souls" are really only mechanistic resonances of our bodies would not have been unfamiliar to John Wesley – or indeed his grandfather!

Classical and Medieval Unbelief

We saw above how Psalms 14 and 53 spoke of scepticism in the time of the Old Testament, although we know very little about its origins or its nature in that world. But once one enters the speculative world of the Greek philosophers, then names, specific writings, and arguments appear for our examination. In fact, one of the extraordinary things about the intellectual freedom of classical Greece is that not only did you have writers such as Hesiod inventing theology and discussing the nature of the myths, attributes, kinships, and reputed antics of the Homeric gods in his *Theogony* (circa sixth century BC), and – centuries later – Roman scholars such as Cicero exploring the relationship of the Greco-Roman pantheon with those of Egypt and elsewhere, but you had all sorts of divergences from orthodoxy. We saw how the idea of the "Logos", 500 years before Christ, spoke of one great intellectual principle beyond the gods of Olympus. And there were also classical thinkers who argued that religion in its entirety was a human invention.

Philosophical schools, such as the Sceptics and the Cynics, have bequeathed their names and styles of thinking to the modern world, especially in the West, and have become embedded in the phraseology of everyday speech. For, religion apart, who is not *sceptical* about the claims of high-pressure salesmen and *cynical* about the promises of politicians? Pyrrho, Diogenes, Critias, Prodicus of Ceos, and others taught us how to articulate doubt, and, if we value freedom of thought, we should be eternally grateful to them. Yet by the same argument, we must be *sceptical* about the pronouncements of agenda-driven ideologists of all kinds (including religious ones) and healthily *cynical* about those pundits who loudly affirm that man is the measure of all things.

The school of atheistic thinking which had, perhaps, the longest-running presence in scientific thinking is that of the atomists. Somewhere about 440 BC, the Greek philosophers Leucippus and Democritus challenged the prevailing ideas about the nature of matter. For what if things did *not*, as thinkers such as Heraclitus, Empedocles, and others suggested, all derive from water, air, earth, or fire? Or, as Aristotle (after Empedocles) would argue in his *De Caelo* ("On the Heavens") around 340 BC, from all four of these primary principles of wetness, windiness, heaviness, or fieriness combined, and interacting together? Water, however, did seem the best candidate for being the key element, for it could be a solid, a liquid, or an airy vapour. Yet what if all these men were wrong, and the elements were not manipulated by some Great Principle to form wood, stone, metal, or flesh? What if the visible elements were themselves the concoctions of even more basic units, and what if there were no guiding rules or geometry of combination, and everything happened by chance? And what if our *seeing* order in the natural world were itself no more than a chance, temporary concatenation, with all the bits *seeming* to come together during the brief duration of our lives, and when our bodies just happened to exist?

And no, this assessment does not come from a latter-day New Atheist out to liberate blinkered humanity from the bondage of priestcraft. In fact, St Paul himself could no doubt have read such things in the public library in Tarsus, and certainly when he was in Athens or Rome, had he cared to do so; for this definitive statement on atomic atheism was published by Titus Carus Lucretius as *De Rerum Natura* ("On the Nature of Things") around 60 BC.

Indeed, you only need to read Lucretius to realize how old hat so many assertions of the New Atheists really are. For Lucretius said it all: men invent the gods in their own image, while prayer, sacrifice, public religion, and spirituality are no more than a human contrivance to ease our fears and sufferings. Nature, as a thing of order, is also an illusion. There are no elements or enduring structures "out there", only atoms. And these tiny little objects are all alike (*not* like the atoms of modern chemistry), and the way in which they stick together or fly apart at any one time is due to pure accident. And they make up our bodies and our world, and produce a mixture of semi-permanence or transience depending entirely on the luck of the moment. And we silly humans think it all makes sense!

As with so many ancient books, manuscript copies of *De Rerum Natura* went missing during the centuries following the end of the Roman Empire as a central cultural and administrative entity, as Goths, Vandals, Muslims, and others invaded and desecrated the Balkans, Syria, Palestine, Egypt, and Spain. And, it must not be forgotten, fanatical Christian outbursts against pagan temples and their libraries, such as that of AD 391, made their destructive contribution. Then the caliph Omar set fire to what was left of the great library at Alexandria in AD 642 as part of Islam's original expansion out of Arabia, and goodness knows what vanished in this and other orgies of anti-classical destruction around the Mediterranean. Lucretius survived as a name and as a body of very reprehensible ideas, as did numerous other scholars, scientists, and philosophers.

It says something about the eclectic reading habits of medieval monks, however, that when *De Rerum Natura* did resurface, in 1417, it was in the library of a German monastery. And yes, it was very naughty reading, yet further manuscript copies were made, circulated, and finally printed for widespread distribution in editions of 1473, 1495, 1500, and thereafter. And *De Rerum Natura* has been in print ever since. So much for uniform church suppression of ideas in the Middle Ages! Indeed, sceptical ideas were even known in the Islamic world, where the twelfth-century Spanish Muslim philosopher Averroes, a disciple of Aristotle, denied that God had created the world and even argued that individual human souls perished after death. Though the unorthodoxy of Averroes's ideas meant that he was to have little influence upon Islamic thought, he was soon translated into Latin by Michael Scot in the early thirteenth century, to be avidly debated in the universities of medieval Europe, invariably causing great controversy.

28

Where we differ from the classical and medieval world, however, is in our use of the term "atheism" in its literal meaning. Nowadays it is taken to signify a rejection of any belief in a supreme being. Yet in his *Apologia* around AD 140, the early Christian theologian Justin Martyr made the seemingly incredible claim that all Christians were accused by the Greeks of being *atheists*. So what on earth could he mean? Very simple, in fact. In the Greek, the word "atheist" (*atheos*) meant "denying the gods" in the plural. So in the strictly literal sense, a devout Christian might, after Justin, consider himself to be an atheist, because in his declared following of *God* in the singular, he rejected the idea of there being many gods. An interesting definition, in fact.

It would be incorrect to assume, however, that the early Christian church was one simple, unified happy family where everyone thought the same. Indeed, as early as the time of St Paul's letters to the young churches of Corinth, Ephesus, and Thessaly in the AD 50s, within twenty years or so of the crucifixion, Christians were up to various activities that were not canonical, and which St Paul chose to correct in his powerfully argued letters. Christians, for instance, could *not* slink off to pagan temples or feasts, or combine their faith with trying to keep on the right side of false heathen gods. And by the fourth century AD, the leaders of the church were holding summit meetings in Nicaea and elsewhere to formulate what was and was not canonical Christianity, based upon careful critical studies of the New Testament books. One could not, for instance, give Satan a power equal to that of Jesus, or believe that ancient secret rituals, occult insights, or extra-Christian forms of *gnosis* – wisdom – would get you into heaven, as the Gnostics had claimed. Only faith in Jesus would do that, as the Gospels tell us.

And then, when the great universities of twelfth- and thirteenth-century Europe began to teach the intellectual techniques of first Socrates and then Aristotle, using reason, logic, and debate to get at the truth, all manner of interesting ideas began to spring forth. And what if logic and debate led you to unbelief, as it did with the followers of Amaury of Paris, who died around 1207? For Amaury came to deny the immortality of the soul, and argued not for the creator–sustainer

29

God of the Judeo-Christian tradition, but for a pantheistic world-soul deity. Yes, you got into serious trouble, and if you persisted, you got burned, as did his followers, the Amalricians, in 1210. But the stark fact of the matter is that medieval Europe was in no way innocent of unbelief, even before Lucretius was rediscovered in 1417. Yet as long as a medieval academic avoided a direct confrontation and a denial of God, Christ, or salvation, what he said could often be absorbed into a wider philosophical picture. And while we no longer burn heretics in the West today, we are by no means as free or as liberal as we might like to think. Try, for instance, holding onto your research funding and career prospects if you are a modern-day earth scientist or independent film-maker who dares express serious scepticism about global warming! (And let me emphasize that I am not in this context making any remarks about global warming as such, but rather about what happens to "heretics" who express dissent from certain modern-day orthodoxies.)

And when one enters the sixteenth century, one finds not only the word "atheism" firmly rooted in the English language, but even various personages being designated sceptics and mockers of religion. Queen Elizabeth I's reign saw a veritable rash of them. The poet Christopher Marlowe was rumoured to be one, as also Sir Walter Ralegh and the supposed members of his "School of Night". The area around Sherborne, Dorset, was believed to contain a nest of atheists, for that is where Sir Walter had a country seat. In 1568, the English Bible translator Miles Coverdale condemned in his *Hope of Faithfull* these contemporary unbelievers who lived only to eat, drink, and have a good time "for tomorrow we shall die: which all the epicures protest openly, and the Italian *aetheoi*". And by "epicures", of course, Coverdale meant followers of the Greek sceptic Epicurus, whose school of thinking found its fullest expression in Lucretius.

One wonders, indeed, how far Elizabethan atheism was in itself a product of the shock of fresh knowledge, coming either from new geographical discoveries or from the burgeoning number of books – including *De Rerum Natura* – which the printing press was making generally available. The Tudor and Jacobean lawyer and philosopher Sir

Francis Bacon seemed to think so, suggesting in Book I, Section 3 of his *Advancement of Learning* (1605) that "a little or superficial knowledge of philosophy may incline the mind of man to atheism, but a further proceeding therein doth bring the mind back again to religion".

And Tudor England, along with Italy and Germany, saw a mushrooming of magic and spirit communication, especially among the educated classes. Sir Walter Ralegh's associate Dr John Dee openly attempted to commune with spirits in spite of explicit biblical condemnation of the practice. For in summoning up the spirits of the dead, or the primordial spirits of the earth, was not one denying the saving grace of God, as when King Saul persuaded the Witch of Endor to illicitly summon up the spirit of the deceased prophet Samuel in the Old Testament book of 1 Samuel?

Nor did the Bible lack its mockers. Sixteenth-century sceptics, including those of Ralegh's school, expressed doubts that the world could have been made from nothing in a spontaneous act of creation as described in Genesis. For does not everything come from something else? Likewise, the textual and narrative anomalies and ambiguities of Scripture were readily pounced upon. Where, for instance, did the women come from who married the sons of Adam and Eve, so that they could beget the patriarchs? And where did all the waters that occasioned Noah's Flood suddenly come from and go back to? And who had ever seen a dead man or woman come back to life?

So all these matters, and many more, were in discussion in avant-garde circles long before 1600, and to give the impression that atheism, scepticism, materialism, and unbelief did not exist until modern times is patently incorrect.

Thomas Hobbes, Materialism, and Man the Machine

Seventeenth-century Europe was the birthplace of materialism and of mechanism. From the precision astronomical measurements of Tycho Brahe in Denmark over the last thirty years of the sixteenth century to the founding of the Royal Society in London in 1660, European thought about the nature of the material world changed fundamentally. The universe of 1600 was still the classical cosmos of the fixed earth surrounded by the planetary spheres, whereas the post-telescopic universe of 1660 was infinite, and very largely empty, except for the orbiting planets and the stars. Material substance also was coming to be seen less as a combination of earth, water, air, and fire, and more as changing agglutinations of atoms. And what seemed to hold everything together were law-like regularities which could be expressed mathematically: exact regularities that governed the motions of the earth and planets around the sun, the behaviour of magnets, the hues and unchanging colour sequences produced by white light when passed through thick glass or water, and the combination of chemical substances in reactions. For whereas the physical world of ancient and medieval scholars could be visualized as a sort of sentient *organism* responding to stimuli, that of the seventeenth century was increasingly seen as analogous to clockwork, in which one part pushed another to move the planets around the sun on the one hand, or drive the blood around the body under the mechanical action of the heart on the other.

The mechanical clock bedazzled the imagination of the age in much the same way as the computer bedazzles ours, producing many largely speculative analogies devised to explain all manner of things. For were not the entire material world, the astronomical cosmos, and the bodies of both humans and animals just component parts or sub-systems of one gigantic piece of precision clockwork, namely, the universe? The radical new physics of René Descartes in France came to be known as the "mechanical philosophy", and claimed to explain everything in terms of self-acting, self-responding mechanical motions. And for a quarter of a century down to his death in 1650, the *Christian* Descartes would wrestle with the problem of how the immaterial immortal soul and mind could relate to the physical body and wider material environment, so that thoughts and physical actions synchronized perfectly. For this is the origin of that science-driven "mind–body" problem which is still with us today, and which the New Atheists do their best to claim is an irrelevance, in their strident insistence that there is really no "mind" in a spiritual sense:

only a programmed survival instinct deriving from the material circumstances of our physical bodies.

Yet when it comes to positing theories of pre-programmed materialist determinism to explain human thought and action, the New Atheists are Johnny-come-latelys, for Thomas Hobbes beat them to it by some 300 years.

I personally would love to have met Hobbes, for evidence suggests that he could have been jolly good company. Hobbes had a sense of humour and a gift for forging long-lasting friendships. The son of an outrageously eccentric Wiltshire parson (given, among other things, to gambling and heavy drinking), Thomas Hobbes was an abstemious, frugal, and well-off bachelor. Educated at Magdalen Hall, Oxford, he once became one of the secretaries to Sir Francis Bacon, Lord Chancellor (perhaps the most influential British philosopher of all time), and after 1608, he found a comfortable lifelong home as tutor and friend to the families of several successive Earls of Devonshire, living on their estates, and in London, Paris, Italy, and elsewhere. He so impressed and entertained the young King Charles II (whom he had once tutored) that Charles gave the elderly Hobbes "free access to his Majesty" and permission to drop in at Whitehall Palace whenever he pleased. Hobbes, moreover, either knew personally or corresponded with most of the great minds of the age, including Descartes and Gassendi, and had even visited the elderly Galileo at Arcetri near Florence in 1638. Active to the end, writing, talking, and playing "real tennis" into his seventies, he died peacefully at ninety-one, in 1679.

Familiar, like so many scholars of that age, with Lucretius, atomism, atheism, and scepticism, the young Hobbes searched for a clear unchallengeable truth, and believed, like the ancient Greeks, that he had found it in geometry and logic. For who could falsify the demonstrable proofs of Euclid's geometry? Having established this principle, he then aspired to build upon it, with further chains of logical proofs about everything. And in his *magnum opus* of 1651, *Leviathan*, he asked how we might establish a stable and efficient political system. And here is where he became notorious, for he began by arguing that before we can talk about government, we need a full analysis of what individual human beings are like; for each person, one might say, is a sort of atomic unit of the total state or nation. So know your "atoms" before talking about society as a whole!

Like a logical reductionist, Hobbes broke "Man" down into his or her most basic functional units. For what are our bodies but self-acting machines?

> For seeing life is but a motion of Limbs... why may we not
> say, that all *Automata* (Engines that move themselves by
> springs and wheeles as doth a watch) have an artificial life?
> For what is the *Heart*, but a *Spring*; and the *Nerves* but so
> many *Strings*; and the *Joynts*, but so many *Wheeles*, giving
> motion to the whole Body, such as was intended by the
> Artificer? (*Leviathan*, Introduction)

And from the natural machine of Man, Hobbes proceeds to build up the *artificial* machine of the state.

Yet no one before had spoken of human beings in these stark, mechanistic terms. And from the machine body, Hobbes next went on to develop mechanistic models for cognition, thinking, and behaving that – substituting clockwork and wheels for neurons and brain circuitry – were astonishingly similar to the speculative psycho- and neuro-babble of modern-day reductionists, albeit, in Hobbes's case, expressed with much greater clarity, elegance, and wit.

For Hobbes, Man exists solely to preserve his own skin, for as long as possible, for we are all pre-programmed, or "hard-wired", self-preservers. Indeed, we are locked into preserving our individual selves just as rigidly as a clock is locked into striking twelve when the mechanism is triggered. Morality is an invention of the social group, devised simply to stop us killing each other, and hence extending our individual lives and "Felicitie" (Hobbes's term for happiness): a sort of tribal insurance policy, for we only form "society" as a way of protecting ourselves *individually* from surprise attack. For "society" and public-spiritedness are in fact illusions: individual skin-saving is all that matters in the long run. No one, moreover, can know the mind or feelings of another person. All we can do is pick up on physical clues, and think something like: "How would I act if this were happening to me?" Then we would *ratiocinate* or calculate how best we might gain a survival advantage over that person: calculating the odds, just like a computer! Or, in the mid-seventeenth century, like one of Sir Samuel Morland's early geared calculating machines.

Our mechanical programming is founded on two basic drives: "Vainglory", or advancing our individual selves as far as we can; and "Fear", or calculating the odds of what will happen to *me* if I miscalculate. What if this person is a bit cleverer than me, and will kill me when I am not on my guard? Or can I really gain an ascendancy here, and make *him* fear *me* to the point where I have full control? Self-sacrifice and altruism were no more than madness, or defects in the mechanism: a sort of self-destructive aberration. Indeed, as brutal and as mechanistic as anything dreamed up by a modern-day bio-reductionist.

And what was all this eventually in aid of? Answer: the abovementioned "Felicitie", or personal security.

And while Hobbes had no notion of evolution in 1651, he certainly was fully aware of man's close physical cousinship with the beasts. No doubt, during his many years in Continental Europe, he had witnessed human and animal cadaver dissections in Paris, Montpellier, Padua, and Bologna – major centres of research in anatomy and physiology – for attending dissections was considered part of a seventeenth-century learned gentleman's education. In London, moreover, Hobbes was a friend, and in 1658 a beneficiary in the will, of Dr William Harvey, the discoverer of the circulation of the blood under the systolic (contractive) force of the heart. For as even the most devoutly Christian anatomists knew, the joints, blood vessels, muscles, and mechanical actions of human and animal bodies shared numerous structural and functional features in common. And Hobbes was by no means unique in recognizing that humans could often be savage and bestial in their behaviour as well.

Where he was unusual, however, was in the seemingly horrendous conclusions he came to in seeing humans as mechanically determined super-beasts who only really differed from dogs, wolves, and monkeys in the wider repertoire of tricks and subterfuges they could perform. For what separated the dog from his master was the master's vastly greater command of language and conceptual manipulation. To Hobbes, words were "wise men's counters", enabling them to calculate, think, and impose their "Vainglory" upon the less intellectually agile creation, both human and animal, with greater efficiency. Dominance, therefore, came through mankind's greater intellectual sophistication and ability to deal with more complex situations. But the bottom line was that humanity's superiority was no more than a survival tool. It was even said that Hobbes's thoroughgoing materialism led to his being more afraid of ghosts when he concluded that they might be physical than when he believed them to be mere incorporeal spirits – for a material ghost might do him physical harm!

From 1651 until into the nineteenth century, the term "Hobbist" came to be synonymous with "atheist"; yet was Hobbes an atheist? It is true that in chapter 47 he discoursed on a "Comparison of the Papacy with the Kingdome of Fayries" and "of Darknesse", but in many respects this is an English Protestant airing well-established national prejudices against perceived Roman Catholic "superstition". On the other hand, one can scarcely turn a leaf, especially within the last 400 pages of *Leviathan*'s 700, without encountering a profound and intimate knowledge of Scripture, and of biblical, Old and New Testament, history. Nowhere more so, in fact, than in his massive and deeply theological eleven-chapter section entitled "Of a Christian Common-Wealth".

And this could not have come about from a 63-year-old – as Hobbes was in 1651 – dimly recollecting his long-dead father's sermons in Malmesbury Parish Church, or his own undergraduate lectures in divinity at Magdalen Hall, Oxford. No: such detailed knowledge could only result from a lifetime's regular study of the Scriptures. Far from being an atheist, moreover, Hobbes sees God as the "Artificer", the master clockmaker or grand mechanician, who had built the great cosmic engine and set it in motion. And there is nothing chaotic in this vast and orderly creation, any more than there is in the going of a fine watch. Hobbes's system is *not* about greed or self-conscious nastiness. Rather, it is about the neutral actions of a mechanism, no more a product of evil or cruelty than are the parts of a watch which in their normal going strike, bounce off, and push each other in an endless cycle. And all sixteen of the *Leviathan* chapters in his large section entitled "Of Man" are intended to serve as a preliminary to his greater purpose of analysing humanity's political condition, and exploring the roots of natural loyalty and disobedience.

So Hobbes, I would argue, was no atheist, in spite of what both Puritan and Royalist contemporaries might have called him. Much more likely, he was a deist, who believed in a divine creator God who had set his creation in motion, but then had left the world and all that it contained – including us – to run by its own mechanical laws.

Hobbes is vital to our discussion for two reasons. Firstly, because he trumps the materialist New Atheists in pretty well everything, 300 years ahead of them, in matters ranging from man's relation to the animal creation to the self-seeking roots of morality to the resemblance of all our actions to those of automatic pre-programmed machines. And secondly, Hobbes is very largely ignored in the modern-day literature dealing with science, Christianity, belief, and unbelief, perhaps because he has slipped almost entirely into the domain of the political scientists, and is now studied primarily by students of either politics or the English Civil War. But when we *do* pay attention to his scientific ideas, we are reminded that there is nothing new under the sun, especially as far as materialist notions are concerned.

Atheists, Deists, and Unbelievers

By the mid seventeenth century one finds a remarkable mixture of unbelief, and the word "atheist" often used as a term of abuse against persons whose beliefs differed from one's own. We saw in the section on classical and medieval unbelief how "atheist" was sometimes bandied between early church Christians and classical pagans – depending upon whether one believed in one God or in many gods – and this recurred in the seventeenth century. The entertainingly acidic Oxford diarist and antiquarian Anthony à Wood included "atheists" in one of his spectacular catch-all sentences to express his disapproval of the times in which he lived:

> ... Whores and harlots, pimps and panders, bawds and buffoons, lechery, treachery, atheists and papists... (*Life and Times of Anthony Wood*, II, ed. A. Clark (Oxford, 1892), p. 125: under 1st December 1667)

Wood was not especially interested in science, though it is true that as a young man in 1659 he had paid to attend a course of private subscription chemistry lectures in Oxford, delivered by John Clerk. He was by instinct a conservative and a traditionalist, treating both Puritan fanatics and Roman Catholics with equal rancour and staunchly defending the Church of England and the king. And for Wood, like so many of his fellow Oxford dons, the term "atheist" could be justifiably flung at anyone believed to be rocking the boat of church and state. In Wood's world of Oxford, Cambridge, and London learned gentlemen, however, there was a growing number of persons whose spirituality was considered to be suspect. They might "worship" the Pope (and be led down the same treasonable path as the Yorkshireman Guy Fawkes); or be like Socinus or the "Mohammetans", and believe that God was a singular and distant being, with Christ no more than a natural man, and grace and the Holy Spirit a fiction; or they might worship their own spiritual conceit like the Puritans, or their own cleverness, or even – as in the case of drunkards and gluttons – "their bellies". They might even openly proclaim their admiration of Thomas Hobbes! And all of them would qualify for the insult "atheist" from Anthony Wood and men of his ilk.

Yet insults apart, the seventeenth century saw burgeoning shades of unbelief around the traditional Judeo-Christian tradition, and many of them derived from new scientific styles of thinking, if not necessarily from science itself. Massively influential here was the Iberian-Dutch former Jewish philosopher Baruch Spinoza. Far from his being an atheist as such, however, what made so many people see red regarding

Spinoza was his actual conception of God. For Spinoza's deity was neither the God of Abraham nor Christ nor the Holy Spirit. Rather, it (not he) was *everything*. Nature itself was divine, and everything was connected to everything else in a sort of pantheism. And while this might seem benign given the stridency of many modern-day secularists, it offended both Jews and Christians in the seventeenth century, primarily because Spinoza depersonalized God and turned him into a universal yet amorphous thing.

And if many saw Spinoza as already well down the slippery slope towards atheism, they were no happier with the deists proper, with their insistence that reason must be the sole arbiter of religion, and that all forms of revelation were no more than outdated folk delusion. Hobbes probably belonged to this category in so far as he seems to have been happy with a creator and probably even a designer of the universe, but probably not with a being who was actively engaged with the running of his creation. For surely, if God were kind and answered the prayers of the sick or shipwrecked, he must have got the big design of the universe wrong in the first place, otherwise he would not need to intervene and tinker with it to save lives or relieve distress. The God of the deists, therefore, was a remote being who had drawn back from his creation and let the great laws of his devising have full play, and regarded the deaths of children as just minor anomalies in the magnificent scheme of things. A God who was especially appealing to well-off, healthy, tidy-minded intellectuals who already had it all. And he still is!

The seventeenth century saw much debate about miracles, and the deists were firmly convinced that such things could not take place. For even if God were tender-hearted and heard the cries of suffering humanity, he could do nothing about them, for the sheer perfection of his original creation, seen in its grandest form in the iron laws of planetary motion and physics, placed an impenetrable wall of glass between God and the creation. Indeed, this was one of the points discussed between the great German mathematician Gottfried Leibnitz and Newton's protégé Samuel Clarke in the early eighteenth century. And as in the case of Spinoza, while the deists did not deny the possible existence of God, he was nonetheless a vastly diminished figure when seen alongside the psalmist's God who rode on the wings of the wind, or the compassionate Suffering Servant of the Gospels. And because of this, it was not infrequent to find deists regarded as little better than "atheists".

Emerging in the seventeenth century, and closely related to deism, is what came to be called "natural religion", a form of spiritual expression, indeed, not to be confused with "natural theology" and the argument from design. For while natural *theology* grew up very much within scholarly Anglicanism, was deeply theistic, and was encapsulated in that style of Christianity displayed by the Hon. Robert Boyle, Bishops John Wilkins, Seth Ward, and Thomas Sprat, Archbishop John Tillotson, and other leading Fellows of the Royal Society – arguing that one could trace the hand of a loving creator in the carefully designed structures of the natural world – natural *religion*, by contrast, went far beyond traditional Christianity.

Instead of devoutly "tracing God's thoughts after him" in nature, natural religion put man and the rational human intellect at the heart of religion. For did not the scientific men of the late seventeenth century, knowing things about the cosmos, the earth, and the microscopic realm undreamt of by the simple followers of Jesus, have insights into the *truth* that made miracles, spiritual wonders, and even grace seem redundant? Rather, should not the critical rational intellect set the standard?

In the 1690s, one writer in particular published a book that gave this natural religious deism something of a new profile for English readers. John Toland's *Christianity not Mysterious* (1695) argued that what appeared miraculous to the writers of the Bible really derived from inadequate observation and understanding. Toland did not deny that miracles existed as events; rather he argued that they were the product of natural agencies operating by complex laws unknown in the days of Moses or Jesus. In short, both God and his revelation were comprehensible by means of human reason, and mystery and miracle were no more than the products of ignorance and priestcraft. And as a baptized Irish Roman Catholic who had become a Protestant on his way towards rationalist deism, Toland was keen to attribute all manner of "priestcraft" subterfuges and mischiefs to the Catholic Church.

In the wake of Toland's controversial writings came another high-profile English deist: an ex-Oxford don, sometime Roman Catholic convert, and full-time controversialist, who at the age of seventy-five published a work which was to become the "Bible" of English deism and natural religion. For even the title of Matthew Tindal's book leaves you in no doubt where he is coming from: *Christianity as old as the Creation, or the Gospel a Republication of the Religion of Nature* (1730). In it Tindal argues that there is an unchanging law running through all things, Reason, which can set us free from superstition, and that the Christian Gospels do no more than reiterate this ancient law. The Gospels, to Tindal, added nothing new to natural reason and natural goodness, and, needless to say, miracles were no more than misunderstandings of nature, or plain superstitious deception.

It was this unfolding of scepticism in its various forms – much of it apparently stimulated by recent scientific discovery – that led the Hon. Robert Boyle to found and endow an annual lecture to be delivered in St Mary-le-Bow Church, London, with the explicit purpose of refuting atheism and demonstrating the harmony of the Christian faith with modern scientific discovery: the "natural theology" of the early Royal Society. Indeed, as the so-called "father of modern chemistry" and an experimental scientist whose name and discoveries still get into today's science textbooks, the devoutly Christian Boyle was well placed to review the relationship between science and Christianity. And in his theological and scientific writings, and afterwards in the lectures which he endowed, Boyle became one of the first great apologists for Christianity in the face of "scientific" atheism and deism.

The lectures were extremely well endowed by seventeenth-century standards, paying the lecturer £50 and intending to attract speakers of the highest talent and integrity, and were administered through a trust. Richard Bentley delivered the first Boyle Lecture in 1692, appropriately entitled "A Confutation of Atheism" (before in subsequent years going on to attack the English freethinker Anthony Collins). The Boyle Lectures continued pretty well every year for over 200 years, dealing with a variety of topics in Christian apologetics. Then in 2004, after being redundant for much of the twentieth century, they were restarted and re-endowed through Gresham College and the Worshipful Company of Mercers in the City of London, and have continued with vigour, packing the large and spacious church of St Mary-le-Bow, often to standing room only. (I have attended all the post-2004 lectures, and can testify both to the intellectual distinction of the lecturers and to the topicality of modern confutation of atheism.)

So let us be *sceptical* and *doubting* when the New Atheists try to hoodwink us into believing that what they have to say is especially new or radical. In fact, a very great deal of it is little more than a rehash of the deist/atheist speculation that Robert Boyle and his fellow FRSs would have heard being bandied about quite openly in the coffee houses of late seventeenth-century London. With the exception, that is, of the monkey origins of the human race, which we will address shortly.

3

The Origins of Unbelief
Part 2: Dreams of a
Brave New World

We saw above how atheism, from its classical philosophical roots, developed new strands of thinking in the wake of medieval and Renaissance Europe's growing fascination with self-acting mechanical devices and the new scientific discoveries of the sixteenth and seventeenth centuries. But by the second half of the eighteenth century further circumstances were providing fertile soil for potential atheistic thinking: most notably, the increasing economic and social complexity of European society, with an expanding class of educated, comfortably off, and relatively leisured people. And then there was the growth of a large industrial workforce by 1850, with the rise of working-class political and self-help movements.

Romantic and Revolutionary Atheism

We are often led to think of the "Romantic" movement of the late eighteenth to early nineteenth centuries as positive and life-enhancing, with its emphasis on freedom, beauty, compassion, and liberation. We tend to think of Jane Austen, Wordsworth, Byron, Coleridge, Burns, Keats, and the Brontë sisters, of polite country-house society, passionate young ladies, and maybe daffodils. Vicarages and cathedral cities play a prominent role in much of the literature of the age, while its greatest visual artists, J. M. W. Turner and John Constable, depicted the English landscape – containing a good few churches – in a way that is most familiar to many people today from reproductions on biscuit-tin lids and table-mats. Real "Old England", in fact. A time of peace, prosperity, and social goodwill to all men. An age, alas, soon to be blighted by railway trains, coal mines, and *On the Origin of Species*!

Yet also part of Romanticism was the ditching of traditional standards, along with a love of being outrageous and shocking: a sort of trial run for the 1960s, including a cult of youth. And one of the things that some Romantics rebelled against was traditional Christianity. A few of them, moreover, could well be considered the true founding fathers of "spoilt brat", "me" culture. Shelley and Byron immediately spring to mind in this respect: elite young men, with private money behind them and no real need to seek paid employment, they had all the time in the world to articulate lofty disdain. And while Shelley may have laughed at the Sermon on the Mount, and derided the idea of the meek inheriting the earth, some openly fawned on the ideals of the French Revolution and even idolized the military dictator Napoleon Bonaparte. Generally speaking, however, they preferred to do this from the "safe" side of the English Channel – where their outrageous ideas wouldn't get them arrested, where they were free to publish their books, and where stable banks and prosperous agriculture ensured that their private incomes were paid on time. Occasionally, though, they fled to the Continent to escape escalating debts at home.

I emphasize, however, that by no means all the great creative spirits of the "Romantic Age" were of this type. William Blake – my own personal favourite – was a working artist, engraver, and illustrator whose eccentric yet inspired Christianity suffused most of what he wrote and drew. Yes, radical Blake rightly attacked the social injustices of his day, but he also had transcendent visions of angels and saw England as the New Jerusalem:

> And did those feet in ancient time
>> Walk upon England's mountains green?
> And was the holy Lamb of God

On England's pleasant pastures seen?
And did the countenance divine
  Shine forth upon our clouded hills?
And was Jerusalem builded here
  Among those dark satanic mills?

And John Constable was a man of modest background whose spirit remained embedded in the traditions, folk ways, and visual beauty of his native Suffolk.

Percy Bysshe Shelley was the Romantic who most clearly declared his contempt for Christianity, although without putting his name on the title page! *The Necessity of Atheism*, by Shelley and his friend T. J. Hogg, caused uproar when published in Worthing in 1811. At the time Shelley, the son of a landowner and MP, Sir Timothy Shelley, was an undergraduate student at University College, Oxford, inspired by various currents of deistic and radical thinking, while enjoying an annual allowance of £200 (in itself an income that would have maintained a modest middle-class family in comfort for a year) from Dad. In short, he dismissed Christianity as lacking evidence, and while he was not saying anything that was especially novel in freethinking circles (for as we have seen, atheism was no less "old hat" in 1811 than it is today), it was the circumstances of his statement that put the cat among the pigeons.

While their tract did not carry its authors' names – Shelley and Hogg – they did send copies to all the bishops and the heads of every college in Oxford University. And let us not forget that in 1811 Oxford and Cambridge were, legally and constitutionally, *Anglican* Christian universities, and to "matriculate", or enter the academic community, Shelley and Hogg would have been obliged to swear an oath of assent to the Thirty-Nine Articles of the Church of England.

In short, their *Atheism* pamphlet was a clear act of challenge and provocation. An undergraduate act of bravado that went wrong and got them both expelled, and which so outraged the good churchman Sir Timothy that he wrote "Impious" across his own copy of young Percy's pamphlet. Yet it shows how widespread atheistic or "advanced" deistic ideas were by 1811 for them to have been so warmly trumpeted by a rich, clever nineteen-year-old. Even in an official Anglican institution such as Oxford University, radical ideas were clearly accessible and being openly discussed, though not necessarily advocated with such stridency, or so publicly, as by Shelley and Hogg. After all, the natural religious writings and other aspects of the philosophy of Oxford's John Locke were normal undergraduate reading, and David Hume's own sceptical writings of eighty years before would have been on the shelves of the Bodleian and many college libraries – not to mention the works of Toland, Tindal, and others.

Of far more powerful and enduring impact than Shelley's 1811 *Atheism* squib was positivism. Drawing upon deistic and atheistic traditions going back into the seventeenth and eighteenth centuries and the perceived infallibility of the scientific method, and fuelled by the radical (and often violent) anti-Roman-Catholicism of the French Revolution, positivism was given its classic original formulation by Auguste Comte, who in turn built upon the earlier writings of Henri de Saint-Simon. Comte's *Course in Positive Philosophy* volumes, published between 1830 and 1842, saw objective truth as purely scientific in its basis. And as one of the major influences upon all subsequent secular thinking, Comte effectively founded what we now often call *scientism* – or the worship of science and the scientific method as an infallible guide to absolute truth in itself. Matter and motion were at the bottom of everything, and religion and other non-physical activities belonged to earlier and more primitive stages of human development. Truth, however, had to be *positive*, and amenable to physical testing by the experimental method and mathematical analysis.

As a natural system-builder, Comte interpreted human history in three great phases. Firstly there was the *theological*, in which human beings believed in fanciful spiritual beings. Secondly, came the *metaphysical*, in which philosophers studied great abstract systems of ideas: rather like castles in the air. Then thirdly, in the modern age, came the *positive*, or scientific. Each epoch transcended the limitations of what went before. Comte was, needless to say, deeply influenced by the extraordinary speed with which science had developed over the previous couple of centuries, and it came to be seen in radical circles as the liberator from theological and metaphysical darkness, and positive *progress* became the touchstone of the human condition. Science, reason, and universal laws based upon physics became the articles of the positivist creed.

Comte's positivism would spawn a whole series of movements in the nineteenth century. One of these would be a new religion of humanity: man, the measure of all things, would become the key principle of ethics, morality, idealism, and social policy. There would even be a new positivist religion, with a priesthood of *cognoscenti* who would teach the principles of physical truth and the morality of being nice to people, to the *hoi polloi*. Naturally, this new religion, and the positivist temples through which it was hopefully to be relayed to the masses, would wholly supersede the superstition and ignorance of the Christian churches, which would die away under the weight of their own pointless mumbo-jumbo, as people would begin to see reason.

A more enduring offshoot of positivism was sociology, or the study of humanity by purely scientific, quantitative methods: were not people and human society themselves governed by great laws, and could we not restructure and improve society by applying the great principles of science to changing the human condition for the better? From religious darkness to positivist light, in fact. Many of the late nineteenth-century founders of sociology, such as Max Weber and Émile Durkheim, were influenced in their thinking by Comte's ideas, even if they did not accept them in their entirety. Positivism, in short, was all set to become the control freak's paradise, as a self-selecting elite of "superior" intellectuals earnestly went about their business of making the world what they saw as a better place, with the common folk following like sheep obediently behind.

Comte's ideas, while nowhere near as widespread as they were in France, did have their followers among the British intelligentsia. And for those who couldn't read French, Harriet Martineau translated him into English in 1853, and others such as George Lewes, John Stuart Mill, and Frederic Harrison were actively presenting his ideas to English-language readers by 1865. Comte also had something of a following among the American intelligentsia well before the Civil War, as the Anglo-American physician–chemist–astronomer Darwinian "Christianophobe", Prof. John William Draper of New York, became his prophet on the East coast. Indeed, the arguments of the atheistic philosophers mentioned so disapprovingly in Louisa M. Alcott's *Little Women* (1868–9), chapter 34 (entitled "Friend"), seem to have been along German metaphysical or positivistic lines.

And how, you may ask, do Comte and his followers differ from the human clockwork of Thomas Hobbes? In fact, the two have a lot in common, given the 200 years of new discoveries that separate them: both are quintessentially materialist, and both see humanity and society as driven by unchanging *physical* laws or principles. On the other hand, there are significant differences. For one thing, Hobbes was writing more by way of a deductive "thought experiment" driven by geometry and logic, and there is no evidence that, as in the case of Comte, he was trying to change the world and rewrite the human condition. Hobbes, moreover, was astonishingly "democratic" or egalitarian, as his "Leviathan" or supreme ruler got the job by the luck of the draw, and not by being especially superior to all the other clockwork humans. Hobbes also, while perhaps a deist, or a rather eccentric Christian, certainly seems to have believed in God – even the God who manifested himself in Scripture – whereas Comte sees no greater being than the elite human. And very importantly, I often wonder, reading the rolling prose of *Leviathan*, how seriously Hobbes *really* took himself. How far is he, the dinner-table performer, enjoying himself in advancing an outrageous argument that he knows will delight some, while causing apoplexies in others? There are places in *Leviathan* where you almost catch the mischievous twinkle in his eye. Comte, on the other hand, comes over as deadly serious in his new vision of what the world will inevitably become, as science and reason sweep the demons of blind faith away. I see one man as something of a wit, and the other as an ideologue.

But all the above is very intellectual, representing the thought of highly educated figures. On the other hand, the Romantic, or English Georgian, age had its share of popular mockery of religion, which totally destroys the received image of a docile and obedient "lower orders" cowed by an authoritarian Church of England. After the French Revolution, for example, the British authorities were rightly concerned with the propagation of both subversive political *and* religious literature in England. The French Revolutionaries manifestly failed to practise the *"Liberté, Égalité, et Fraternité"* that they preached, and were often savage to the Roman Catholic Church, murdering priests, monks, and devout laity, raping nuns, burning churches, and even smashing open the royal tombs in the St Denis Basilica to drag out and destroy the mummified remains of French kings. So the British government kept a watchful eye on "Jacobin Clubs" of Revolutionary sympathizers on this side of the English Channel, along with their generally anti-Christian secularist sentiments. Yet because blasphemous pictures lacked the legal specificity of blasphemous printed text – which often made it harder to punish the perpetrators – there came into being a small yet notorious genre of potentially blasphemous prints.

Of course, some prints, and their accompanying texts, were not theologically offensive as much as laughably naughty in the twentieth-century seaside postcard sense: well-fed bishops – invariably complete with lawn sleeves and mitres – snug in bed with pretty young women, or groups of obese parsons tucking into gargantuan dinners while poor beggars looked on through the window. (And yes, some parsons *were* greedy; yet the historical record shows that many good-living vicars, such as James Woodforde and Sydney Smith, also gave liberally to charity, acted in lieu of a local doctor, and were popular among their people.) One instance of such boisterous anti-clerical humour is G. A. Stevens's and T. Colley's rollickingly funny *The Vicar and Moses*, published in several versions after 1782. In these pictures, the inebriate parson and his boozing companion Moses, the parish clerk, roll along laughing merrily to conduct a funeral. But, so the accompanying text tells us, the Reverend Gentleman and his clerk are so slewed that the funeral becomes a shambles (shades, perhaps, of Thomas Hobbes's own bibulous parson dad!).

Far more vicious, however, were the prints and texts of Richard Carlile, for which he sometimes served spells behind bars for blasphemy and subversion. His *An Address to Men of Science: Calling upon them to… Vindicate the Truth from the Foul Grasp and Persecution of Religion* (1821) is a title that, without benefit of a second glance, could well appear on a present-day bookstand as the work of any modern Christianophobe. And Carlile's print and text *The God of the Jews and Christians. The Great Jehovah* (1825) – a visual parody of the descriptions of God in the Psalms, Revelation, and elsewhere in the Bible – is so grotesque in its blasphemy that I am sure many a modern-day atheist would feel embarrassed by it. It is reproduced in Vic Gatrell's *City of Laughter* (2006), page 543.

So when we look at "Romantic" era literature, from Shelley to the early positivists, to the mocking prints and texts of Richard Carlile and his radical atheist friends, what do the modern-day atheists have to say that we have not heard centuries before? Deism, scepticism, secularism, science-worship, anti-religious mockery, and self-congratulatory self-electing intellectual elites were around long before the New Atheists decided to save us from our superstitious selves.

Robert Owen, George Holyoake, and the Victorian Secular Atheists

In many respects Victorian Britain was a much more robust, tolerant, and relaxed society than the one we have today. True, there were vast and glaring disparities of wealth; and while the urban working-man householder got the vote in 1867, the same right would not be extended to women until the decade after 1919. Yet Victorian Britain had a pride, a self-confidence, and a sense of destiny which leaves us moderns wringing our hands and apologizing – for its missionary activities, for the British Empire, for its legacy of industrialization, hymn-singing, and even cricket. The Common Law, for example, punished actions, and *not* peacefully articulated thoughts, prejudices, or opinions (contrary to what interpretation of European Union Law sometimes makes possible today). Declaring yourself an atheist might get your name struck off the vicarage tea-party invitation list, but unless your views came to be associated with republicanism, subversion, or treason, and were proclaimed at rowdy or inflammatory public meetings during times of national crisis, the law would do nothing. It is true that things were rather more fraught during the troubles of the "Hungry Forties" – a time of food shortages, a shamefully neglected famine in Ireland, and labour unrest – but if you did not openly mock or ridicule the Christian faith, the monarchy, and the rule of law, were not seen to be promoting sexual obscenity, and did not declare an approval of French Revolutionary principles, then a philosophical irreligion was not likely to lead to criminal proceedings.

By 1880, the good people of Northampton – including many God-fearing Christians and supporters of our most Christian of prime ministers, William Ewart Gladstone – had enthusiastically voted in the freethinking, secularist, Republican-sympathizing Charles Bradlaugh as their Liberal Party MP. Even after his initial unwillingness to subscribe to a Christian Oath of Allegiance meant he was unable to take his seat, his constituents kept voting him back, until in 1886 the Speaker of the House did allow him to sit, and in 1888 a new Act permitted a secular affirmation.

Indeed, the Bradlaugh affair gives us a remarkable insight into the way that popular opinion and tolerance could lead to peaceful constitutional changes in the more stable and comfortable 1880s, enabling a popular figure, in spite of his "outrageous" views, to be serially elected and confirmed as an MP by Methodists, Baptists, Pentecostals, Unitarians, and even Anglicans. Because, clearly, they liked him and thought he was a good MP.

A far cry, indeed, from the prevailing secularist myth (still rehearsed by fans of the "Enlightenment", as I know from personal experience) that modern freedom only became possible when a few inspired and courageous unbelievers dared to seize power from a reactionary Christian elite; for there were certainly not enough radical secular atheists in Northampton in 1880 to return an MP single-handed. But there *must* have been a lot of Christians who felt that Bradlaugh had won his seat fairly in an open contest, and had a right to sit in it.

It is in this context of remarkable freedom of expression that "modern" atheism and secularism were born in the late Georgian and Victorian era. Their first major advocate, in many respects, was the idealistic Welsh-born self-made industrial millionaire and public philanthropist, Robert Owen.

Moving from Wales to Manchester, then on to Scotland, Owen was in the thick of the first Industrial Revolution, when "Cotton was King" and great fortunes could be made in the textile trade. Most mill-owners treated their workers barbarously, like "white slaves" it was sometimes said; but Owen was a kindly, good-natured, and naturally affable man who also realized that well-treated, well-housed, well-fed, and regularly rested workers were a better investment than angry half-dead ones. He built a new industrial town, New Lanark, in southern Scotland, which possessed, among other amenities, schools, medical care, decent sanitation, and a clean water supply. For Owen was an idealist socialist, freethinker and secularist. And believing that man could be socially engineered into perfectibility once separated from excesses of the bottle and the Bible, he even went on to found a utopian colony, New Harmony, in America in 1825, although, predictably, disharmony set in, and it failed.

But Owen had a fascinating mix of traits that placed him firmly in the tradition of great British eccentrics: he was an amazingly generous philanthropist, an idealist capitalist yet a believer in cooperation rather than competition, an advocate of socialism, a creator of harmonious master–worker trades union relations, a pioneer of the cooperative movement for working people, and a secularist. And honest to his principles, he put his money where his mouth was, and used his own resources to establish, in the late 1830s, a Rational Religion and Rationalist Society, propagated by lectures, meetings, and celebrations aimed primarily at working men. Yet Owen did seem to come to a sort of religious understanding when, in 1854, he became a spiritualist. His boundless zeal for making the world a better place never deserted him, however, continuing right down to his death at the age of eighty-seven in 1858.

Owen's impact on English secularism and early socialism was enormous, especially as he was one of the few people of his persuasion not to live in an intellectual bubble, but to take a hands-on approach and spend considerable sums of his own earned money in pursuit of his ideals: astonishingly similar to contemporary Christian evangelicals and Christian socialists, in fact.

But it was George Holyoake who really got the British secularist movement off the ground in the 1840s, serving six months in Gloucester gaol for blasphemy in 1842 when, during a radical lecture, he made contemptuous remarks about Christianity. But this period, let us remember, was one of great political unrest: shots had recently been fired at the young Queen Victoria in London, the country was disturbed by widespread rioting, and the economy was in what we would now call "recession", so that noisily proclaimed allegiances to atheism, secularism, French Republicanism and socialism could get one into trouble. And Holyoake was one of the leading lights in the British secularist and freethinking movement from the early 1840s to the 1890s, as a lecturer, writer, and propagandist.

Holyoake seems to have coined the term "secularism" around 1851, and while it was, and remained, generally associated with a non-religious approach to life, it did not necessarily have to be so. Secularism could, after all, be taken as a purely social creed, meaning that while a person might sincerely believe in God, he or she nonetheless recognized that certain parts of life were theologically neutral. This was probably why Bradlaugh kept winning parliamentary elections in Northampton, as a spectrum of Dissenting Christians no doubt resented what was seen as Anglicanism's privileged position in national life, and wished to end that privilege. In spite of their own personal atheism, both Holyoake and Bradlaugh were associated, like Owen, with a string of popular social justice and humanitarian causes, including, in Bradlaugh's case, championing the rights of the ordinary people of India in the Westminster Parliament.

And finally, by way of a coda, let us also be aware of the myth that says British trades unionism and popular working-class social improvement campaigns were products of secular radicals overthrowing Christian control. The true picture is far from simple and clear-cut. Yes, there undoubtedly were radical, secular influences present in British working-class movements, as one sees with Robert Owen and the "Owenites", and with Holyoake, Bradlaugh, and others: movements drawing on

"Rights of Man" and republican ideas. Yet Victorian Britain, let us not forget, was a deeply Christian country, from the archbishops sitting in the House of Lords to the vibrant Dissenting chapel communities of working people that stretched from Cornwall to Scotland, along with the newly founded Salvation Army, and were especially powerful in the industrial towns. One has only to travel across Great Britain today to see these occasionally small but more often imposing chapels, some still in use as places of Christian worship, and others turned into warehouses or theatres. The Welsh valleys and my own native industrial Lancashire in particular were full of them: "Bethesda, 1875", "Elim, 1880", along with "Happy Land", "Reheboth", "Mount Sion", "Peniel", and so on (often named after places where God had revealed himself to mankind in the Old Testament), some dating from the late eighteenth century, but invariably with new re-foundation stones, proudly proclaiming "Rebuilt and extended 1885" or words to that effect.

Indeed, a rapidly growing population after 1840 led not only to waves of chapel-building, but to the building of hundreds of new Anglican churches as well, as Methodists, Baptists, Anglicans, and other denominations competed to win the souls of the expanding working and lower middle classes. And this phenomenon of indigenous local multidenominational Christian revivalism, complete with its penny-a-week insurance "sick clubs", adult literacy Sunday and other schools, and Mechanics' Institutes, had far more to do with the growth of working-class self-help movements and trades unions than had the Marxist, German revolutionary, or anarchist movements of the age.

Very important when considering the chapels was the fact that they often – along with the pubs – acted as centres of working-class life, and were built, paid for, and managed by subscriptions from the coal-miners, mill-workers, and working men *and women* themselves. Wesleyan and Primitive Methodism, Congregationalism, and after 1907 American Pentecostalism in particular made extensive use of lay ministers: ordinary working people who were not only literate but often astonishingly widely read. (I have come across Victorian working-men lay ministers who taught themselves Greek, Latin, and German, not to mention natural science.) Some scrimped and saved to train for the full-time Methodist ministry – always poorly paid – often while doing a full-time day job. My own father had two late-Victorian uncles, one of whom, after finishing his apprenticeship as a mechanic, trained as a full-time Methodist minister and became a noted scholar and bibliophile, while the other, also a working man, became an Anglican lay reader.

And what has all this to do with trades unionism? Well, the skills of oratory and exhortation which enabled a man to spellbind 1,000 people in a large galleried chapel on a Sunday could also be used for addressing a union meeting on a Monday. A powerful working-class minister who could dramatically argue Satan back into hell from the pulpit on Sunday might also be able to beat a mill- or mine-owner into submission when negotiating for better pay and conditions – just as Jesus did with the Pharisees and Sadducees. A far more effective way of improving the people's lot, indeed, than bloody revolution with its recurrent cycles of political instability!

The great ex-coal-miner labour leader and effective founder of the Labour Party in 1900, James Keir Hardie, had much affinity with this tradition. Cutting his teeth as a lay preacher in the Scottish Evangelical Union, and subsequently becoming a convert to *non*-Marxist socialism, Hardie seems to have regarded himself as a radical Christian throughout his life, making reference to his saviour in Gethsemane as the horrors of World War I began to unfold in August 1914. As he recorded later in life, "The impetus which drove me first of all into the Labour movement and inspiration which has carried me on in it… has derived more from the teachings of Jesus of Nazareth than all the other sources combined."

So what, you may ask, have socialism, rationalism, secularism, and trades unionism to do with science and religion? A very great deal, I would argue. Many of these ideas claimed a sort of scientific basis: in positivism, in early secular or "rational" sociology, in the view that we were now living in a post-religious era of "science", and, by the 1860s, in a Marxist model of "dialectical materialism", where matter, conflict, and progress were the sole engines of social change. It is true that in the British radical tradition of Owen, Holyoake, and Bradlaugh there was a beneficence and a kindly idealism that wanted to make the world a better place, and might almost be considered a sort of "secular" Christianity. And this contrasted sharply with the much more brutal revolutionary and often murderous atheistical schemes more common in Continental Europe, from the French Revolutionaries after 1789 to the German anarchists and Marxists of the 1880s, and on to the horrors of Russia after 1917.

What we see here, therefore, is the emergence, in the nineteenth century, of an attempt to understand and control human beings in a way that often dismissed revealed religion as belonging to a more backward phase of social development. And once again, we find another clear contradiction to the myth that superstition and church dogma reigned supreme in their control of thoughts and actions until the modern atheists stepped in to save the world.

The Myth that Simple Faith Was Destroyed by Darwin in 1859

I hope to have shown in this chapter that, on the eve of the publication of Darwin's *On the Origin of Species*, the world was, theologically speaking, a much more complex place than some people might lead us to believe. Doubt, scepticism, and unbelief were anciently established in the world of philosophy, and "atheism" had long been a term of abuse. The idea of humans as programmed machines responding to stimuli had been around for over two centuries by 1859, while "scientific" social theories were already being actively propagated at the time of Darwin's sailing away on HMS *Beagle* in 1831. There were also those who openly mocked the Bible – and *occasionally* ended up behind bars – long before Darwin was even born. Since the late seventeenth century, too, devoutly Christian scientists such as Robert Boyle had been actively engaged in arguing against those who believed that the new science must inevitably make a person an atheist.

So what can we say about the widespread notion that until brave evolutionists dared to challenge the church, everyone did as they were told and dissent from its authority was effectively non-existent? The answer is simple: it is pure myth!

4

The Historical Roots of Anti-Christianity
Part 1: Two Persistent Myths

We saw in the previous two chapters how those ideas now being presented by modern-day atheists and secularists as undermining traditional Christian belief, far from being new, original, and shocking, are in most cases many centuries old. But what I want to do now is trace some of the arguments and myths that have led to so much attack on the Christian faith, especially in the twentieth century.

The Myth of the Medieval "Dark Age"

In spite of a massive body of original research from the nineteenth century onwards, undertaken by scholars across Europe and America, into the documented history of the medieval centuries, and the rich, vibrant, and ingenious culture that it has revealed, the popular myth remains that the centuries between AD 500 and 1500 were "dark". It is a myth that has been fed into the Western imagination by nineteenth-century "gothic" novels (complete with cackling monks), paintings of deranged alchemists, and, most of all, by Hollywood and television (the Monty Python comedies and *The Name of the Rose* spring to mind as examples). An age not only dark, but also filthy, in which only heroes and heroines ever washed – and usually had "orthodontically perfect" smiles to boot! Monks in particular got it in the neck from anti-medieval fantasists. Evil fellows, the lot of 'em, obsessed with making décolletée maidens "confess" their lustful thoughts, plotting nasty deeds, or perhaps shuffling around subterranean laboratories full of bubbling retorts in search of the philosopher's stone or trying to conjure up the legions of hell. Alternatively, they might be overweight buffoons, as in the popular cinematic depictions of Friar Tuck.

In this popular way of thinking, the medieval world is a place as alien as Mars. Sandwiched between the sunny glories of Greece and Rome (and if you are religious, the time of Jesus) and the "Renaissance", which dawned when the skies cleared once again after 1500, it is a foreign place of superstition and repression. And worst of all, for a Protestant, it was Catholic! Indeed, it became a hell-sent playground for atheists, mockers, and secular "progressives" of all shades, for what horrors of backwardness can you *not* project back onto the "Dark Ages"?

As an extenuating circumstance for the Christianity-haters, however, one has to admit that they did not invent vilification of the medieval, but found it as a tempting brickbat all ready to throw! For the Protestant Christians got there first. Indeed, it was the anti-medieval, anti-Catholic Protestant rhetoric, going right back to the sixteenth-century Reformers themselves, that began the task of darkening the 1,000 years that had rolled before then. For were not the Protestant Reformers seeing the Gospels in a light that had been dimmed since the days of the apostles, and which "the church" of the medieval centuries had almost snuffed out? Indeed, you had only to look at such things as popes, the seven sacraments, transubstantiation (the bread and wine miraculously being transformed into the body and blood of Jesus by the priest during Mass), Purgatory, elaborate vestments, crucifixes, and other "idols", the "worship" of the Virgin Mary and the saints, liturgical ceremonies, monks and nuns, confession, and a host of other things that had never been mentioned in the New Testament, to realize how "superstitious" the Roman Catholic Church had made the simple teachings of Jesus!

So some early Protestants smashed church decorations, burned "Popish" books, dissolved religious communities, and, between 1535 and 1680, barbarously executed, often by hanging, drawing, and quartering, well over 100 English Roman Catholic bishops, priests, monks, nuns, and laity as "traitors". Their treachery, however, in the vast majority of cases (barring Spanish-inspired fanatics) rarely lay in anything more serious than refusing to assent to King Henry VIII's Act of Supremacy of 1534, which made the king supreme governor of the English Church and formally excluded papal authority from England. They were executed simply for continuing in their loyalty to the Catholic faith of their English and European ancestors – a faith which King Henry himself had passionately defended up to 1533. It was this new Act of Supremacy that led to Lord Chancellor Sir (Saint) Thomas More (*A Man for all Seasons*) losing his head in 1535, and to the barbarous judicial murder of numerous Jesuit priests such as St Edmund Campion and St Ambrose Barlow who, over the ensuing century, would go to the butcher's block for nothing more wicked than taking the sacraments to beleaguered Catholic households around England.

Of course, one is not denying that Protestantism had its own equally brave martyrs, burnt during the Catholic Queen Mary's short reign in the 1550s and immortalized in John Foxe's *Book of Martyrs* (1563). And Protestantism had its own great strengths and great glories, most notably the use of vernacular languages in worship and in accessible printed Bibles. But what is relevant to my argument is that the Protestants began the job of vilifying the Middle Ages through their vilification of the Catholic Church. And when science began to occupy an increasingly prominent place in the cultural agenda, the Middle Ages came under especial attack, for why had science not "progressed" in the days between the last Greeks and us "moderns"? This way of thinking, moreover, was natural to Robert Hooke, the pioneer of experimental science and a leading early Fellow of the Royal Society, in the early 1660s. As he spelled out in the surviving manuscript of a lecture which he delivered to the Royal Society on 4 December 1689, these times were backward. Indeed, Hooke, the son of an Isle of Wight clergyman and educated at Westminster School and Christ Church, Oxford, with an array of bishops, senior Anglican clergy, and learned laymen among his friends (including the devout Robert Boyle), was a Protestant to his fingertips, with no love of the Church of Rome. In his lecture he writes off the entire medieval age – "the Darknesse of those times" – as a scientific wilderness, with only two exceptions. One was Pope Sylvester II (elected AD 999), a French mathematician and supposed designer of clockwork; while the other was Friar Roger Bacon of Oxford, the alchemist and optician. For Hooke, science proper came into existence not much before he himself was born in 1635, when the telescope, magnetic devices, and other new instruments began to change the world through experimental knowledge. And Hooke was by no means unique in his day, for what impressed him was how knowledge of geography, optics, astronomy, mechanics, physiology, and practically everything else had advanced by leaps and bounds since the end of "the Darknesse of those times".

Yet the more modern historical scholarship investigates the culture of medieval Europe, the more sophisticated and elaborate that culture becomes. For while Hooke was correct in finding very little *experimental*, inquisitive, research-driven science in the Middle Ages, this could hardly in fairness be used as an accusation against the culture of that time. Not until the great oceanic voyages of discovery after 1480, and their knock-on effect on the problem of interpreting new knowledge and devising new instruments to make sense of that knowledge, was European science *forced* to confront a mass of fresh facts never dreamed of by the ancient Greeks. Such as why there are vast oceans and continents on the earth never mentioned by the Greek geographical writer Ptolemy, and why there are animals, birds, and reptiles never described by Aristotle, and winds and tidal currents never discussed by Pliny.

Science in the Middle Ages was not backward, so much as about other things. What drove it was not so much experiment, as mathematical geometry, taxonomy, logical deduction, and philosophical theology. On the other hand, let us be clear about one thing: no medieval scholar of any worth thought the earth was flat, and no educated person in 1492 believed that Columbus or the other early navigators would sail over the edge of it. (That seems to have been a folk myth propagated by American writers such as Washington Irving in the early nineteenth century.)

Indeed, one needs only to read the astronomical literature of the Middle Ages to realize that the spherical nature of the earth, about 6,000 or 8,000 miles across, was standard knowledge, and taught to university students from Salamanca to Prague. One has only, too, to read the first medieval astronomical treatise to be written in English, Geoffrey Chaucer's *Treatise on the Astrolabe* (c. 1381), to find that the spherical, mathematical geometry of the earth and the heavens was also standard knowledge. Inherited in unbroken succession from the Greeks, in fact, taught by the Venerable Bede to the young monks of Jarrow Abbey in AD 710, and encapsulated in John of the Holy Wood's (Johannes de Sacrobosco's) Latin textbook *De Sphaera Mundi* ("On the Sphere of the Earth") of c. 1240. All of these writers, moreover, told how the round shadow of the earth that fell across the lunar disk during a lunar eclipse could only be produced by a sphere.

"Aha!" I hear someone say by way of contradiction, "What about those flat-earth maps, such as that of c. 1300 preserved in Hereford Cathedral, showing the earth as a flat disk, with water around the edge?" These "Mappa Mundi" charts, however, were symbolic maps, placing Jerusalem at their centre, with countries such as the British Isles and Spain squeezed into the edge. They were *not* scientific teaching or direction-finding maps so much as spiritual maps, showing Christ crucified at the centre of the world. Just compare them to a map of the London Underground. Do the straight, curved, and diagonal coloured lines on the Underground map look like London? Of course not: it is a schematic representation of local stations and their relationships with each other. Ditto for the disk-like distortions of the "Mappa Mundi". On the other hand, if you look at the "Portolano" navigational charts of the Middle Ages, you find the countries and regions from the Baltic to North Africa drawn to an amazing standard of geographical accuracy. From the fourteenth century onwards, in fact, Europe developed a rich tradition of *scientific* cartography, as our museum collections testify.

No medieval undergraduate, moreover, could take his degree without demonstrating his knowledge of astronomy, mathematics, and geometry; while the medical faculties of Paris, Montpellier, Padua, and other great European universities regularly dissected human and animal cadavers as part of the MD degree.

But one major area where medieval Europe initiated experimentation was in the science of optics. Starting out from Aristotle's and Ptolemy's optical writings, which were further developed by Alhazen of Cairo in c. AD 1000 (whose Arabic *Optical Thesaurus* was soon translated into Latin), Robert Grosseteste, Roger Bacon, Theodoric of Freiburg, and others pioneered original researches into the refraction, reflection, and colours of light by 1350. Why, they asked, did the white light from the sun and stars become coloured when it passed through glass or water? And let us be quite clear that while Sir Isaac Newton after 1672 did fundamental work on the light spectrum, it was the classical Greeks, medieval Arabs, and, most especially, the medieval Europeans who made and publicized crucial breakthroughs in our understanding of light.

Roger Bacon, perhaps when living in Oxford around 1250, made a detailed study of the optics of the rainbow, and came to realize that the bow was simply part of a geometrical cone of light, with the sun at the apex of the cone. And taking measurements with a brass astrolabe, Bacon discovered what I have been bold enough to call the earliest law of experimental physics: namely, that the coloured light coming out of the clouds producing the rainbow unfailingly does so at an angle of 42° to the white sunlight going into the cloud. Bacon even found that the same geometry applied to "artificial" rainbows made by the spray thrown up by water wheels. You can get the same effect from a modern lawn sprinkler. Try it, with the sun directed behind you, and the spray going up high.

Then Theodoric of Freiburg took the idea further, discovering that it was not simply the cloud or mist of water that produced the colours and the 42° angle, but each individual droplet of water – perhaps many millions – each one both refracting and reflecting the sunlight. He even devised a "lab" experiment in optics: one of the earliest times a scientific researcher had tried to "model" a piece of nature under controlled conditions. And once again, it is so easy and safe that even young children could do it. Simply take a plain cylindrical drinking glass or jam-jar full of water, and place it on a piece of white paper in a darkened room. Prepare a good torch with a mask, so that it only emits a single narrow ray of light. (Theodoric probably used sunlight coming through a small hole in a window shutter.) Make sure your eyes get thoroughly dark-adapted, then shine the narrow torch beam along the table top with the light glancing into the glass of water. You will then notice a thin band of colours coming from the glass. And if you use a simple school protractor, you will find that the exiting "rainbow" on the paper forms an exact 42° with the white torchlight going in. In short, you are replicating the optical geometry of the rainbow on a table top. And if anybody tries to tell you there was no science in the Middle Ages, and that everyone superstitiously believed that one could find pots of gold at the end of a rainbow, you can confidently proclaim "Myth!"

Optics, light, and lenses were close to the heart and intellect of the Middle Ages, for not only did they provide elegant, geometrical demonstrations of meteorological phenomena, but they brought science and faith intimately together. For divine light was a luminous emanation of God. Genesis tells us that it was present at the creation, when it penetrated the darkness and illumined the world; Psalm 104 further tells us that God decked himself "with light as it were a garment", while Jesus came as "the Light" into the world.

And by the 1320s, the wonders of that newly devised technology, clockwork, were being applied to demonstrate God's glory. Around 1326, Richard of Wallingford, abbot of the great Benedictine house at St Albans and already a mathematician of European standing, designed and built the most sophisticated machine of the entire Middle Ages. This was not merely a clock to tell the time, for these weight-driven geared machines were already being used to mark the hours and ring bells, but a working model of the *universe* as it was then understood.

At that time, the best geometrical and observational evidence pointed to the hypothesis that all the astronomical bodies rotated around the earth. (There would be no physical, measured proof that the earth moved in space until 1728.) So Abbot Richard used gears, weights, ratchets, and levers to set up a machine that depicted the sun, moon, and stars rotating accurately around a central earth. Indeed, for 200 years it was one of the mechanical wonders of Europe, and pilgrims coming to the Shrine of St Alban the Martyr were fascinated to see how human intellect and hands could mirror the geometrical perfection of God's cosmos. Tragically, the great clock vanished at the Reformation – almost certainly smashed by Protestant zealots as a Popish bauble. But luckily, descriptions and drawings of its ingenious gearing survive, and a replica now ticks away in the monastic church which became St Albans Cathedral in the sixteenth century.

Finally, it was medieval scholars who touched upon concepts that would not really re-emerge – albeit in a different context – until the "new physics" of the twentieth century. For example, in Oxford around 1330, Thomas Bradwardine was asking questions about infinity, for could not an infinitely powerful God create an infinity of worlds if he chose to do so? Did time exist in heaven? Or, as St Augustine had argued, was it restricted to the cosmos governed by orbiting astronomical bodies? So were the dead outside time? And how could God create everything from nothing – which he clearly had done? What was matter really made of? And Nicholas of Cusa and Nicole de Oresme in Europe, and the famous Merton College Oxford geometers, pursued all kinds of ideas about time, space, and relative motion.

It is true that none of these men had telescopes or cyclotrons as twenty-first-century scientists do. Rather, they came to their ideas from philosophy, geometry, and "thought experiments" based upon trying to deduce what powers an infinite, loving creator God might choose to exercise. It was, indeed, a world of extraordinary breadth and ingenuity, in which classical and contemporary science, the properties of nature, the perfection of mathematics, logic, philosophy, and theology all came together.

And surely, they must have got into serious trouble with "the church" for entertaining such ideas? The answer is that none of them did.

Thomas Bradwardine and Nicole de Oresme became Roman Catholic bishops, and Nicholas of Cusa was a cardinal. But the plain fact is that, unless they doubted the nature and powers of God, academics in European universities enjoyed a remarkable degree of freedom in the pursuit of ideas, for surely (and most scholars in the universities were friars, deacons, or priests) these intellectual explorations could only *add* to mankind's awareness of the glory of God.

And also let us remember that, in firm contradiction to standard modern mythology, the medieval church was in no way biblically fundamentalist. For St Augustine – perhaps the most influential early theologian in the thought of medieval Europe – had pointed out in his commentary on Genesis after AD 401 that the physical world described in Genesis – with its flat earth and tent-like sky – was not the same as the spherical physical world and sky known to the Greeks. But this did not invalidate the Bible, for the Bible's primary message – about God creating everything from nothing, humanity being in God's image, God's love, and the saviourship of Jesus Christ – remained unchanged.

I am aware that I have spent a great deal of time on the Middle Ages and its rich intellectual culture. But I have done this in the hope of countering one of the most pervasive and grotesque myths in the whole history of the relationship between science and Christianity.

The Myth of the "Enlightenment"

In diametrical opposition to the myth that the Middle Ages were dark and repressive is the myth that with the "Enlightenment", so called, came an age of light, freedom, self-expression, justice, and modernity. And central to this liberation was the naming and shaming of traditional Christianity, and especially – no prizes for guessing correctly – the Roman Catholic Church. And while maybe not quite as bad as the "Papists", the Church of England, with its rich bishops sitting in the House of Lords and well-beneficed clergy who trampled on "the people", did not follow far behind. More laudable were the "Dissenters", who stood proudly free from the big, oppressive denominations – Baptists, Congregationalists, some Presbyterians, and Methodists – but especially approved were the hard-working, un-superstitious, peaceful Quakers, and the rationally minded Unitarians.

Separating the Enlightenment from the Dark Ages was the "Renaissance", the great reawakening of the Western mind from its 1,000-year-long medieval slumber. And what a star-studded era this Renaissance was, complete with giants such as Leonardo da Vinci, Michelangelo, Sir Francis Drake, and Shakespeare! It was also during this reawakening (the term "Renaissance" was first used in its present-day sense by the Swiss cultural historian Jacob Burkhardt in 1860) that real art was rediscovered, from its lost Greek prototypes, as well as science.

Of course I am not undermining for a moment the genius of the Italian and wider Renaissance of the late fifteenth and sixteenth centuries. Its brilliance is beyond dispute. But what I am challenging is its perceived surgical separation from what had gone before. And there are, moreover, two features of this Renaissance movement which sit incongruously with the imagined "liberation from the Middle Ages" ideal of the age. First, much of the patronage of the Italian Renaissance in particular came not from anti-medieval proto-secularists but from popes, cardinals, bishops, and devoutly Catholic lay patrons. You only need to visit Rome or Florence to have that plain fact hammered home. And secondly, we often forget that the "Renaissance" was deeply Christian and theological at heart, in spite of its fondness for playing with Greco-Roman pagan motifs. And that north European phenomenon which we call the Protestant Reformation, with Luther, Calvin, and Queen Elizabeth I, and then the Roman Catholic Counter-Reformation, were just as much an integral part of that same age as were the secular Mona Lisa, Shakespeare's *A Midsummer Night's Dream,* and Claudio Monteverdi's sensuous madrigals. And as far as science goes, those inspired evangelical Catholics, the Jesuits, not only made significant scientific discoveries, but taught the new sciences in places as far-flung as Peru and China.

On a more careful historical inspection, therefore, the nice, clean break which popular mythology would have us believe took place between the end of the Dark Ages and the Renaissance turns out to be non-existent. And how does this Renaissance lay the foundations for a supposed "Age of Reason" or "Enlightenment"? The answer is simple: it does not. Just as the notion of "the Renaissance" as a historical category really made its appearance in the mid nineteenth century, so "the Enlightenment" likewise transpires to be the creation of scholars with their own cultural and usually anti-Christian axes to grind. The *Oxford English Dictionary*, for instance, ascribes the word "Enlightenment" as specifically describing the aims and methods of the eighteenth-century philosophers to J. H. Stirling in his *Secret of Hegel* (1865), page xxvii: "Deism, Atheism, Pantheism and all manner of *isms* due to Enlightenment", and "Shallow Enlightenment, supported on such semi-information, on such weak personal vanity".

In short, therefore, the terms "Middle Ages", "Renaissance", and "Enlightenment", along with "English", and "Industrial" and "Scientific" "Revolution", have very little to do with the perceptions of the real people who lived in the periods to which they are applied, but are *post-factum* historians' categories, imposed by the present upon the past. (Designations including the suffix "Revolution", while of established usage for dramatic political events, when applied to intellectual changes were generally the invention of twentieth-century Marxist historians, for such scholars tended to interpret history as a series of clashes and turnabouts in which the radical, modern, and "freethinking" ideas overrode the more traditional and Christian to supposedly bring about "progress".)

The "Enlightenment" age is generally thought to run from around 1650 to 1800: from the time when "science" began to replace "superstition" as a yardstick of authority. Yet when one analyses this subsequently crowned "Age of Reason", one finds that the popularly perceived progressive *versus* backward, scientific *versus* superstitious, and libertarian *versus* enslaved categories dissolve away, as grand theory is corroded by the potent acid of plain historical fact. Let us start by looking at science and religion within the period, and in particular, the bogey of Roman Catholicism.

One thing that rapidly emerges from the evidence is that Roman Catholics were not only fully active in the scientific advances of the day, but many of science's leading practitioners were in holy orders. The popes, for instance, from 1582 had maintained a full-scale, state-of-the-art astronomical observatory within the Vatican City itself. Father Christopher Clavius and several other Jesuit priest-astronomers worked there, and became pioneers of telescopic astronomy after 1610. This observatory produced front-rank published research right through the seventeenth and eighteenth centuries, and in the nineteenth century Father Angelo Secchi, SJ, became one of the founders of the new science of the spectroscopic chemical analysis of the sun and stars. In the twentieth century, the observatory moved out of the Holy City, due to increasing atmospheric pollution, to the Papal Summer Residence at Castel Gandolfo a few miles away (which I have visited), although the Vatican's main research observatory today is located under the pristine skies of the Arizona desert. Over four centuries this observatory has produced world-class science, and simply took the "Enlightenment" in its stride.

In addition to devout Catholic scientists, ordained and lay, in a variety of disciplines ranging from natural history and medicine to astronomy, physics, and geology (the Danish-born Nils Steno, anatomist, physiologist, and pioneer of fossil geology, died a cardinal in 1686), the "Enlightenment" period produced legions of sincere Christian scientists who were Protestants, some surprisingly ecumenical. One finds them in Leiden, Berlin, Geneva, Copenhagen, Stockholm, and all over Scotland. And perhaps nowhere does one encounter more Protestant Christians in science than in the Fellowship of the Royal Society of London, for from its foundation in 1660 until well into the Victorian age not merely sincerely religious, but even ordained, scientists – including some bishops and even Roman Catholics – abounded in the Society. Some held top official positions in the science establishment, such as the Astronomers Royal and Directors of the Royal Observatory, Greenwich. And with the exception of the layman Edmond Halley, who held office as Astronomer Royal at Greenwich between 1720 and 1742, all four of the other men who directed the Royal Observatory between 1675 and 1811 were Anglican priests. Likewise, the professors of astronomy and experimental philosophy (physics) at Oxford and Cambridge during the "Age of Reason" were invariably Anglican clergymen, while in Scotland many ministers of the Presbyterian Kirk were actively involved in academic science. And the "parson naturalists", or Anglican and other Christian-denomination clergymen who were noted authorities on botany, zoology, and meteorology, were everywhere. The Revd Gilbert White was a renowned example, and his *Natural History of Selborne* (1789) remains a classic, while the Revd Stephen Hales, Minister of Teddington, was not only an FRS and Royal Society Copley Medallist – the "Nobel Prize" of the age – but undertook, and published, fundamental research in gas chemistry, chemical statistics, and experimental physiology. Hales was, among other things, the first scientist to demonstrate experimentally the cardiac systolic blood pressure. The Oxford Doctor of Medicine who successfully treated King George III for mental illness in 1788–9, moreover, was the *Reverend* Dr Francis Willis, who held jointly both clerical and medical qualifications. And the next time you take an aspirin-related medicine, just remember the Revd Edmund Stone, of Wadham College, Oxford, whose researches into the "fever-breaking", or anti-pyretic, properties of willow bark, first tried out upon his Oxfordshire parishioners, were published in the *Philosophical Transactions* of the Royal Society in 1763. Indeed, parson-doctors were a common feature on the British "Enlightenment" landscape, for the physical cure of body and the spiritual cure of soul were seen as inextricably connected.

Devout laymen were even thicker on the ground. Dr Thomas Willis in the 1660s (no relation to the Revd Dr Francis Willis) laid the foundation for our modern understanding of the functioning of the brain, yet saw no incongruity between his neurophysiological researches and his deep High Church Anglican faith, as we will see in Chapter 8. And even 160 years later, between 1810 and 1860, the Oxford physician and professor of chemistry, Dr Charles Daubeny, was a devout Christian and a regular attender of his college (Magdalen) chapel.

Over the years I have collected details of the names and researches of quite literally *scores* of devoutly Christian men of science, lay and ordained, who were active throughout the "Age of Reason", and who saw no conflict whatsoever between their faith and their science. Indeed, quite the reverse; for many explicitly stated how they saw their science as complementing and enhancing their belief in a beneficent deity.

And I have even found a small but growing number of women, especially wives of clergymen, who had an active and intelligent interest in medicine, and often ran free – and very competent – medical services for the poor. Mrs Elizabeth Tillotson, wife of Archbishop of Canterbury John Tillotson FRS, in the late seventeenth century, was one such female medical practitioner. Her famous purgative ale was praised, and consumed in considerable quantities by the hypochondriacal Robert Hooke FRS, when visiting his archbishop friend in Lambeth Palace and elsewhere.

Now while there were ordained men of science engaged in the very front rank of scientific research, I am not claiming that *all* of them were "scientists" in the modern sense. Many ordained FRSs, rather, would have been enthusiastic scientific amateurs, and most notably, they would have been active *friends* of science. As such, they would have promoted scientific understanding, encouraged others to look at the stars, collected exotic creatures, maybe dissected cadavers, contrived useful inventions, conducted chemical researches, or run a free dispensary from the vicarage. But most of all, they would have seen their science and their Christian faith as melded inextricably together, and in no way in conflict. And all of this in sharp contradiction to the secular "Enlightenment" story of science needing to break free of Christianity, which we must knock firmly on the head and expose for the myth that it is.

But, you might ask, what about all those great men who strove to set humanity free from bondage and superstition during the "Age of Reason", such as Voltaire, Rousseau, or Diderot? Who can deny the wit and brilliance of Voltaire, the seemingly deep humanity of Rousseau, and the visionary scholarship of Diderot and his *Encyclopédie*? But with the exception of the great scholarly enterprise of the *Encyclopédie* (1751–80), which would inspire *Encyclopaedia Britannica* (1768–71) and other works that aimed to marshal the whole of human knowledge for universal consultation, what did the predominantly French *philosophes* of the "Enlightenment" actually achieve? They certainly talked a great deal, corresponded, and published. They looked with hungry eyes at the free press with its openness to ideas in England, which the autocratic monarchs of their own countries in Europe, sometimes assisted by powerful Catholic bishops and ecclesiastical politicians, often did their best to control. For we must remember that the Roman Catholic Church was never a unified whole, and that French, Italian, German, and Spanish cardinals and their respective monarchs often politicked furiously against each other, and with pro- or anti-Vatican factions within the church. And the Jesuits were often in trouble with the "hierarchy": intellectually radical, cleverly argumentative, and often on the side of the poor, as in Latin America, where the Jesuit missionaries sometimes championed the rights of the Indians against the new Spanish colonial landowners. For were not *all* people equal in Christ?

But it is probably Jean-Jacques Rousseau that most people have come to see as typifying the "Enlightenment". Born in 1712 the son of a Protestant watchmaker in Geneva, he ran away, became a Roman Catholic, and thereafter a freethinker. Yet with the best will in the world, it is hard to think of him as other than an opportunist and a hypocrite. Starting out as a musician and composer in Paris, his charm and winning ways with aristocratic ladies seem to have obtained for him something of a livelihood. But it was his atheist friend Diderot who suggested that Rousseau should compete for the Dijon Prize Essay with a novel idea. Instead of following the usual line of going on about science and progress, Rousseau's winning essay argued a "back to simple nature" approach. For simple folks were more "true" than sophisticates. Indeed, the idea propelled him into celebrity – and the company of even more aristocratic ladies. For was not man "born free, but everywhere in chains", as kings, priests, and traditional Christian morality cramped our natural human goodness with its power-serving rules and regulations?

The shock waves of Rousseau's thinking still reverberate in modern liberal society, where they have inspired all manner of movements, such as "the child is always right" educational psychology, and (mixed in with strands drawn from subsequent revolutionary philosophies) the middle-class student "drop out" culture of the 1960s, and even the anti-capitalist campsite protests of 2011.

But where Rousseau's spectacular hypocrisy and self-conceit were perhaps best seen was in his views on child-rearing and the simple life. His massively influential educational treatise *Émile* (1762) advocated no school or formal education for children, but just letting the little innocents be natural in the woods and fields, for this was the logical development of the anti-high-civilization stance that had won him celebrity. And to complete his new celebrity image, the harpsichord-playing, countess-seducing Rousseau now took what might be called a "trophy" peasant mistress, Thérèse le Vasseur, with whom he had five children. Yet far from being lovingly brought up as sons and daughters of nature, nurtured in some carefree cottage in the woods, all of them were promptly dumped in orphanages, so as not to impede their father's career as an anti-establishment, anti-clerical, freedom-loving son of nature! We will meet Jean-Jacques again in Chapter 13.

I write much about Rousseau because the myths he generated about freedom and nature went a long way towards colouring our modern-day picture of "Enlightenment". They were also influential, after 1789, in framing French Revolutionary ideals of *"Liberté, Égalité, Fraternité"*. But when the traditional bonds of French society broke down under the impact of revolution, what rapidly replaced them was not Romantic idealism and universal beneficence, but savagery, fanatical ideological intolerance, and then military dictatorship.

Yet if you look at humanitarian culture during the "Enlightenment" age, you *do* see genuine progress. The only problem is, as far as the standard "Age of Reason" line runs, it happened not in a secular, but in a deeply *Christian*, context. And it happened in the British Isles, not in France.

Take, for example, the issue of slavery, which was a trade of enormous economic importance in the eighteenth century, as black people were shipped out by the million from the Congo region of Africa to Portuguese Brazil and the British and French Caribbean. Yet the first to condemn that trade were Christian Quakers. By the 1760s a movement had begun to grow in England – encompassing Anglicans and Methodists as well as Quakers – that would lead to William Wilberforce and Thomas Clarkson getting the trade outlawed in 1807. Yet in the midst of the windy libertarian rhetoric of the French Revolutionary and early Napoleonic period, Wilberforce was unable to get the "Enlightenment" French Assembly to outlaw the trade in their own vessels. Indeed, in 1791, when French-owned slaves in Haiti, hearing of revolution back in France, rose in bloody rebellion against their owners and declared their own freedom, the French government sent shiploads of soldiers to put the revolt down by force – and failed. Conversely, what Wilberforce and the British Christian evangelicals did was to legally buy land in West African Sierra Leone, and found Freetown, a new settlement to which liberated slaves could be repatriated and live on equal legal terms with white people.

And was not the Methodist movement of John and Charles Wesley in eighteenth-century England a force for liberty? Methodism encouraged ordinary folk to study and propagate the gospel, empowering miners and milkmaids. It has been suggested that Methodism was one of the major reasons why French Revolutionary ideas never took much hold in England, for it gave a self-respect, courage, and campaigning Christian spirit to believers. And by the time of the Napoleonic Wars, in Nelson's time, Methodists, Anglicans, and other evangelicals formed an influential body of opinion within the armed forces – both men and officers. Sir Charles Middleton, Admiral Lord Barham, whose global naval strategy made possible Nelson's victory at Trafalgar in 1805, was a powerful Anglican evangelical voice in Parliament, a friend of Wilberforce, and a passionate slave trade abolitionist.

And on into the early nineteenth century, *all* of the great movements of social reform – from prison reform to factory reform, from the abolition of child and female labour in coal mines to movements to punish cruelty to animals – came *not* out of "the Rights of Man" rhetoric, but out of a Christian conscience.

So let us lay aside the myth that the "Enlightenment" somehow liberated humanity from ignorance and oppression. Great scientific discoveries continued to be made by Catholic and Protestant Christians across Europe, and the great humanitarian movements, all of which helped make the world a truly better and more just place in practical terms, were largely triggered by the Christian conscience and not by "Enlightenment" idealism.

What the "Enlightenment" really was, however, was a great elite talking-shop in which gentlemen in brocade coats and ladies in rich silks, it was said, "talked about freedom and the Rights of Man once the servants had gone to bed"!

5

The Historical Roots of Anti-Christianity
Part 2: Myths of Changing Circumstances

In the previous chapter I confronted two of the most deeply entrenched myths that are still wheeled out with monotonous regularity to demonstrate the "backwardness" of Christianity and the "progressiveness" of so-called "Enlightenment" values. But what I shall do now is look at some of the less well-known intellectual developments that have also been seen as striking blows at the roots of Christianity.

The Problem of Eternal Damnation

Christ spoke to many audiences and individuals in the Gospels, including simple working folk, Jewish academics and liturgical lawyers, Roman officials, self-righteous rich men, tax collectors, lunatics, prostitutes, and thieves. And if one is not aware of the context and the circumstances of the person to whom he speaks on a given occasion, one could end up being confused, for, in most of his encounters with people, Jesus tailors his teaching to the understanding and actions of those to whom it is directed, rather than enforcing inflexible rules.

One body of teachings which had become something of a problem by the nineteenth century was that relating to eternal damnation. Was damnation for *ever*, or for a finite period? And was it not unfair for sins committed *in time* to be punished *in eternity*? For in many places in the Gospels, as well as in St Paul's letters, the message comes across loud and clear that if you repent and turn to God, you will be saved, no matter how vile your former sins. Yet how does this sit with the parable of Lazarus and the rich man in Luke 16? Here Jesus is approached by a self-satisfied, wealthy man requesting spiritual advice, and Jesus tells him a parable of a rich man who in life cared nothing for the welfare of Lazarus the beggar, but after death found himself incapable of repentance because he was now in hell, and no good intentions would get him out. So is Jesus saying that if you die unrepentant you will burn for evermore, irrespective of how much the scorching flames make you cry out for mercy, or how you may long for temporary release in order to warn easy-living relatives?

It did, after all, seem so very harsh, and to many Victorians in particular it was a matter for much soul-searching. When Charles Darwin's generous and genial freethinking father, Dr Robert, died in 1848, powerful surviving strands from his old Christian upbringing, and, no doubt, the sincere Christian faith of his wife Emma, caused Charles agonies of depression and spiritual malaise, in spite of the fact that he had largely abandoned formal Christian belief by that time. Could the good Doctor be damned eternally for his honest and peaceable beliefs, and could Charles find a similar fate awaiting himself when the time came? The terrors of hell, it seemed, could still haunt those who no longer believed in it!

But why was eternal damnation more troublesome to the Victorians than to medieval people? There is no simple answer, although I would suggest that much came from the sheer starkness of a Protestant death: especially if your faith – or former faith – contained more than a trace of Puritan hellfire, which was not uncommon for many English people. For a Roman Catholic, however, be he or she medieval or Victorian, prospects after death could be much kinder. Instead of a sudden Protestant switch from deathbed to awesome reckoning before the potentially stern and searching Judge, the newly passed-over Catholic soul had more options available. There was First Judgment, in which your sins were weighed, and a sentence of purgation was prescribed in Purgatory – unless you were a manifest saint, in which case your soul passed directly to heaven to sit at God's right hand.

And while Purgatory was not at all meant to be a pleasant place – for here the ordinary mortal burnt off, as it were, his or her earthly sins – it was not the end. After Purgatory the soul faced the Last Judgment, which would take place at the end of time. Only then would you go to heaven or hell, depending in part on how you had weathered Purgatory. If your sins had been properly and repentantly "shriven" or cleansed away, then you could find felicity with God and the saints, in eternal bliss. Indeed, not unlike the way in which an earthly prison sentence could hopefully lead a former criminal to repentance, reform, and a new life upon release.

And the Catholic Church possessed an array of spiritual instruments whereby Purgatory's pains could be ameliorated. Gifts to the poor during life, or pilgrimage, for example, could soften impending punishment for the sinner, while the prayers of the living for the souls of the departed could help ease the sufferings of those in Purgatory. And also in the hope of warding off an uncomfortable Purgatory, rich men and women might fund schools, hospitals, almshouses for the poor, or Oxford and Cambridge colleges, to give free social and medical care, accommodation, or education to generations yet unborn. And in return, the beneficiaries would say daily prayers for their benefactors' souls across the years or centuries to come. (Most Oxbridge colleges still say "Founder's Prayers", centuries after their founder's death, and 500 years after the Protestant Reformation officially outlawed prayers for the dead.) In this way, a rich benefactor could look forward to being spiritually cleansed after death, so that at the last he or she might enter the full glories of heaven. (A beautiful practice in my view, linking the living and the dead, benefactor and beneficiary, past, present, and future, the world and heaven.)

But to a Protestant, none of this comfort was available, for the sixteenth-century Reformers had reinterpreted or dismissed those biblical passages of Judas Maccabaeus in 2 Maccabees in the Old Testament Apocrypha, and in Matthew and St Paul to the Corinthians in the New, which seemed to speak of a cleansing taking place between death and Final Judgment. Instead, so the Protestant theologians argued (at least, until the nineteenth-century Anglo-Catholic Tractarians), the dead went straight to an eternal heaven if they were lucky, or else to an eternal and unameliorated hell directly following their last earthly breath. And this seemed especially cruel if all you had done wrong was think honest, sceptical thoughts, while at the same time being kind and generous to others, as old Dr Darwin had always been.

Yet even after the Reformation had dismissed Purgatory and intercession for the dead as a "Popish superstition", the ancient Christian tradition of founding almshouses, colleges, and hospitals continued. In part, of course, it was the acting out of gospel teaching that it was the duty of those who had much to give to those who had little, added to which the founding of educational charities in particular served as a useful mechanism through which the teachings of the Reformers could be securely handed on to the brightest of the next generation to establish and institutionalize Protestantism.

Coming from a separate direction, however, I would suggest that new and predominantly Protestant thinking about law and personal freedom also played a significant part in understanding humanity's spiritual destiny. Since Reformation times, Protestant jurists and legal thinkers had discussed the problem of how far a good Protestant had a right or even a duty to rebel against a Catholic monarch. Then in the 1640s and 1650s, as the world was "turned upside down" in the English Civil War and its aftermath, all manner of radical social ideas began to emerge – all of which were based on biblical texts, teachings, or examples. As we are all the children of Adam and Eve, and all in need of redemption from sin, are not all human beings equal? This equality is in many ways implicit in the writings and recorded speeches of the radical Protestant Levellers, "Free-Born" John Lilburne and Richard Overton and others in the 1640s, and would find a more philosophical expression in the second of John

Locke's *Two Treatises on Civil Government* (1690). Were not humans intended by God to actively seek godly happiness and social justice in this world? Indeed, as in so many currents of thinking, it was in the Middle Ages that radical Christian egalitarianism had found early expression in England, when, in the 1370s, the itinerant priest and political preacher John Ball popularized the jingle "When Adam dalf [delved] and Eve span, Who was then a gentilman?"

Of course, on the one hand it is easy to see how this kind of thinking stimulated many new currents of ideas by 1800. It could, for instance, when robbed of its Christian spiritual dimension, be adapted to justify the secular "Rights of Man" movements of the eighteenth century. And there again, in its Christian context, it could inspire and inflame the movement to abolish slavery. For justice could be seen as possessing a human, worldly, and political, as well as a spiritual, dimension.

So when one adds this largely secular approach to justice and fairness to the growing power of the science and technology of the age, plus anti-spiritual, future-oriented physical philosophies such as positivism, one begins to see why eternal damnation came to repel so many well-meaning people. And one sees how that repulsion could help to drive one away not only from thoughts of hell, but from Christianity itself, as the old ghost of eternal damnation still haunted increasingly secular minds like that of Charles Darwin, in times of crisis or bereavement. And it still does today.

Biblical Criticism, "Myth", and Early Biblical Archaeology

Biblical criticism, as a term, has often given rise to much misunderstanding. It does not, in its proper academic sense, necessarily imply that the Bible is being criticized in a nasty, sneering, or unbelieving way, for "criticism" in this context means analysis and elucidation – making clearer, in fact. On the other hand, it has to be admitted that some honestly conceived criticism (often styled "higher criticism"), especially over the past two centuries, has fed currents of unbelief. For certain aspects of "higher criticism" thinking have been gleefully seized upon by atheists, who have used them to present the Bible as no more than made-up Jewish fairy tales, with "the church" hoodwinking simple folk into believing nonsense as a way of furthering its unscrupulous grip. But more of this myth shortly.

In fact, biblical criticism is as old as the Bible itself. The pre-Christian Jewish rabbis applied critical thinking to their own Hebrew books, while early church scholars, such as St Athanasius, Eusebius, St Gregory, St Augustine, and St Jerome, analysed the Old and New Testament texts with critical minds. First, they had to decide which sections of the Jewish Bible, with its rich traditions of prophecy, vision, law, historical narrative, and wisdom, should go into the Christian Bible. For it was by no means a simple or an obvious task, especially as the four Gospels and the Epistles had, by custom, come into fairly standard liturgical use by the early second century AD. Indeed, sorting through the enormous manuscript literature about Jesus generated within decades of the crucifixion, and deciding what was canonical and of a piece, and what was aberrant and should be excluded, was a mammoth undertaking. The four Gospel narratives, Acts, St Paul's letters, and Revelation tied in with Old Testament messianic prophecies, such as those of Isaiah, Daniel, Ezekiel, and others and the Psalms, and could thus be viewed as authentic; whereas others, such as the later "Gnostic" gospels of Judas and Mary Magdalene, clearly came from a different, often much later, Greek philosophical speculative tradition.

No one has ever claimed that the Bible, unlike the holy books of some other religions, fell down from heaven perfect and in one piece. Indeed, right from the word "go", its production was first a customary and then a collaborative scholarly exercise. And very much in keeping with the Greco-Roman democratic "civic virtue" tradition within which Christianity grew up, the hammering out of the biblical canon of texts was done by inspired, devout, and critically minded learned men who worked together and held meetings and "councils" of the early church, such as at Nicaea and Chalcedon. And very crucially, these men prayed to God for guidance in their deliberations.

It was also by this process of scholarly analysis, discussion, and meetings that the great doctrines of Christianity, such as the incarnation, the resurrection, and the relationship between Father, Son, and Holy Ghost in the Trinity, were elucidated. For another myth frequently trotted out by secularizers is that all the church's key beliefs were made up centuries after the events to which they purported to relate. But once again, this only exposes the ignorance of the atheists, for these doctrines, even if not formulated *canonically* until centuries after the events described (such as the adoration of the Virgin Mary), can be traced back to specific passages in Scripture, to particular textual principles, or to well-recorded early church usage, for all doctrines were, and are, intended to provide clearly thought out mental and spiritual hooks upon which people could anchor the Christian message.

And perhaps the greatest of these early church scholars was St Augustine himself, writing between c. AD 390 and 430. His great commentary on Genesis, AD 401–15, for instance, provides an excellent example of how *un*-naïve these men were, for, among other things, he looked at the cosmology of the Mosaic books, with its flat earth and curved sky, and related them to the spherical earth and sky of Greek learning. In this context, however, one must remember that St Augustine was not what we might now call "writing about science". Rather, he was trying to prevent fellow-Christians from looking ridiculous when talking to well-educated pagans by defending ideas about cosmology which had long since been superseded and were known to be physically incorrect (a lesson of which many modern-day fundamentalists might profitably take note).

But what mattered was not the physics of Genesis, but the book's proclamation of the fact that God the Father was the source of all creation, that he had made the world from nothing, had created humanity in his own image, and loved his creation. A well-argued counter to simple fundamentalism, in fact.

And this tradition of elucidating "criticism" continued through the centuries. It continued through the supposed "Dark Ages", and was there at the Reformation, as the early Protestants came to exclude the

Jewish Apocryphal books from the official inspired scriptural canon, though the majority of the Reformers accepted the Apocrypha's value as a source of historical and edifying reading. Most of the Apocrypha was included as a useful Appendix to the Lutheran, Geneva, and 1611 Authorized Version Bibles, although the Puritans were instrumental in excluding it from later seventeenth-century printings, and it is still excluded from most "Protestant" Bibles today.

Martin Luther, the effective founder of Protestantism, moreover, expressed scholarly doubts about the full canonical status of James and Hebrews, and perhaps even Revelation, because they did not, in his view, contain a full expression of the doctrine of justification by faith. And some years later, in Geneva, John Calvin argued that St Peter had not actually written the second letter ascribed to him in the New Testament (it does, after all, argue more like a Greek philosopher or Greek-educated rabbi than a simple Galilean fisherman); while he also suggested that Psalms 74 and 79 were very late, dating from the Jewish Maccabean period of the second century BC, rather than from the Priest Asaph (to whom the Bible ascribes authorship) of the Davidic Kingdom of 700 years before.

Yet all of this, and what was to be written and argued by scholars over the next few centuries, is not what most people now think of as biblical criticism, for this "lower criticism" of textual details never questioned the essential uniqueness of the Christian revelation, but set out rather to clarify specific points. What so many people in the nineteenth and twentieth centuries *did* find disturbing, however, was the "higher criticism", which really began in the early nineteenth century.

For centuries the German universities, especially Tübingen, had enjoyed a high theological reputation. And it was to be there that higher criticism would be born: very much the child of German metaphysical philosophy. Engendered in part from the secular philosophies of the "Enlightenment", and in part from ancient Christian mystical traditions, higher criticism was by definition highly philosophical and often abstract, as it began to explore secular lines of thinking and attempt to apply them to theology. One such line was that of "mythos": did the ancient cultural narratives of the Greek poet Homer, Moses, or Jesus actually describe real people and real incidents, or were they – in the kindest sense – made up? Perhaps no less so than were the Germanic folktales of the kind being collected by the devoutly Protestant Brothers Jakob and Wilhelm Grimm, or those studied by Sanskrit and other Orientalist scholars who were beginning to translate into European languages the religious and cultural narratives of India and China?

And in addition to the "mythos" school of ancient history interpretation, there was the incalculable influence of German metaphysics, beginning in a serious way in the eighteenth century with Immanuel Kant, but especially taking European thought by storm in the teachings and writings of Georg Wilhelm Friedrich Hegel by 1820.

Legendarily difficult to understand, Hegel postulated a developmentalism in the world of ideas: an early, abstract philosophical expression of that way of looking at life which decades later would be seen as "evolutionary". But Hegel did not deal with people or animals so much as with abstract philosophical ideas. For an idea rarely rested for long without challenge. First, in Hegel's system of thinking, would be the *thesis*, or original argument; next would come the *antithesis*, to challenge it; and from this conflict would emerge the *synthesis*. It was, in many ways, a radical new development of the logical system of Aristotle.

Hegel's intellectual techniques could be used to envisage or analyse all sorts of philosophical situations, creating as they did methods or patterns for thinking. Yet when they were applied to religious texts, they could give rise to all manner of curious ideas, many of which alarmed more orthodox Christian scholars. The Revd Canon Edward Bouverie Pusey, Regius Professor of Hebrew at Christ Church, Oxford, was concerned when his warnings to his own students about the dangers of the new German philosophy proved counter-productive, and only stimulated them to read German metaphysical theology and, in some cases, to undertake periods of study in Germany!

But the Tübingen theologian and disciple of Hegel who sent unintended shivers through Victorian Christendom was David

Friedrich Strauss, for the ideas contained in his *Das Leben Jesu* (1835–6) would come, for many people, to epitomize the essence of biblical criticism with all its horrors. In this work, Strauss analysed the life of Jesus from a non-transcendent, naturalistic, historical viewpoint. Rather than being the genuine incarnation of God, the Jesus of the Gospels was a character of late Jewish myth, built up by storytellers somewhere between the crucifixion and the supposed – very late – composition of the Gospels in the second century AD. To Strauss, the primitive church of Galilee and of St Paul could be interpreted in terms of the Hegelian dialectic, as the Jesus myth countered the pagan myths to produce a new dominant myth – Christianity.

Of course, Strauss's book was an exercise in Hegelian speculative philosophy, but it cost him his professorship. Then, some thirty years later, the French seminarian Ernest Renan lost his faith after reading German Hegelian philosophy and in his *La Vie de Jésus* (1863) produced his own explanation of the Christ story: was not the historical Jesus what we might now call no more than an attractive and charismatic local preacher, whose brief story got blown up out of all proportion by legend-builders? After all, positivistic styles of thinking in mid nineteenth-century Europe were coming to argue (as we saw in Chapter 3) that scientific naturalism was the only yardstick of truth, and notions such as miracle, transcendence, God-given morality, and salvation were really the outdated cultural fossils of a more primitive, unscientific stage of human progress. A nearly 200-year-old line of argument, indeed, that the New Atheists of today are so busy trying to convince us is daring and original!

There were, however, two home-grown British examples of biblical criticism that did cause serious ructions in the 1860s, which, in our modern-day obsession with men and monkeys during that decade, we have tended to lose sight of. The first of these was the publication, in 1860, of *Essays and Reviews*, a volume of essays written by seven eminent theological scholars which argued for a less rigid and more context-related interpretation of Scripture than was acceptable in certain quarters at that time. And included within the book's wider argument, and relating to the preceding section of this chapter, was a textually related plea for a less rigid interpretation of the doctrine of eternal damnation. Several thousand clergy, however, were quick to sign a petition *affirming* their belief in damnation, and there were successful legal attempts to have some of the essayists removed from their posts.

The second came in 1863 when, in good faith, John Colenso, bishop of the new Anglican Diocese of Natal in South Africa, published a work suggesting that the Pentateuch and Joshua, constituting between them the first six books of the Old Testament, might not actually have been written by Moses and Joshua, and might not be wholly authentic as historical sources. Colenso's Pentateuch study came, moreover, in the wake of his controversial 1861 commentary on St Paul's Epistle to the Romans, where once again eternal damnation had been called into question. It is clear, however, that Colenso – a popular and hard-working missionary bishop – had many supporters, both ordained and lay, and petitions and fighting funds to finance his legal resistance to being deprived of his see accumulated.

On the other hand, *Essays and Reviews*, Colenso, eternal damnation – and, to some extent, even responses to Darwinism – must be seen within the context of the wider Anglican politics of the mid nineteenth century, for at the time, the Church of England was neither a unified nor an especially happy institution. The new and powerful spiritual forces that had swept through late Georgian Britain had not only re-energized the once slothful church, but had also divided it. The Anglo-Catholic Oxford Movement of the 1840s, for example, had brought a sacramentalism and an approach to scriptural interpretation into Anglicanism which made many Low Church evangelicals, with their more "back to the plain word of Scripture" approach, see red, while the more liberal "Broad" Churchmen frequently angered them both. A modern reader might, therefore, be forgiven for being confused about how different groups of sincerely Christian scholars could rail at each other about the literal or more figurative interpretation of a particular passage of Scripture or ensuing doctrine. But all of these disagreements could, and still do, provide ammunition for those atheists who will gleefully seize upon any brickbat they can throw against Christianity, and that is why they must be addressed in a chapter attempting to trace the roots of anti-Christianity.

Yet there is one aspect of nineteenth-century Christian history that receives surprisingly little attention from present-day scholars and writers: the burgeoning Victorian fascination with the study of the Holy Land. Phasing in almost exactly, chronologically speaking, with the new Hegelian "higher criticism", yet running in diametrical opposition to it, was a growing passion to study, visit, and even excavate the Holy Land. Almost as if wanting to overturn the "myth" theory of biblical interpretation by actual physical proof, people began to descend in increasing numbers on the lands between Egypt and Mesopotamia, but most of all Galilee and Jerusalem, especially from about 1850 onwards.

Of course, at that time, a century before the foundation of the state of Israel, there were few Jews living in the Holy Land, although there were pockets of Coptic and Nestorian Christians which had hung on since antiquity. But since the seventh century, and particularly following the destruction of Christian Byzantium in 1453, the whole region had been overwhelmingly Muslim. By the late eighteenth century, however, and especially after the establishment of a Franco-English presence in the Middle East following Napoleon in the 1790s and the destruction of his fleet by Nelson in the Battle of the Nile in 1797, Egypt had become the first "Holy Land" country to open up to tourism. And by the 1860s, with steam boats on the Nile, growing numbers of well-to-do Europeans and Americans were coming, often Bibles in hand, to find the "Land of Goshen", where the Jews of the captivity had lived, or to explore the Sinai peninsula and try to identify the places described in Exodus. Arthur Penrhyn Stanley, Queen Victoria's future Dean of Westminster, and a group of gentlemen went to Egypt and then to rough it in the wastes of Sinai over the winter of 1852–3, and Stanley's resulting book, *Sinai and Palestine* (1856), became a major bestseller, going through over twenty editions by the early twentieth century, and stimulating others to follow in his footsteps.

It had been the American biblical scholar Dr Edward Robinson and the Arabic-speaking missionary Eli Smith, however, who received permission from local rulers to travel in Palestine in 1838, and got the ball rolling. Smith's book *Biblical Researches in Palestine* (1841), with its attempt to identify key scriptural locations, whetted Christian appetites on both sides of the Atlantic for tangible *evidences* of their faith. Indeed, it is my argument that at the same time as German higher criticism was apparently undermining faith, so the new scheduled steamships, hotels, organized tourism, and a growing well-off and leisured Euro-American middle class was fuelling a passion to show the Bible to be based on physical fact. Not myth, not a product of Hegelian or positivistic dialectic, but demonstrably *true*.

And these Victorians were willing to put their money where their mouths were. In 1864, for instance, a private subscription began the Palestine Exploration Fund, to use the latest scientific techniques to survey, measure, and excavate the Holy Land. (Egyptian archaeology was already in full swing by 1864.) And nine years after his first visit, Stanley returned to the Holy Land, in a party to show the holy places to the Prince of Wales – the future King Edward VII.

Tourism hit the Holy Land in a big way after 1869, when Thomas Cook of Northampton, an already highly successful package holiday and travel promoter, took his first group of middle-class English folk to see the Bible lands with their own eyes. Seeing the River Jordan for the first time, it was reported, Cook, a devout Baptist, waded in and immersed himself fully clothed, frock coat and stovepipe hat included, as did others. For were they not reliving the very act that the Bible said the historical John the Baptist had done to Jesus himself?

It has been estimated that Thomas Cook, along with his rival tour promoters in Europe and America, took more Christians to the Holy Land between 1869 and the early twentieth century than did all the crusading armies of the Middle Ages. Cook's first expedition accommodated travellers in a hired, sumptuous Bedouin-style travelling camp, complete with large tents, beds, chairs, portable kitchen, and servants, over the course of several weeks. But it was the growing volume of Western tourists that gave Palestine, just like nearby Egypt, its first modern hotels, with sanitation, hopefully clean water, and electric light well before the time of World War I. And what all the visitors wanted to see was Jerusalem, Bethlehem, Galilee, and the Jesus-related holy places, for, quite frankly, if all you wanted was sunshine and sea, by 1880 there was no shortage of package tours to take you on a comfortable train journey to the south of France or the Italian Riviera. It needed commitment to do the Holy Land, with its flies, camp beds, and necessity for armed guards.

Needless to say, these Holy Land package tours did not come cheap, but were aimed at that growing body of comfortably off middle-class folk who were not stuck for a hundred guineas or so, and could afford to spend a couple of months travelling abroad. And Great Britain, northern Europe, and America were producing such people in ever increasing numbers, as professional, mercantile, and industrial fortunes burgeoned. And these were exactly the same people who, so some argue, were losing their faith because of Darwinism, positivism, or biblical criticism, as they read Comte (or his English disciple Frederic Harrison), Strauss, or Renan in English translation. Yet no matter what, there were sufficient of these middle-class people not only to sustain Holy Land tourism, but also to subscribe to research and archaeological bodies such as the Palestine Exploration Fund.

Of all branches of archaeology, however, that of the Bible lands has probably received the most adverse criticism, on the assumption that you do not have an "open mind" if you go with a preconceived agenda. It is true that early claims to have found the ruins of Sodom and Gomorrah, direct evidences for the Flood of Noah and the plagues of Egypt, and Christ's tomb in the Garden of Gethsemane raised critical eyebrows, and rightly so, for one cannot properly archaeologize with a Bible in one hand and a shovel in the other. Yet what the real fruit of biblical archaeology has been is its provision of a wider context for the biblical world: from Sir Austen Henry Layard's discovery of the genuine ruins of the biblical Nineveh and Babylon in the 1840s, to Sir Leonard Woolley's 1920s excavations at Ur of the Chaldees in modern-day Iraq, to Dame Kathleen Kenyon's later digs in Palestine.

What archaeology has shown is that the world of the pharaohs, Sennacherib's failed siege of Jerusalem in the days of Isaiah, and Nebuchadnezzar's successful assault 130 years later were events in real time, as recorded in written texts, stone relief pictorial carvings, and archaeological artefacts. And while no one can reasonably expect that the three-year ministry of Jesus would have left any visible impact on Roman Palestine, archaeology nonetheless reveals a world that is congruent with New Testament narratives, as is the Romano-Greek world with that described in St Paul's travels.

Suffice it to say, however, that just as Heinrich Schliemann's excavations in Victorian Greco-Turkey disproved the then parallel classical orthodoxy that the world of Homer was one of myth, so the excavation of the Holy Land, from the Pyramids of Egypt to the ziggurats of Babylon and Ur in Mesopotamia, showed that the world of the Old and New Testaments was real, and a credible backdrop to what was described in the Bible.

So in a way, one might argue that what the higher criticism with its philosophical theories at first undermined, so later archaeology and evidence-hungry travellers helped to restore, as the "mythical Bible" *itself* became an outdated cultural myth.

Nationalistic Christianity

It is hard to calculate the damage Christianity suffered during the first half of the twentieth century through its association with specific nationalistic agendas. This is especially paradoxical when one bears in mind that from its very beginning Christ's message of peace and love was for *all* people: Jews and Gentiles – Galileans, Greeks, Romans, and by extension Africans, Asians, and then indigenous Americans, and the rest of the planet. And it was the nineteenth century that took Christianity to the furthest corners of the world via Protestant and Catholic missionaries. Missionaries who were no doubt wary of each other, nonetheless, as they remembered 200- or 300-year-old grudges, which included the York-born Catholic convert traitor Guy Fawkes on the one side and Sir Francis Drake's burning of the Cadiz fleet along with Spanish settlements in the New World on the other. Guy Fawkes was destined to become one of the enduring bogeymen of English culture, and is still burned in effigy on 5 November today (the date in 1605 when he attempted to blow up Parliament), while it was said that long after his death, in 1596, Spanish mothers would try to frighten naughty children into obedience by threatening them with "El Draco", or Drake!

But on the whole, Christendom was at peace with itself by the nineteenth century, as hostility between Protestants, Catholics, and Orthodox became largely limited to name-calling, tract-writing, depriving men of university chairs, and the occasional black eye. What came to matter much more was taking the faith to all people in all places, and by 1910 this enterprise had been a spectacular global success. And perhaps nowhere more than in Africa, as the peoples of the southern half of that vast continent in particular became passionate in their new faith. And they still are, as Islamic jihadi persecution produces modern-day Christian martyrs in Nigeria, Somalia, Ethiopia, and elsewhere. Persecution still steels the Christian soul, just as it did in the days of Nero and Diocletian. Rome now has its black, Asian, and Latin American cardinals; while by 2010 two of the Church of England's most popular, plain-speaking and controversial bishops were the Ugandan, the Most Revd Dr John Sentamu, Archbishop of York, and the Pakistani-born former Bishop of Rochester, the Rt Revd Dr Michael Nazir-Ali: the spiritual children of former missionaries, and now themselves missionaries in "secular" Britain, and both of them victims of anti-Christian and anti-libertarian persecution in their home countries.

But what circumstances led to Africans and Asians becoming missionaries to Christian Great Britain and Europe? Back to that small piece of the earth's surface, in fact, which little more than a century ago was the missionary powerhouse of the planet? We will be returning to this subject in Chapters 8 and 9, but suffice it to say at present that full-scale warfare between two of the great Christian nations and their allies in 1914 played a major part.

No one in 1901 could have reasonably foreseen World War I, for in that year Queen Victoria's son, grandsons, and one close relative by marriage either already ruled, or would soon rule, three countries which, with their empires, controlled millions of square miles of the earth's surface. They were King Edward VII and King George V of Great Britain, Kaiser Wilhelm of Germany, and Czar Nicholas of Russia. Three deeply Christian countries, two with the most advanced technological economies in history, and a third which was struggling to reform and "come up to date".

London and Berlin had so much in common. Both were essentially Protestant, yet with sizeable integrated Roman Catholic and Jewish minorities. And in addition to long-standing royal ties of blood and religion, Great Britain and Germany had many other links in business, science, technology, education, art, culture, and general understanding. Rather more, in fact, than Great Britain did with France, against whom she had fought regularly across the previous 800 years. We had never exchanged a shot in anger with Germany, and in several previous wars British troops had stood shoulder-to-shoulder with the Germans – and the Dutch – against Philip II of Spain, and Louis XIV and XV and Bonaparte of France. A war with our devout, hard-working, and honourable Teutonic cousin and friend seemed impossible.

And then all suddenly went mad in August 1914, as the two nations began to blow each other, and each other's allies, to bits in the fields of northern France. Then Russia came in, was beaten by the Germans, its royal family summarily murdered by the Bolsheviks, with Lenin, Trotsky, and others proclaiming atheism, communism, and Marxist Revolution.

It is hard for us, a century later, and almost desensitized by the subsequent genocides of Stalin, Hitler, Mao, and the other hordes of hell, to fully appreciate the numbing horror of the years 1914–18, when high Christian civilization suddenly seemed to commit suicide. And apparently out of a clear blue sky!

But it is not my purpose here to explore the causes of World War I, so much as to emphasize its spiritual damage. Why had God let it happen, people asked? Was not God a good Englishman, a good German, or the heavenly Father to the "Little Father", the Czar of Holy Russia, depending on the flag you flew? Had he not empowered his earthly children in northern Europe, and their cousins in North America, to take the light of the gospel to the "darkest corners" of creation, and in most cases, had not the inhabitants of those lands come to embrace it with a passion? And would not a global Christian Europe be an insurance policy for peace and prosperity into the future?

So *what* had gone wrong, when scarcely a single family on either side of the North Sea had not lost one or more of its beloved sons in the madness? Were the atheists right after all? Was it to freethinkers like Arthur Schopenhauer, Ludwig Andreas Feuerbach, Friedrich Nietzsche, or Bertrand Russell that we should be turning for fresh direction? To philosophical pessimism, to the "Will", to dialectical materialism, to scientific rationalism, to atheism? For the Christian imperial insurance policy had apparently crashed in our darkest hour!

This "nationalistic Christianity" and its sudden failure to maintain peace even within heartland Europe, I would argue, would become a major feature of anti-Christianity in the twentieth century.

The Growth and Power of Science

In addition to all the factors discussed above that may, for whatever reason, have fed a current of anti-Christianity, one cannot overestimate the sheer explanatory and life-transforming power of modern science. What might once have been ascribed to the direct finger of God, such as a lightning strike or a fortuitous recovery from the jaws of death, can now, in many cases, be explained by measured sequences of natural processes. And over the past 200 years in particular, these scientific explanations have grown too numerous to count.

On the other hand, while science's advancing power, from Newtonian gravitation theory to antibiotics and DNA, has been truly stupendous, its province is what might be called the "how" questions. *How*, for example, do the planets move? *How* is disease altered by scientific medicine? *How* do the components in the DNA double helix make us the individuals that we are?

Yet in addition to *how* things work, human beings are driven to ask "*why*" questions, for humans are interested not just in processes – *how* things happen – but in *why* they happen. From "Why am I the person that I am?" to "Why am I curious about the universe, when knowledge of the universe plays no part whatsoever in what I eat, or how safe I may be when walking down the street?" In short, matters that have no biological survival value at all!

And science, while triumphant in answering the *how* questions, cannot even begin to answer the *why* questions, for they belong to a non-physical category best dealt with by philosophy or theology. So when an atheist tries to convince you that *why* questions are a delusion, an irrelevance, or a waste of intellectual energy, then simply ask him or her, "Then *why* are you trying to convince me that you are right?" The bottom line is that spiritual and religious questions, and why we still search for answers to them, remain untouched by science. But more of this in Chapter 10.

6

Some Popular Myths about Science and Religion

We have seen in the previous chapter how very old hat and unoriginal the ideas of the New Atheists really are, and how they invariably repeat, in modern form, what has been around for centuries. But where, historically speaking, does the idea of science and Christianity in particular being in *conflict* actually come from, and why?

Christianity and Science in "Conflict": Two Nineteenth-Century American "Atheists"

During the last quarter of the nineteenth century, two distinguished American authors put their cards on the table, with a pair of books, whose pugnacious titles leave one in no doubt about what they are going to say. The first was Dr John William Draper's *History of the Conflict between Religion and Science* (1874), and the second Andrew Dickson White's *A History of the Warfare of Science with Theology in Christendom* (1896). Indeed, this seems plain fighting talk, reminiscent, perhaps, of that of Shelley's *Necessity for Atheism*, but written not as an anonymous piece of undergraduate bravado, but by two mature men of the highest intellectual standing, who were not afraid of putting their names on their title pages.

Draper was an eminent physician and professor of chemistry at New York University. The English-born son of a Wesleyan minister, he emigrated to America aged twenty in 1831, where members of his mother's family were already settled. Qualifying as a doctor, he not only went on to become a prominent academic physician in New York Medical School, but was a significant figure in both chemistry and astronomy. He took, for example, the first ever photograph of an astronomical body, the moon, in 1840. His deceased father's Wesleyan Methodism had long since been a thing of the past, however, as he had read Comte and become a positivist and an ardent devotee of the religion of scientism. For Draper, science became The Truth. He also developed his own "take" on positivism, which in 1859 he infused with the newly published evolutionary ideas of Charles Darwin, to produce a philosophy of biological and social progressivism.

Andrew D. White was an eminent academic historian and educator, co-founder and first president of Cornell University, and later US ambassador to Germany. He was a passionate believer in science and progress, who early in his career came to associate religious belief with anti-modern, anti-scientific values.

Both Draper's and White's books are replete with scholarship, ranging from classical and early church history to the latest advances in modern science. Furthermore, both men were committed to making the world a better place. So what made them so bitter about Christianity, and what led them to interpret history as a saga of conflict between foolish blind faith and ignorance on the one hand and enlightened scientific optimism on the other?

Of course, positivism coloured both. And like so many people of a positivistic turn of mind, Draper and White were inspired not only by Charles Darwin's *On the Origin of Species* in 1859, but also by his *The Descent of Man* of 1871, in which Darwin explored the human–primate connection.

One does not need to proceed very far into either author's book, however, to detect a distinct animus against Roman Catholicism. And I would suggest that the conservative Pius IX, pope from 1846 to 1878, was regarded with especial distaste, and seen as an anachronistic autocrat by the progressives. The contemporary promulgations of the

Vatican Council, and most of all its new 1870 doctrine that the Pope was theologically infallible, aroused them to fury. Indeed, Draper rehearses this whole scenario in his chapter XII, "The Impending Crisis", where he discusses "the dogmatic constitution of the Catholic faith" and "its denunciation of modern civilization".

Irrespective of how a person may regard Roman Catholicism and its history, no one can deny that the Catholic Church was facing political crisis in the nineteenth century. But this is perhaps best seen in the context of wider history. Since first the French Revolutionary and then the Bonapartist armies "liberated" and invaded Italy in the 1790s, the country had been in a state of political ferment, with outbreaks of civil war and efforts to found a largely secular Italian state after 1871. So Italy's history and apparent "progression" from a Catholic land in 1790 to a secular government and intelligentsia with the Vatican in visible retreat enthused many abroad who not only sympathized with the plight of "backward", un-industrialized, "priest-ridden" Italy, but also harboured their own animus against Christianity, which they saw epitomized in Pope Pius IX.

Andrew D. White, who very clearly in his writings, lectures, and actions saw himself as a crusader against Christian theology's involvement with science, acknowledged the work of Draper in his "Introduction", as well as making subsequent text references to his writings. White, however, may not have been an atheist as such, but rather someone who believed that science and religion occupied distinct spheres and should not be mixed. And interestingly enough, he presented himself as a "myth-buster". Indeed, in Volume Two, chapter 18, he lays into the "mythologies" not only of Christianity, but of Judaism, Islam, and Buddhism, and even into European folk tales. The message he sustains throughout the *Warfare* volumes is that mankind lay for centuries in the dark bondage of religious superstition, and that now, at last, science has come to illumine all!

Yet nowhere in this undoubted masterpiece of scholarship does he ask the question "Am I as blinkered in my materialist scientific adulation as peoples of the 'Dark Ages' were in their religion?" Time and again, he piles erudite bare fact upon fact to show how the superstitious ignorance of the past crumbled before the relentless power of science.

None of White's facts are in themselves incorrect, and it is all too easy for a reader to be beguiled by his meticulously marshalled notes and references, as to some degree I was myself when I first read his *Warfare* as an undergraduate! Yes, there really were unwashed monks who died from sundry pestilences; there were some ignorant Christians who thought the earth was flat; and there was a belief that mental illness could be ascribed to demonic possession. But that was not the whole story, and it was in the undisguised one-sidedness of White's argument that I first began to smell a rat. While, in fairness, White does mention medieval people who did not hold "superstitious" views about the natural world, he presents them as besieged minorities in a surrounding culture of darkness. But very often, his exceptions prove the rule. Having, for example, discussed superstitious flat-earth views, he goes on to cite Augustine, Ambrose, Bede, Albertus Magnus, Aquinas, Dante, Vincent of Beauvais, and others who argued that the earth was *spherical!* Only the most distinguished and influential thinkers of early Christendom, no less – *none* of whom suffered punishment for their views!

His presentation of medical "backwardness" is similarly one-sided. Yes, there were ignorant monks who thought soap and water were wicked luxuries, but there were lots of other monks and clergy who did not. What about the Cistercians, whose twelfth-century monasteries had the most advanced plumbing and clean water supplies of the age? Or the Benedictines, who treated hygiene as a necessary prerequisite for proper communal living? Mental illness was also understood to have organic causes, dating back to the much-lauded Hippocrates, as well as a demonic one. And while White mentions eminent medical men, such as William of Saliceto and Guy de Chauliac (a devout papal physician, incidentally), he sets them in enlightened isolation in an ocean of medical mumbo-jumbo! In spite of the abundance of classically based university medical faculties across Europe!

It is ironic, therefore, that two books, each written with the express intention of displaying the myths and fallacies of Christianity and its supposed antipathy to science, should themselves become foundation stones for one of the greatest myths of the modern world; namely, that science and the Christian faith must of necessity be at war with each other.

All Christians Are Really Biblical Fundamentalists

Time and again when engaging with anti-religious people one encounters the old notion that everyone *knows* that to be a Christian you have to believe every single word in the Bible. And preferably in the Authorized Version of 1611, complete with all the "thees" and "thous". But this is patent nonsense. It was certainly never a part of historic Christendom, for as we saw in Chapter 2, not only was the Bible in the form that we know it the result of careful sifting and scrutinizing of both ancient Jewish and Christian writings, but different parts of it have been re-evaluated and re-understood in the light of new knowledge over the past 2,000 years. This is what textual "criticism" has always been about, from the first century AD to the discovery of the Dead Sea Scrolls after 1948.

What the attackers of Christianity persistently fail to take on board is that Christian understanding has developed – and evolved – over 2,000 years. This does not mean that the church has "changed its mind" or become fuzzy, as the secularists like to claim, so much as that insights have deepened as Christian spiritual experience has broadened. The centrality of Christ's incarnation, resurrection, or saviourship has in no way been "explained away"; rather, we now know far more about the world in which Jesus lived and ministered and how language was used than we did in AD 1000 or 1800. And this means that we read texts differently, and more deeply, and can give them a better context than before linguistics, archaeology, Egyptology, Assyriology, and new studies into the Greco-Roman world began in their modern form in the 1790s. Likewise with geology for our understanding of natural phenomena in the Old Testament, for until the seventeenth century we had no real insights into earth-forming processes other than what was said in Genesis.

On the other hand, we should remind atheists who go on about fundamentalism or Christians "changing their minds" that scientists are always changing theirs. In 1500, for instance, the leading astronomers in Europe believed that the spherical earth was fixed in the centre of the universe, while in 1820 the best doctors believed that cancerous lumps (Greek *onkos*, "mass" or "bulk", hence *oncology*) were caused by fluid blockages within the body. Of course, these views changed in the wake of newly discovered *evidence*, as is implicit within the very nature of science.

Yet why, if our ever-deepening knowledge of the world of matter allows us to develop new interpretations in the light of new evidence, should a sincere Christian not be granted the same privilege? And just as the exploring scientist never doubts the fundamental laws of matter, why should the exploring Christian doubt the eternal guidance of God? It seems blatantly unfair that scientists should be allowed to deepen their understanding of matter, while the validity of Christians' attempts to deepen their knowledge of the spirit is denied. And this is especially significant where interpreting ancient texts and languages is concerned.

Biblical literalism can be attributed in part to the Reformation, when much of the apparatus of Catholic thought and spirituality was thrown out, and "the plain word of Scripture" put in its place. Yet all the great Protestant thinkers, from Luther and Calvin onwards, fully acknowledged that a critical caution should be exercised when reading the Bible, for none of these men were fundamentalists.

Indeed, fundamentalism in its modern form is really a twentieth-century phenomenon, originating in America in the 1910s among independent Protestant communities, and people who were angered by Darwinism and especially the higher criticism of the Bible. This movement in its various shades, however, "went global", especially from the 1960s onwards, appealing as it did to millions of people who felt at odds not only with Darwinism and higher criticism, but also with what seemed like a liberal sell-out to secularism.

Yet the fact is, to many atheists and secularists, the strict, literalistic Bible faith of those early twentieth-century Americans who insisted that they were going back to "the fundamentals" has become synonymous with "Christianity". It is, however, a wholly false analogy, though one must admit that it has been cleverly used by the atheists to form a hypothesis which runs: "Christianity is simple-minded and locked into out-of-date texts, whereas atheism is sophisticated and scientific."

The basic fact remains, however, that the great majority of Christians worldwide – Protestant, Catholic, and Orthodox – while seeing God's inspiration, creative power, and love fully at work in Scripture, are *not* fundamentalist. Spreading the myth that all Christians are fundamentalists, therefore, only indicates how ignorant of history the New Atheists are.

The Church Has Always Persecuted Science and Scientists

We saw at the beginning of Chapter 2 the absurdity of the popular belief that there was no science in the Middle Ages, and how the myth of the medieval church's persecution of scientists is exploded by sheer historical evidences to the contrary. Not only were classical Greek astronomy and geometry taught as standard in the medieval universities of Europe, but it was monks and priests in pursuit of a deeper understanding of divine light who first began the process of unravelling the mathematical physics of the rainbow. Moreover, a succession of monastic alchemists from Friar Roger Bacon in the thirteenth century to George Ripley in the late fifteenth were free to undertake major researches into reactive and metallurgical chemistry, while burgeoning medical schools in Paris, Montpellier, Bologna, and Padua taught human and animal anatomy and even dissected human corpses before students. The papal physician Guy de Chauliac investigated the new fourteenth-century scourge, bubonic plague – he caught it himself, and survived – as well as producing his formidable clinical masterpiece *Chirurgia Magna* ("Great Surgery"), the greatest single treatise on surgery from the entire Middle Ages, in 1361. In the fourteenth and fifteenth centuries, moreover, Merton College, Oxford – all the dons of which were in holy orders – became a European "centre of excellence" in the study of the mathematics of motion and acceleration. Merton's William of Heytesbury's research into the acceleration of falling bodies, in the "mean speed theorem" of around 1360, even preceded Galileo's, and William pioneered, and may have invented, the use of block graphs as a means of representing increasing mathematical proportions. Several brass instruments of the "Merton Geometers" are still preserved in Oxford. So if this was persecuting science, one wonders what encouraging it would have looked like!

But four names are always wheeled out in the persecution litany: Copernicus, Bruno, Galileo, and Darwin. So let us look at them one by one, although we will save Darwin for Chapter 9.

Copernicus, so the mythology goes, dared to break silence and state the truth that the earth rotated around the sun in the teeth of the church's suppression of the fact. But he only dared to publish his great book declaring the truth as he lay on his deathbed in 1543, for otherwise the Inquisition would "get him". I have probably heard this tale more times than I have eaten the proverbial hot dinners, and it is pure nonsense, dispelled by the hard facts themselves.

For one thing, the Catholic Church had no doctrinal statement one way or the other on cosmology in 1543. Yes, the geocentric (earth-centred) cosmology was the accepted one, but only because it was the system that accorded with (a) common sense, and (b) the writings of the pagan Greek astronomer Ptolemy, whose mathematical cosmology was taught across Europe, and (c) it was implied on a common-sense level in Scripture. For does not the earth *appear* to be rock solid and stable, and do not all the heavenly bodies *appear* to rise and set around it? And if the earth were rotating on its axis, would we not all be flung off into space?

The well-documented Nicholas Copernicus of history was a churchman: a canon of the Polish cathedral of Frombork, probably a lay canon and a Church lawyer. He came from a high-status family, being the nephew of a bishop, and had been educated first in Cracow, then in several leading Italian Renaissance universities, before taking up his canonry. He was a sincerely devout man with a lifelong passion for astronomy, and by his thirties had become concerned about the problems implicit in the geocentric cosmology because the observed motions of the planets often differed from the predicted ones. His sun-centred system, one should not forget, had, as he reminded his readers, classical Greek antecedents; and he was discussing it in writing with friends as early as 1510–13, probably including his bishop friend, Johannes Dantiscus. It had clearly come to be known across Europe by 1536, for in that year Cardinal Schönberg in Italy wrote a friendly and admiring letter to Copernicus requesting technical details. And Copernicus was so clearly delighted with this request that he printed it in full as part of the prefatory pages to his *De Revolutionibus Orbium Coelestium* ("On the Revolutions of the Heavenly Bodies") in 1543. And far from there being a backlash, Copernicus's Lutheran disciple, Joachim Rheticus of Wittenberg, further published a printed synopsis of the sun-centred system, *Narratio Prima* ("First Account"), in 1540, with a second edition in 1541. And no one, Catholic or Protestant, got arrested or punished!

So why did Copernicus wait until he was dying before he published his *magnum opus*? The truth is that he did not. While his health was already deteriorating the sixty-nine- or seventy-year-old Copernicus seems to have suffered a stroke as yet another Lutheran disciple, Andreas Osiander, was seeing *De Revolutionibus* through the press in Nuremberg, and he was within a few days or even hours of death when the first copies arrived after their over-600-mile journey across eastern Europe.

But there were probably two other factors involved in the delay: firstly, Copernicus was a perfectionist, and all too aware of mathematical anomalies in his sun-centred theory. Secondly, being a quiet man, he probably feared ridicule, as he realized that his theory seemed to fly in the face of common sense. We must never forget that *De Revolutionibus* was a deeply mathematical book, dealing with problems in technical astronomy, and in no way conceived as a challenge to established ideas. Copernicus was too much of a conservative figure for that. Yet very importantly, from our point of view, the church *did nothing whatsoever*. And a second edition went peacefully through the press, in Basel, in 1566.

Giordano Bruno was a very different kettle of fish, however, for he was openly provocative, often downright insulting to Christianity, and what might be styled a triple-starred "Grade A" heretic, who was *not* an astronomer, but did become fascinated by certain philosophical ideas which he drew from Copernicanism. Born in Naples in 1548, and becoming a Dominican friar, he abandoned the doctrine of transubstantiation – where the bread and wine become the body and blood of Jesus at the Eucharist – and went to Geneva. But he was too outrageous for the Calvinists, and had to get out. He then caused uproar in Toulouse, Wittenberg, and Oxford – where he poured contempt on the university and its Aristotelian philosophy.

In many respects, it was the dominant teleological philosophy of Aristotle of the European universities which, along with wider Christian thought, was Bruno's main target. He had moved away from the orthodox position of a God–creation separation to a sort of classical pagan pantheism in which God was *everything*, and *everything* was divine. It was, of course, quintessentially heretical in so far as it erased any distinction between God and humanity, and did away with Jesus as saviour, and with sin and grace, making Christianity (along with Judaism and Islam) an irrelevance.

The appeal of Copernicanism to Bruno was *not* scientific, but metaphysical. If the earth were not at the centre of creation, cosmologically and spiritually, then could there not perhaps be myriads of other worlds and beings unmentioned in Scripture, throughout a pantheistic infinity?

And Bruno cherry-picked ideas not only from the devout Copernicus, but even from the mid fifteenth-century German Cardinal Nicholas of Cusa, whom many see as a founder of the north European Renaissance. Some of Cusa's ideas on relative motion, moreover, had even influenced Copernicus, and had themselves been coloured in turn by the fourteenth-century Oxford don Thomas Bradwardine, who had asked whether an infinitely powerful creator God could have created an infinity of worlds *if* he had chosen to do so. And to give some idea of the openness of debate in "High Medieval" academic

Christendom, not only was Cusa a cardinal, but Bradwardine had died in office as Archbishop of Canterbury.

Yet whereas Bradwardine, Cusa, Copernicus, and the Merton College geometers had explored relative motion and infinity within the context of their common Christian faith, Bruno did so within a pagan metaphysic. And while he could well have got away with that in itself, he tipped things over the edge of tolerance when he began to lash out and treat traditional learning and Christendom with ridicule. And it was that, *not* astronomical science, which really brought him to the stake in Rome in February 1600.

Traits similar to those found in Bruno figured prominently in Galileo Galilei, although the "martyr of science" myth adroitly sidesteps them.

Galileo's first brush with the Roman Inquisition had come in 1604, when he was forty years old, and a professor of mathematics at the great Italian University of Padua. Yet the brush had not come from his defending truth against mumbo-jumbo: quite the opposite, in fact, for he got into trouble for calculating horoscopes! For at that time Galileo was trying to support a lady friend, Marina Gamba, and their three love children on a small academic salary, and whatever earnings he could pick up besides. And oh, how he wanted fame, wealth, and position!

His opportunity came in 1609, when, hearing of the invention of the telescope in Holland, he made one himself, got a reward from his employers, the Serene Republic of Venice, then between November that year and January 1610 used the telescope to discover that the moon was rough and mountainous, Jupiter had four moons, and the stars seemed to recede to infinity. By 1612, moreover, he had also discovered spots on the sun and the phases of Venus – all in contradiction to existing cosmological ideas.

Yet far from getting into hot water, Galileo found the celebrity he desired. Everyone wanted to meet him, including great churchmen, and Cosimo II Medici, Grand Duke of Tuscany, made him his court philosopher. Central, however, to Galileo's getting into trouble were two factors. Firstly, his acrimonious dispute with Jesuit astronomers about the nature of sunspots; and secondly, his often adversarial and mocking style of argument, for Galileo could be formidable in debate and, it was said, resembled a lion among sheep. Of course, there was nothing wrong with that in itself, for the universities of medieval and Renaissance Europe often ran on fierce intellectual confrontation, as had been the case with Bruno. But things could easily get out of hand if one misjudged the time, place, and context.

By 1610 Galileo had become firmly convinced of the *physical* and not just *philosophical* truth of Copernicanism, and felt that his recent telescopic discoveries, which had made him famous across Europe overnight, tipped the balance of evidence in favour of the sun-centred cosmology. What was still missing, however, were crucial mathematical measurements to clinch the moving earth argument. The Jesuit mathematicians, being cautious men, and many others too, were well aware of this lack, and did not like it when, instead of solid physical and mathematical proofs, Galileo could supply only analogies from his telescopic discoveries – and even resorted to ridiculing his questioners.

This led to his being formally warned by the very learned Cardinal Roberto Bellarmine and the Inquisition in 1616. But then in 1623, Galileo's patron and friend Cardinal Maffeo Barberini became Pope Urban VIII, which truly gave him friends at the Vatican Court, for Urban was a sophisticated thinker who fully understood all the astronomy involved. Feeling by 1631 that the Vatican might be more sympathetic, Galileo produced his famous *Dialogue on the Two Chief Systems of the World*, Ptolemy's and Copernicus's. Yet far from coming over as an even-handed debate – conducted between three philosophical characters – it could be read as blatantly one-sided. The fixed-earth philosopher Simplicius invariably comes off worst, and Galileo even uses denigrating phrases like "mental pygmies" and "dumb idiots" about the anti-Copernicans.

Pugnacious men like Galileo never lack enemies, and once the Pope and the Inquisition had become riled at Galileo's advocacy of Copernicanism in the light of his warning of 1616, then the skids were under him, and things quickly went to trial and condemnation. Yet let us be quite clear about why Galileo was on trial, for, unlike Bruno, no one ever questioned his Catholic Christian orthodoxy. Galileo's heresy, rather, was the relatively minor one of effectively breaching the conditions of the 1616 restriction not to teach the Copernican theory as true, especially as he was still unable to prove it. His views about God, Jesus, the Virgin Mary, salvation, and redemption were never once called into question. His heresy was technical, and about obedience, not Christian belief.

Indeed, in 1615, he had published his *Letter to the Grand Duchess Christina*, which still stands today as one of the most powerful arguments in print on the subject of the profound compatibility of science and Christian theology. In it, Galileo argued that God had written two books: his word (the Bible) and his works (nature), and these could never contradict one another when read and interpreted correctly and prayerfully. He also cited his contemporary Cardinal Boronius, who said that the Bible is to teach us how to go to heaven, not how the heavens go.

Of course, it would be false to claim that there were not churchmen who did attack Galileo's interpretation of Scripture to accommodate a moving earth – such as the Dominican Fra. Tommáso Caccini, who preached furiously against him. On the other hand, Galileo had many clerical defenders, and was even sent an apology from Fra. Luigi Maraffi, Master General of the Dominican Order, who admired him. For the church as a body was *not* fundamentalist on the matter of scriptural interpretation.

Many factors came together in the Galileo affair, including factional politics between the Roman Catholic religious orders, the Vatican–Spanish political stand-off (the *Spanish* Inquisition, of all bodies, refused to condemn Galileo), the overweening pride of Pope Urban VIII and many cardinals, Vatican Court politics, and the international stresses across Christendom caused by the Reformation and Counter-Reformation. And perhaps to top it all was Galileo's love of academic rough-and-tumble, name-calling, and rival-ridiculing, which were just about permissible when directed against conservative Aristotelian philosophers in Padua, but could have horrendous consequences when indulged in throughout high-ranking international ecclesiastical circles.

Yet all of this was quietly overlooked by the anti-Christian myth-builders of the eighteenth and nineteenth centuries, who ignored Galileo the vigorous wrangler and saw only Galileo the pitiful old man confessing before the cardinals.

But all other circumstances apart, let us not forget Galileo's genuine standing as a scientist, and as a physicist and astronomer of the very front rank. Yet equally importantly, let us remember that Galileo lived and died an obedient if disputatious son of the church, and that to see him as a martyr striving to make the world a cosy place for secularist ideologists to live in is pure mythology.

Religion Causes the World's Troubles: Only Secularism Can Bring Peace

Since the horrors of 11 September 2001 (9/11), the London Tube and bus bombings of 7 July 2005, and other Islamic jihadi mass murders, many atheists and secularists have come to argue that such atrocities provide clinching evidence that religion is by its nature tribal, backward, and capable of appalling sectarian brutality. And going further back in time, the more historically aware atheists like to point out that Christianity had its own bloodbath in the Catholic *versus* Protestant "wars of religion" that followed the Reformation. And they also like to trot out the collective guilt Christians ought to feel for the awful Crusades in the twelfth century: horrible, unwashed, cross-wielding thugs stampeding into the sophisticated peace-loving Middle East! (On the other hand, they rarely bother to look into why the Crusades occurred in the first place. And while it is true that relations were not good between the Roman Catholic and Eastern Byzantine churches, had not the fanatical Caliph Hakim begun to slaughter Christian pilgrims and destroy customarily permitted churches, had not the militant Seljuk Turks then seized Jerusalem from its current Christian-pilgrimage-tolerant Arab rulers in 1071, and had not decades of diplomatic negotiation failed to reopen the routes, then Pope Urban II would never have needed in 1095 to preach a Crusade in the first place.)

But either way, this is all grist to the mill for the proponents of the myth that religion is inherently violent, and that not until religion has been banned or ridiculed out of existence will the world know true and lasting peace. This cloud-cuckoo-land analysis, however, misses certain rather important facts, starting with "How do you define a religion?" Christianity naturally comes top on the villain list, not only because of its formative influence upon Western civilization, but because it is, as we saw in Chapter 1, the only religion the atheists and secularists can openly and publicly mock and attack without fear of legal, social, or physical reprisals – at least, in present-day Great Britain.

Yet if you define a religion as a passionate loyalty to a collective group interest which provides meaning and purpose while often serving no obvious survival advantages, where do you draw the boundaries? After all, insisting that a religion must include worship of a divine being is a bit arbitrary. Why not worship abstract concepts, such as triumph or victory as some Greeks and Romans did?

Take football as an example, a secular religion to those who eat, sleep, and live "the beautiful game". Could one not think of the supporters as a committed laity, the team as priests who manipulate the "magic", the stadium as the church, the goalposts as the altar, the ball as a sacred object that must be defended from rival "priests" (the opposing side), the winning goal as an ecstatic sacrament, sending the faithful into raptures of delight, and heaven as your team coming top of the League and winning the Cup Final, to give a kind of earthly bliss. Football even possesses a powerful evangelical aspect, in so far as the leading teams, with their vast commercial infrastructures, aim to win over the loyalty and the cash of rival team supporters. And what happens when you are faced with nasty, chanting heretics – supporters of a successful rival team who won't be "converted"? Why, you punch the living daylights out of them, of course!

And this is only one of a variety of worldly pursuits that can take on a religious dimension. Even avid gardeners and dog or budgerigar breeders can become fiendishly competitive: knobbling each other's prize blooms or marrows, or surreptitiously opening a rival's cage door on the night before a crucial show. Human beings don't need God as an excuse to be nasty to each other, for conflict is "in the genes".

And when you come to religions proper, i.e. *transcendent* divine belief systems, they vary enormously not only in how they respond to violence, but also in how they evangelize. Some religions are predominantly contemplative, and try, within the limits of human frailty, to spread peace, inner calm, and love among all people. Others were born of the sword, and are propagated by the sword, though even they, in some cases, still nurture inner contemplative traditions within themselves. Christianity has always tackled the seemingly Herculean task of turning natural brutes into angels by recognizing that even the vilest brute is a child of God, and that the grace and love of Christ can transform the grossest base metal into the finest gold. A thing which spiritual alchemists such as St Paul, St Ignatius Loyola, George Herbert, John Newton, General William Booth, and many others both recognized and even achieved over the centuries. Yet despite the fleshly limitations of its followers, and their tendency to lapse into nastiness, Christendom has always possessed the courage to face up to its own inner demons, and try to do better next time. And to aspire, in each generation, to be a channel for the love of God, and to strive against all apparent odds to make the world a better, fairer, and kinder place, in spite of our often brutish instincts. But it is really a form of "running repair", for while we mortals can be transformed by the Holy Spirit as individuals, the next generation is always a fresh challenge.

Yet if religion per se is inherently trouble-causing, let us now look at what atheism and secularism have achieved in the last couple of centuries since Revolutionary France became the first country to "liberate" its people from Christian tyranny.

Things began fine and rosy in July 1789, when young English idealists such as William Wordsworth proclaimed the joy of witnessing a new, free world being born in France. For most of the early "Revolutionaries" were essentially honest, educated, public-spirited French gentlemen who wanted to give their country a stable, balanced, liberal political constitution such as they saw in operation in England. But it did not stay like that for long, as the liberal honeymoon, as we saw in Chapter 3, had begun to spiral into ideological brutality by 1792. Soon, the liberal gentlemen had either fled or perished, as the guillotine became the real symbol of "liberty".

And subsequent efforts to frame or change a society in accordance with secular atheist principles did no better. The late nineteenth-century German and other anarchists saw terrorism and murder as legitimate political techniques, while the apotheosis of Marxist dialectical materialism after 1917 drew part of its inspiration from secular "social science" and part from a virulent anti-Christian current. Russia under Lenin and Stalin, China under Mao after 1948, and other satellite Marxist regimes in Eastern Europe or the Far East all acted in accordance with goals and doctrines which were perceived as "scientific", "rational", and as delivering mankind from bondage to outdated religious beliefs. And all rapidly became brutal and repressive beyond description!

How, therefore, can religion, and Christianity in particular, be accused of causing the world's troubles when on the key occasions when secular atheists have gained absolute control of governments and nations, as in France in 1791, Russia in 1917, and China in 1948, they have acted with such consummate barbarity? (Nazism, while equally anti-Christian and equally savage, was in some ways less of a social science philosophy and more of a pagan cult, seeking part of its inspiration from Nordic mythology, although it did attempt to use eugenic "science" to justify the Master Race's right to rule and to annihilate other human groups.)

Arguably, what makes such barbarity more likely in secular social systems is an absence of those moral brakes – the prospect of judgment after death – which can, hopefully, make a Christian think twice before committing an atrocity. A secular dictator, on the other hand, with only his own ego to answer to, can quite literally get away with murder, at least until a *coup d'état* sees him off.

"What a cheek", I hear the honest unbeliever say, "to assume that only people who believe in God are moral!" And I entirely agree, for there are countless secularists who are honest, humane, and fair-minded, as we all know from daily experience. Likewise, my critics will validly argue, what about those well-run, just, and prosperous modern-day countries where religion plays no formal part in public life – France, Sweden, and Finland, for example? And others, with secular constitutions, yet with overwhelmingly Christian populations, such as the USA or Poland?

I would be so bold as to argue, however, that modern secular states take many of their moral values, sense of public justice, and most of all, equal human rights, from the Judeo-Christian tradition. Some time ago, a Christian friend who sits in Parliament told me of a debate on religion and the state, in which a secularist atheist said that he disliked religion (Christianity), and wanted a just society where the poor were helped, people had value and their rights were respected, the sick were cured, and strangers and victims of persecution found comfort. My friend said he responded by telling the atheist that he had just unknowingly cited some of the key principles contained in Christ's Sermon on the Mount!

Even when such ideals have been filtered through secular "Enlightenment" or socialist values, and their spiritual origins stripped away and even strenuously denied, the Christian principles remain. And although Thomas Hobbes put his finger on an important point when he said, as we saw in Chapter 2, that being nice to each other is really no more than a charade to protect our skins and beguile and disarm potential aggressors, we must not forget the *hundreds* of biblical quotations in *Leviathan* (1651), which indicate how deeply this Wiltshire parson's son was steeped in Christianity, in spite of his mechanistic outrageousness.

Nor should we forget that when seventy years of Soviet communism came to an end after 1990, many Russians and East Europeans in formerly occupied countries could not run away from the state "religion" of atheism quickly enough, as churches suddenly filled, new ones were built, and incoming Western missionaries found ready listeners. The dullness, drabness, and brutal oppressiveness of state-enforced atheism had utterly failed to win hearts and minds.

111

And while the dogs of war may never be far below our collective human skin, be it in the army of a Christian nation or in a rampaging crowd of football hooligans, I would humbly suggest that Christian teaching and conscience at least still provides the strongest leash with which the beast in all of us just might be brought to heel.

7

Monkeying around with History: The Myth of the Big 1860 "Oxford Debate" on Evolution

In the same way that everyone knows how the church punished that innocent "martyr of science" Galileo, so few people have never encountered the story of the world-changing clash that took place in Oxford's newly opened University Museum, on the momentous summer's afternoon of 30 June 1860. Almost as a vindication of poor Galileo, whom 227 years before (so the myth goes) the church had driven into submission, so the Oxford evolution debate dramatically turned the tables. In Oxford, a reactionary, anti-scientific, Bible-thumping old bishop had been argued down and publicly humiliated by a vigorous young freethinking "man of science". Mankind had finally been liberated from its ancient bondage to spiritual superstition, and was now free to proclaim its cousinship with noble apes! And the newly liberated Prometheus of science was all set to change the world and bring in "The Truth".

What happened at that momentous encounter, as the myth has it, is that the Bishop of Oxford, Samuel Wilberforce, delivered an uninformed tirade against Charles Darwin's *On the Origin of Species*, published just over seven months previously, and defended the strict literal truth of Genesis. He then made insinuating remarks against the evolutionist Thomas Henry Huxley, by asking from which of his grandparents he was descended from the apes. To which young "Darwin's Bulldog" Huxley retorted, quick as a flash, that he would rather be descended from an innocent ape than from an ignorant bishop. At this irreverence ladies fainted, evolutionists proclaimed victory, and Wilberforce and all his clerical cronies were crushed. The meeting came to a dramatic end. And the world changed!

As the twentieth century progressed, and especially after c. 1950, this heroic scenario progressively ensconced itself in the Western psyche, through books, magazine articles, and bad TV docu-dramas which acted the whole thing out in graphic detail. And as a schoolboy and a student I swallowed it hook, line, and sinker, just like most other people; and only when I began on my history of science research career did I become gradually aware of serious problems in the "orthodox" telling of the confrontation.

One such problem was in the curiously unbalanced nature of the evidence. A research historian naturally expects the most detailed authentic accounts about an event to be found in the records of the time in which it took place, with shades of interpretation, rather than fundamental factual reportage, coming from 100 or so years later. But with the "Oxford Debate" it was the other way round: lots of modern-day references and amplifications yet, when you try to find an authentic source in the publications of around July 1860, you search largely in vain. For the "Debate" was scarcely noticed in the newspapers, magazines, and book literature of 1860, and what little there was failed to square with the "canonical" narratives of a century later, such as that presented in William Irvine's *Apes, Angels, and Victorians* (1956). Yet in 1860, just like today, a world-changing event hit the then mass media of the printed word. But more about the authentic sources of the "Debate" anon: let us first look at the *dramatis personae*.

Central was the Rt Revd Samuel Wilberforce, Lord Bishop of Oxford. Yet far from being an out-of-touch geriatric, Samuel in 1860 was a vigorous 54-year-old, and bang up to date. And far from being a scientific ignoramus, he had a first-class honours degree in mathematics from Oxford, where he had been both an undergraduate and a member of Oriel College before ascending the ecclesiastical ladder. He also had a range of scientific friends, such as the astronomer Sir John Herschel and the physiologist Sir Richard Owen. And if anyone bothers to check the Royal Society registers, as I have done, they will find that by 1860 Samuel had been a full fellow of that society for *fifteen* years (longer than Huxley, in fact). I can, of course, already hear defenders of the "Debate" myth exclaiming "Aha! But in 1845 you did not need to be a full-time working scientist to be elected FRS, as you do now", and I wholeheartedly agree. On the other hand, the Society would never vote you into the Fellowship if you were a scientific ignoramus, or an enemy of modern science. In fact, Sam of Oxford belonged to a long and noble breed of clerical scientists and friends of science that went back to the very founding of the Royal Society in 1660 – highly educated gentlemen, often in public life, with an informed knowledge of science! Indeed, a very useful thing for any civilized society to possess. Men with a breadth of vision, who could relate their science to their religion and social and political lives!

Bishop Samuel was also a brilliant orator, a wit, and a seasoned debater who clearly relished a merry old scrap in the House of Lords, in the universities, or at scientific or religious meetings. Nor is there evidence that he bore long-term grudges – unlike the much stiffer, earnest, and, one suspects, humourless Huxley. He even played along with his nickname "Soapy Sam", saying that while he was often in hot water, he always emerged with clean hands; although we should remember that in Victorian usage "soapy" also meant smooth and polished. Or in today's fashionable lingo, *cool*.

In fact, by 1860 Samuel was one of the most high-profile of all English churchmen, and was further revered because his father, William Wilberforce, was the "national saint" who had spearheaded the parliamentary campaign to abolish the slave trade in 1807. Samuel was also a very popular diocesan bishop, the driving force behind many charities, and a social lion. When the popular magazine *Vanity Fair* did a profile and a cartoon of Wilberforce in July 1869, in its

"Men of the Day" series, it said that should the Church of England be suddenly disestablished and lose its investment revenues, Samuel "assuredly would be provided for by a grateful country as the most amusing diner out of his time", and would never lack for Society dinner tables at which to eat! So one might be rightly forgiven for asking the question "How does this Bishop Wilberforce of historical record square with the fundamentalist buffoon of myth?"

Thomas Henry Huxley was a profoundly different sort of man. He was born in 1825, the son of a far from wealthy schoolmaster, but his brilliance had secured him a scholarship to medical school. After an unhappy Pacific voyage as assistant surgeon aboard HMS *Rattlesnake*, which nonetheless taught him a lot of zoology and natural history, Huxley came to occupy a Chair at the School of Mines in London, and also ran evening classes for working men. A friend of Charles Darwin – himself a wealthy gentleman naturalist – the hard-up Huxley identified himself with that small minority of professional, paid-position-holding academic scientists, rather than with clerical "Grand Amateurs" like Wilberforce, whom he seems to have actively disliked. And while the early widowed Wilberforce was a deeply religious High Church evangelical who could be at ease among scientists, peers of the realm, dons, and the frequenters of Pall Mall clubs and Society dinner parties, the happily married, agnostic Huxley preferred to move among his fellow-scientists and his family.

So who said what to whom on that fateful 30 June 1860? The plain fact is, we don't really know, for there is no official record of a wholly spontaneous, very brief exchange of words, and the best that we have are very partisan private remarks. But we do know this for certain. (1) The "Debate" was part of that annual week-long jamboree of British science, the meeting of the British Association for the Advancement of Science, which in 1860 just happened to take place in Oxford. It was *not* a "special event". (2) The meeting phased in with the end of the Oxford academic year, when, in addition to the scientists (clerical, lay, and amateur), journalists, and pundits up for the jamboree, there would have been numerous mamas and papas, with marriageable daughters in attendance, up to meet their undergraduate sons' friends, attend balls and dinners, go for jaunts on the river, and enjoy all the other delights of the Victorian upper middle classes at play. In short, Oxford was in high holiday. (It is important to note, however, that the fun, games, and courtship are never mentioned in the twentieth-century "canonical" accounts of the "Debate", charged as they invariably are with fanatical anti-religious fervour.) (3) A discussion of Darwin's novel ideas had been tabled for the day in the newly opened University Museum, under the "Section D, Zoology and Botany" part of the Association meeting. (4) The discussion began with Dr John William Draper of New York (whom we met at the beginning of Chapter 6) delivering a paper on his own version of Darwinized positivism as an explanation of modern society. We can infer that it was a tedious beginning to that hot afternoon from the references to cat-calls and animal noises contributed by mischievous undergraduates who were among the 700 people packed into the Museum Lecture Room. (5) Then the audience got what most of them had probably come for, when Bishop Samuel took the floor. Though delivered spontaneously, or at least with no surviving record, Wilberforce's lecture said a lot about Darwinism as a scientific theory, but *nothing*, as far as we can gather, about religion. And then, by way of a throw-away remark, he seems to have asked Huxley the fateful question about his monkey ancestry. (6) And, as we saw above, Huxley replied something about preferring a primate to a Primate ancestor!

The "Great Debate" as a world-changing encounter, however, did not hit the public consciousness until after 1887, when Francis Darwin, Charles's son, published his father's *Life and Letters*. Here we find letters from Huxley, Joseph Dalton Hooker, and other friends who wrote to the indisposed Darwin (who was then taking a water-cure at Richmond) reporting what happened. Primary sources, it is true, but replete with their own contradictions. Huxley tells Darwin how he stood up to the bishop, yet Hooker claims that *he*, Hooker, was the one who had personally "smashed" Soapy Sam, and that Bulldog Huxley did not speak loudly enough to be heard among the bedlam of laughter that had, no doubt, erupted after Sam's quip.

Yet other manuscript reminiscences only add confusion to the clean-kill scenario of the "canonical" account. The Revd Adam Storey Farrar believed the bishop had been improper to ask whether another gentleman's grandmother had been a monkey, while William Tuckwell recorded in his *Reminiscences of Oxford* (1900, 1907) that the bishop seems to have pulled himself up sharp and apologized to Huxley, not meaning "to hurt the Professor's feelings", although this was probably lost in the noise and laughter. Furthermore, both the Scottish physicist Balfour Stuart, FRS, and Mr Henry Baker Tristram recorded that as they saw it the bishop came off best; while Wilberforce himself wrote to a friend a few days later: "I think, I thoroughly beat him [Huxley or Hooker?]."

So whose account can be believed? Let us now refer to the nearest thing we have in the contemporary media to a report on what was said, in the local paper, *Jackson's Oxford Journal*, 7 July 1860, which devotes twenty lines to the "Section D" session among several full broadsheet pages covering the rest of the British Association meeting. The anonymous reporter tells his readers that the bishop "condemned the Darwinian theory as unphilosophical [i.e. unscientific]; as founded not upon philosophical principles [i.e. scientific or experimental induction], but upon fancy, and he denied that one instance had been produced by Mr Darwin of the alleged change from one species to another had ever taken place [*sic*]". Hardly a fundamentalist rant, indeed! The reporter names four other respondents in addition to Huxley, including Hooker, but does not record what they said. But no reference to religion at all. Only what Wilberforce identified as Darwin's *scientific* evidential shortcomings: shortcomings which the honest Darwin fully admitted. So no clean Huxley–Wilberforce kill and no Bible-thumping!

What we see here is not the ignorant episcopal buffoon of legend, but Wilberforce the sharp-eyed FRS, dissecting the scientific work of another FRS – Darwin – and being challenged by yet other FRSs – Huxley, Hooker, et al. For we must never forget that Victorian science was deeply inductive and experimental in its basis, and in that respect, as things stood regarding biological knowledge in 1860, Darwin was on very shaky "philosophical" ground – and he knew it, for neither he nor any other scientist could demonstrate evolution experimentally.

One or two papers covered other aspects of the week-long British Association meeting: *The Athenaeum*, 7 July 1860, for instance, mentioning the "play" and exchanges that took place in the various section meetings. Yet one searches in vain for the "Great Debate" of 30 June. Even the leading satirical paper of the day, *Punch*, which was not averse to publishing cartoons and poems about "Soapy Sam" as a High Tory bishop, is silent about the "Debate". I wonder why? Could it have anything to do with a fleeting humorous exchange being in reality no more than that, yet blown up out of all proportion in the decades after 1887? Wilberforce was killed in a riding accident in 1873, and could do nothing to challenge the tale thereafter, while the "canonical" view is repeated in Huxley's *Life and Letters* (1900) and those of Hooker (1918).

One finds a fascinating perspective on the "Debate", however, in our two "American atheists" mentioned above. While John William Draper had spoken on Darwinized positivism in "Section D" immediately before Wilberforce, and was clearly a witness to whatever else followed, he quite forgot to mention the world-changing "Debate" in his anti-Christian *A History of the Conflict between Science and Religion* (1874). I wonder why? Because the momentous exchange was in reality nothing more than a quip, which he had long forgotten by 1874? On the other hand, when Andrew D. White published his magisterial *Warfare* volumes in 1896, he made what is probably the first independent mention of the "Debate". White, however, had *not* been in England in June 1860, and had the advantage of access to the Huxley, Hooker, and other letters, plus Francis Darwin's interpretation of the "Debate" in his edition of his father's *Life and Letters* (though in 1860 Francis had been a twelve-year-old schoolboy and had not been present at the event).

I have read, and been told, many reasons why the Oxford "debacle" never hit the national headlines in July 1860, usually based upon a "press cover-up" theory. For would not the public humiliation of a bishop make ladies faint and the establishment crumble? Yet such an explanation can only be sustained in blissful ignorance of the workings of the Victorian "mass media". In 1860, England had *scores* of daily and weekly newspapers, magazines, and "scandal rags". There is probably no underhand trick used by modern-day reporters that their Victorian forebears did not use 150 years before – mobile phones notwithstanding – for the Victorian press was big, noisy, and *free*. A thing of national pride, in fact, for it proclaimed to the world that John Bull could speak his mind, unlike the more government-controlled news agencies of Continental Europe.

Reforming papers like *The Times* and *The Examiner* regularly exposed ecclesiastical abuses of various kinds, while Dissenting Christian, freethinking, and radical political periodicals would have had a field day with a bishop who had been made a monkey of in Oxford. Just think of the stick Anthony Trollope gives the self-satisfied Chapter of the fictitious Barchester Cathedral in *The Warden* (1855), and the assault on it by his fictional character Tom Towers, the radical editor of *The Jupiter* newspaper! A veil of polite reverence, indeed!

I have devoted so much space to the Oxford "Debate" myth because it has become so pervasive, and so universally accepted, while in 2010 Richard Dawkins was instrumental in having a memorial stone to the "event" set up outside the Oxford University Museum. Yet, as I hope to have shown from what we know of the *historical record*, as opposed to the cosy fairyland of atheist fantasy, what the stone actually commemorates is a prime example of ideologically motivated "monkeying around with history". What, I have suggested, is *really* the "Great Delusion"!

8

The Myth of the Young Earth and the Origins of Evolutionary Ideas

Perhaps no other branches of modern science have become so fraught in their perceived relationship with religion as geology and evolution. We saw in the last chapter how the so-called "Debate" in Oxford in June 1860 has been inflated into the classic event in the "conflict" between science and faith, to become one of the twentieth century's most persistent myths. But what I want to do in the present chapter is trace the historical roots of geology and evolution. My aim is to show that neither the geological nor the evolutionary ideas that emerged were as new or quite as shocking as we are sometimes led to believe, and to disprove the myth that until *On the Origin of Species* hit the bookshops, in November 1859, everyone obediently believed what the priests told them; namely, that the earth had been created at 9 a.m. on 21 March 4004 BC. Just as it does *not* say in the book of Genesis, in fact. So how did this and other individual dates in 4004 BC come to be put forward?

Dating the Creation

The received mythology tells us that it was the seventeenth-century Church of Ireland Archbishop of Armagh, James Ussher, who pronounced the 4004 BC date. But like so many tales, it is only partially true. Since both Judaism and Christianity have always been faiths that practise the very highest standards of scholarship and critical accuracy in their interpretation of Scripture, it was early rabbis and Christian scholars who first enquired into when key events in the Old Testament actually took place. When exactly did King David reign, when did Jehovah first speak to Abraham in the land of Shinar, and when did the creation itself take place? Good historical scholarship, in fact, considering the factual data that were available 2,000 years ago, and a million miles from superstition.

In the total absence of any naturalistic indicators, such as geological strata, to give guidance, how did the early "chronologists" date the creation? Well, it was argued, the Jewish Scriptures contain some interesting numbers that might yield a clue. Genesis tells us that God made the world in six days, while Psalm 90 sings, "One thousand ages in Thy sight are but as yesterday." So is each creation day meant to represent one epoch of 1,000 years? And then, if you add up the years that have elapsed since Adam and Eve, using the Genesis dates of the patriarchs (Methuselah, for instance, died at 969 years old), you get back to 4004 BC – depending, that is, on how many years you allocate to a generation, for other chronologists came up with different numbers. And this, I would emphasize, in the absence of any naturalistic indications, such as strata or fossils, would have seemed a perfectly reasonable way of approaching the age of the earth.

We must remember, however, that chronologists such as Philo of Alexandria, Julius Scaliger, and Archbishop Ussher did *not* share the agenda of modern scientists, and it is an abuse of scholarship to presume that they did. They were less concerned with the age of our planet as a physical object in space than with tracing divine providence through history, and to attempt to read Genesis as a key to exact scientific facts, past and future, is as misplaced as trying to use modern genetics to discover what the angels are made of.

And when we examine Archbishop Ussher's *Annales Veteris et Novi Testamenti* ("Annals of the Old and New Testaments"), 1650–4, we find that he is *not* trying to do cosmology so much as to date events in the Old Testament, such as the reigns of the kings, wars, or individuals' lives. And he does this just as intelligently as any modern-day historian might, given the limited sources available 360 years ago. He attempts, whenever possible, to establish collateral dates from non-biblical sources, which, in a pre-archaeological age, meant clues in the Greek historical and travel writers such as Herodotus of c. 440 BC, whose *Histories* gave the most detailed information about ancient Egypt available before 1800. Ussher's purpose in dating the creation is primarily to establish the "beginning of the biblical story", as it were; he is *not* engaged in a piece of pseudo-scientific mummery, as many agenda-driven secularists would lead us to assume.

Coming not from a historical but from a physics direction, however, Ussher's younger contemporaries, Robert Hooke and Edmond Halley, were perhaps the first to try to date the creation from naturalistic evidences. In the brilliant and perceptive twenty-seven "Earthquake Discourses" which he delivered to the Royal Society, the first series ending in 1668 and the rest delivered by 1700, and which were sumptuously published in 1705, Robert Hooke effectively founds geological science. He collects data, worldwide, about earthquakes, tidal waves, and volcanic eruptions, as a way of attempting to understand the workings of the globe. But more importantly from our point of view, he draws some remarkable conclusions from the geology of his native Isle of Wight and the British south coast. (1) Judging from the parallel fossil-bearing strata beds across the Solent, the Isle seemed to have once been attached to the Dorset and Hampshire mainland. (2) There were rich beds of marine fossils at the Isle's western tip, opposite Hurst Castle, that were now sixty feet above the high-tide point. (3) There were no known living equivalents for some of these marine fossils found in the strata, such as the giant ammonites. So had they become extinct? (4) Why were there no human or modern animal remains in the strata – only extinct shellfish? (5) Had the Isle of Wight and adjacent mainland once been the bed of a long-dried-up ocean? (6) And, drawing upon evidences brought in by travellers from as far afield as Switzerland, the West Indies, Indonesia, and China, were there not visible physical indicators in the rocks of the earth's antiquity, and endless change? (7) Could it be, therefore, that the earth was *vastly* ancient, and that Noah's Flood, recounted in Genesis, was merely the last of an immemorial cycle of earth-forming geological catastrophes that had taken place long, long before – between the time of God's original act of creation and his replanting of a chaotic earth to create the Garden of Eden, in around 4004 BC, and crown his creation by making Adam and Eve? For after all, so Hooke tells us, recent translations of Chinese literature seemed to indicate an incredibly ancient earth.

Of course, not for a moment did Hooke see his work as challenging the glory of God. Rather, it demonstrated that our God-given intelligence enabled us to fathom out all sorts of things in the world of nature. And if one wants an indication of Hooke's good standing in ecclesiastical circles, one has merely to remember that in 1691, his old friend John Tillotson, Archbishop of Canterbury, conferred a Lambeth MD degree upon him! Further, if you read Hooke's published *Diary*, 1672–80, you can see how many prominent Anglican clergymen he ranked among his friends and dining companions!

And in the 1680s and 1690s, Hooke's younger protégé, Edmond Halley, published a series of brilliant physical studies in the Royal Society's *Philosophical Transactions*, which laid the foundation of modern meteorology and global climatology. Studies, indeed, in evaporation, rainfall, wind movement caused by solar heating, erosion, and continent-changing. Had the earth's surface been formed not just by volcanoes, but also by bombardment of large comets from space? (In 1690, they thought comets were large solid bodies.) Had what is now England once formed the bed of a tropical sea? And all this during those vast eras that had elapsed between the creation and the divine planting of Eden – or the world as we know it today? Could even Noah's Flood have been caused by naturalistic mechanisms? Halley calculated that if the whole earth had been subjected to a constant forty-day downpour that was equivalent to the heaviest measured tropical storm, then far from the sea covering the mountains, the resulting rise above existing global sea levels would be a mere 132 feet! And could this inundation have hit the earth as it passed through the – presumably aqueous –

tail of a comet? It is true that some contemporaries suggested that Halley might be a deist or even worse, but that did not prevent him from becoming Savilian Professor of Geometry in Oxford in 1703, or Astronomer Royal at Greenwich in 1720.

The eighteenth century saw various mechanisms proposed by scientists to explain the development of the cosmos. The Frenchman Pierre Simon Laplace suggested in 1796 that the solar system may have condensed out of matter once ejected from the young sun; while the astronomer Sir William Herschel, as he told the Royal Society on 19 June 1817, saw the universe as revealed in his large telescopes as dynamic, developing, and unbelievably vast. Indeed, as he tried to fathom its "length, breadth, and depth; or longitude, latitude, and profundity" (a phrase curiously reminiscent of St Paul's "breadth, and length, and depth, and height" of Christ's love, Ephesians 3:18), Herschel realized that he was looking into "times past", for it had probably taken centuries for the light of the dimmest visible stars to reach us!

And as they considered the tiny speck of the earth in this vastness, early geologists began to ask whether the earth had been formed by repeated floods (the "Neptunists"), of which that of Noah was merely the last, or by constant volcanic change (the "Vulcanists"). The pioneer Vulcanist was the Edinburgh physician and amateur field geologist Dr James Hutton, who in the 1790s suggested that Edinburgh's Arthur's Seat and Salisbury Crags were the eroded granite plugs of a gigantic volcano, whose surrounding ash cone had once covered the site of modern Edinburgh. The leading Neptunist was Gottfried Werner of Freiburg, who drew attention to the importance of the sedimentary, or water-originating, rock strata in forming the modern earth.

And very importantly, it should be borne in mind that *no one* was punished for expressing these ideas (as we saw in Chapter 4, even the medieval Catholic Church, while punishing theological heresies, had no particularly repressive policies with regard to science itself, nor had the Protestants). What some people had for sometime been suggesting was that the reason why none of these earth-forming events had been mentioned in Scripture was because no human beings, made in the image of God, existed on earth in those days. For the Bible, as Galileo had reiterated in 1615, was to teach us how to go to heaven, and *not* how the heavens (or earth) go! And the man who was to hammer this point home in the early nineteenth century was a senior Oxford clerical scientist, the Revd Canon Dr William Buckland, reader in geology and mineralogy, of Christ Church Cathedral and College, Oxford. Since Scripture was a revelation of God's plan for his immortal-soul-bearing *human* creation, not for ichthyosauri, why should God mention primitive lizards in his Genesis revelation? Let God-given human intelligence unravel *their* history for its own curiosity!

Two major discoveries paved the way for modern geology soon after 1800. The first was when the French Protestant scientist Georges Cuvier realized that he could use his anatomical knowledge to "articulate" scattered fossil bones to re-create prehistoric beasts. And what a sensation that caused in Paris! The first three-dimensional *dinosaurs*, indeed: although the word "dinosaur" ("terrifying lizard", from the Greek) was itself coined by the Anglican English anatomist Sir Richard Owen in 1840.

The second discovery was made by the canal surveyor and amateur geologist, William Smith, around 1815, when he found that the occurrence of fossils in rocks was not indiscriminate: specific fossils only occurred in specific sedimentary rocks. Could it be that God had created creatures in a clear, progressive anatomical sequence, with primitive life forms in the lowest strata and increasingly anatomically sophisticated ones in the higher? And why were there such exact dividing lines between the strata as one excavated them in a rock face? Could it be that, as Cuvier had proposed, God sent great *natural* "catastrophes" to the ancient earth, wiping out primitive species and entombing their remains in the strata, and then repopulated the globe with "higher" creatures? And allowed ingenious men to uncover his plan, millions of years later? And far from being punished, Smith was given an honorary doctorate by Trinity College, Dublin, and Buckland and his clerical friends were blazing a geological trail across the British Isles by 1825.

Indeed, by 1825 geology had become something of a national passion. Could one trace the effects of Noah's Flood in the English landscape? By 1836, however, Buckland was coming to think of the Flood as perhaps *not* universal across the planet, so much as a flood affecting the Middle East – "the whole world" as people in Old Testament times understood it. The rapidly advancing science of field geology did not appear to show traces of a global flood on the landscape. And by the 1840s, influenced by the glaciation studies of the Swiss scientist Jean Louis Agassiz, Buckland was coming to attribute "Flood" damage to an ancient Ice Age. For did not some of the Scottish glens bear a resemblance to the glaciated valleys of Switzerland?

The whole "Catastrophist" school of geology was challenged in 1830 by Sir Charles Lyell, whose *Principles of Geology* put forth an alternative idea. Could not the earth have been formed by endless slow changes, or "causes now in operation", such as wind, water, "normal" earthquakes, and erosion, given *vast* periods of time, have gently, yet inexorably, remodelled the globe? Charles Darwin read Lyell's *Principles* aboard HMS *Beagle* as he sailed out from Plymouth in 1831, and came to see the geology of South America and the Pacific basin as formed not by global catastrophes so much as by endless little changes, over countless millions of years. This slowly changing, stable geological landscape would provide a necessary environment in which, by 1839, he would come to see species gradually evolving.

And what mighty force was infusing European and American culture during this "geological" age? Romanticism. Writers, musicians, and artists were inspired by grandeur and high emotional charge, from the dreamy landscapes of J. W. M. Turner to the bizarre gothic poems of Edgar Allen Poe. And science was seen as intensely "Romantic". Mary Shelley's *Frankenstein* (1818) was inspired by recent discoveries in electricity and physiology, while Sir William Herschel's cosmology seemed mind-blowing in the vastness it revealed. And geology, with its immense time spans, "dinosaurs", and the idea that mountains and continents were but temporary things, fitted perfectly into this way of thinking.

Yet far from viewing these discoveries as undermining Christianity and the Bible, men such as Buckland in Oxford and his Cambridge professorial geological counterpart and Prebend of Norwich Cathedral, the Revd Dr Adam Sedgwick, who taught Darwin field geology, saw them as *strengthening* their faith. For was not the "God of the Fossils" even grander, in the sheer richness and majesty of his creative and sustaining power, than the God of the simpler *complete* act of creation described in Genesis? And had not God given us intelligence to uncover new wonders within his works that Moses on Sinai had never been told of?

Of course, this did not mean that the Bible account of creation was wrong. Yes, God *had* created the earth and the cosmos from nothing, and *had* populated the world with a staggering diversity of living things, and *had* created man in his own image. It was, rather, that he had done so on a vastly greater scale, with all its myriad detail and complexity, than it had been necessary to tell the children of Israel at the foot of Mount Sinai in 1500 BC. This was the natural theology of the original founders of the Royal Society, on a scale of magnificence that even perhaps Robert Boyle could scarcely have envisaged back in 1660. To men like Buckland, Sedgwick, and the majority of their contemporaries, indeed, science and God were intimately bound up together, and one could trace the work of the "divine hand" in the landscape and sky, and in the laboratory. Romanticism and revelation together, in fact! "Philosophers with hammers", as Sedgwick styled geologists.

And as I mentioned above, geology became a national passion, as the well-to-do visited the Scottish Highlands in summer, a geological hammer in one hand and a copy of Sir Walter Scott in the other. Both energetic ladies and working men on their days off took up "geologizing", adding fossils to their cabinets of curiosities; while Miss Mary Anning, of Lyme Regis, Dorset, became such a skilled fossil geologist that she was deferred to by Professor Buckland, himself a West Country man. The devout Christian stonemason–poet, Hugh Miller, made the transition from Scottish working man to famous geologist and author of the best-selling *Footprints of the Creator* (1850) and other books. And swelling the "fraternity of the geological hammer" were country gentlemen, retired military officers, doctors, working men, ladies, and legions of clergymen.

Both Buckland and Sedgwick were charismatic and entertaining men, and had influential "fans" in high places, such as Prime Minister Sir Robert Peel. And for more than a fifty-year period, moreover, both men taught geology to large classes of young gentlemen in Oxford and Cambridge, not to mention giving sell-out lectures at British Association and other convivial meetings – which could be attended by ladies. Geology was always a popular subject for lectures at the Working Men's Institutes, too. So how many *thousands* of people had sat at Buckland's and Sedgwick's feet over the decades, in the universities, in London, in the provincial societies, and elsewhere? How many future clergy, journalists, dons, teachers, lawyers, politicians, colonial administrators, civil servants – and even working people – had been exposed to the latest ideas in geology, science, and religion in their lectures (and let us not forget students of other geological academics in the new London and four Scottish universities, and in Trinity College and Cork College, Ireland)? And then add to that the impact of the widespread publication of popular books and magazine articles!

Yet while no one was questioning the *fact* of the new fossil discoveries, there was, one must admit, an increasingly marginalized constituency of people who did not accept Buckland's and Sedgwick's ancient earth interpretations: the "Scriptural Geologists". When, for example, the British Association met at York, in 1844, the Very Revd Sir William Cockburn, Dean of the Minster, caused uproar by delivering an address condemning the geologists for their failure to interpret Genesis literally! We know from a letter of Mary Buckland that her husband was not sorry to be leaving Oxford in 1845, upon becoming Dean of Westminster; this, however, was not occasioned by any specific persecution of science in Oxford at this time so much as by a perceived indifference, amidst the theological feuds then breaking out in the university between the Anglo-Catholics John Henry Newman, Edward Pusey, and their supporters and the "Low Church" evangelicals, to whom even the slightest whiff of "Popery" was anathema.

Yet to assume that when Darwin's *On the Origin of Species* was published, towards the end of 1859, it horrified and stunned a nation of simple biblical fundamentalists who all swore by a creation date of 4004 BC, is pure nonsense. Mythology set in stone, no less!

The Origins of Life: Pre-Darwinian Ideas of "Evolution"

We saw in the previous section how the idea of an ancient earth was firmly established among most of the formally- and the self-educated classes long before 1859. Yet the development of naturalistic geology from the seventeenth century to the Victorian age had not fundamentally challenged the biblical idea of the uniqueness of the human race; rather, humanity was seen as the crowning glory in an ancient planet.

On the other hand, it is false to assume that before Charles Darwin no one had seriously considered evolution – or, under its older name, "transmutationism". Quite the contrary, in fact: by the time Darwin published *Origin* in 1859, naturalistic species-change ideas had been discussed for almost two centuries. Indeed, on page 291 of his 1668 "Earthquake Discourse", Robert Hooke not only speaks of extinction but says "that 'tis not unlikely also but that there may be divers new kinds [of living creatures] now, which have not been from the beginning". An opinion he repeats in other places. And let us not forget that these "Discourses" were first delivered to Royal Society meetings with clerical FRSs in his audience. Of course, Hooke was not proposing any biological mechanism for this change – just noting the stratigraphic appearance of new forms, whether divinely or naturally created. Yet as he makes clear elsewhere in his "Discourses", every classically educated gentleman was familiar with the notion of species change from Greek mythology, though that, admittedly, was *not* the same thing as science.

I would, however, be cautious about reading too much evolution into Hooke's remarks on fossils and species change. For Hooke was a physicist by instinct, not a natural historian, and was primarily interested in the physics of earth-forming processes, and not so much in living creatures themselves.

All of these ideas and speculations about geology, fossils, and species, moreover, would have been readily available to John and Charles Wesley when they were undergraduates at Oxford. For Hooke, let us remember, like the Wesleys, had been a Christ Church man, and a copy of his *Posthumous Works* (1705), containing the "Earthquake Discourses", has been in the Christ Church library for nearly 300 years (yes, I have checked) – not to mention copies in the Bodleian and other Oxford libraries!

Yet let us not lose sight of the fact, as noted in Chapter 2, that comparative anatomists had been aware since classical times that human and higher-animal bodies shared an enormous number of structural and functional features. Indeed, the Scottish nobleman Lord Monboddo, whom Dr Samuel Johnson encountered when visiting Scotland in 1773, was well known for his opinion that humans were related to monkeys, and there seems to have been jokes doing the rounds about men with tails. But the overwhelming weight of scientific opinion in the eighteenth century, geological timescales apart, was that species were fixed. And that view, on its highest authority, derived *not* from the Bible, but from scientific botany and natural history. For the great Swedish botanist and medical doctor Carl von Linnaeus, of Uppsala University, argued from the best available evidences that while species were incredibly diverse, they seemed to be fixed, although he was puzzled by certain hybrid varieties. And from around 1780 to 1850, every medical student in Europe and America would have known Linnaeus's works on botanical classification, for botany was fundamental to pharmacy.

The first published scientific, albeit speculative, discussion about species change, however, came out between 1794 and 1796, for over those years Dr Erasmus Darwin, FRS, an eminent physician and naturalist of Lichfield, Staffordshire, published the poem entitled *Zoonomia*. And Dr Erasmus Darwin was none other than Charles Darwin's grandfather! In this treatise, written in poetic verse, Dr Erasmus discussed the merging of plants under environmental pressures to produce new forms, or species, inspired in part by his knowledge of plant speciation, and in part by his professional interest in hereditary diseases. For what exactly was it that passed down through the generations to make plants, animals, and humans the beings that they were? Indeed, heredity and the transmission of characteristics was fascinating the doctors of this time, as it would later fascinate Charles Darwin. Why, for instance, earlier naturalists had asked, did the offspring of performing animals in circuses find it easier to learn tricks than ordinary animals? Were they just quicker at learning, or did they *inherit* something from their parents? And what is the cause of biological variation, in so far as offspring never replicate their parents *exactly*? In *On the Origin of Species* chapter 1, Darwin even cites a prominent scientific divine for substantiation of this biological point, for in 1822, and then especially in 1837, the subsequent Very Revd Dean of Manchester, William Herbert, had reported that "horticultural experiments have established, beyond the possibility of refutation, that botanical species are only a higher and more permanent class of varieties": an opinion which he also extended to animals. So there were even deans of the Church of England conducting experiments into species change, were there?

And in the year that Charles Darwin was born, 1809, the French anatomist and zoologist Jean-Baptiste Lamarck published his *Philosophie Zoologique*, which, along with his other writings, proposed the first biological mechanism to explain species variation and transmutation. Could it be that useful traits acquired by the parent stock were passed on to the offspring – the "inheritance of acquired characteristics", as it came to be known? Sadly, we have allowed Lamarck's brilliant researches and biological insights – incorrect as they are now known to be – to be entirely swamped in a focused obsession with Darwin as the only worthwhile evolutionary scientist.

Yet by the 1820s, and in the wake of a growing body of discoveries, many scientists were expressing qualms about species fixity. Dr Robert Edmund Grant of Edinburgh, for instance, who between 1825 and 1827 would exert a profound influence on the student Charles Darwin, was one of them. Grant was fascinated by primitive invertebrates: marine creatures such as jellyfish, with no skeleton and only the most rudimentary form of nervous system. Yet they thrived in their simple lifestyles, and seemed to have relatives in the ancient geological record. Why, though, if the world had been moulded by vast global catastrophes wiping out *all* creatures, to be followed by God restocking the planet with a new, more advanced special creation, had these rudimentary organisms survived? Perhaps geological catastrophes were relatively local, and species survived, varied, and changed depending on circumstances?

And in an anatomical and biological context, German "Naturphilosophie" scientists, such as Lorenz Oken, asked about the nature of life forces. Many were fascinated by "recapitulation biology", or the theory that lower life forms often had features that were "recapitulated" or developed in higher ones, as though an unbroken lineage connected them. Foetuses especially were subjected to scrutiny. Was it not remarkable, for example, that frogs, mice, cats, monkeys, and humans all seemed to go through similar embryological stages? Could it be that all were driven by the same "life force" and that whether a creature was destined to be a frog or a human somehow depended upon a continuing developmental process? Did frogs then stop developing earlier than humans? By 1844, there was no shortage in the literature of research and speculation by scientists and philosophers about the nature of *life*, and organic *development*. They were connected to geology, zoology, embryology, early organic chemistry, and even astronomy – for did not the newly discovered ice ages, sunspot cycle, ultraviolet and infrared radiation, and cyclical changes in the terrestrial magnetic field all indicate that the earth's surface was being bombarded with both internal and external "energy" that might perhaps affect foetuses? And I specify 1844, because that is when the first "transmutationist" bombshell hit the English-speaking, then the European, popular press. And it so alarmed the 35-year-old Darwin that he put his own maturing evolutionary ideas on the back burner.

The Vestiges of the Natural History of Creation was the bombshell. Published anonymously in Edinburgh, it was the literary sensation of the year. For its author, the Scottish publisher and widely read scientific "amateur" Robert Chambers, no doubt sensed that it would be a bestseller long before he even sent his manuscript to the family printing factory.

Written in the accessible style of a seasoned journalist, *Vestiges* caused an uproar. Its anonymity further fanned the flames, as a whole array of eminent public men with known scientific tastes, including Prince Albert and even Charles Darwin, were suggested in the newspapers as the possible author. And drawing on his science editor's extensive knowledge of contemporary British and European publications across a gamut of sciences, this, in a nutshell, is what Chambers said. (1) Could not life on earth have originated in an oxygen, hydrogen, carbon, and nitrogen chemical "soup", activated by electricity? (2) Could not the resulting primitive life forms have been gradually modified by natural forces? (3) Are living forms the products of countless natural-forces-induced foetal changes, taking us, over vast ages, from microscopic blobs (the function of *cells* as biological agents was not properly understood until after 1858) to modern creatures? (4) And have the oceans, continents, and their animal populations come about not by catastrophes, but by endless, gentle "causes now in operation" forces? And by implication, who knows what will happen in the countless millennia that lie ahead?

On the other hand, Chambers was *not* denying that there had been an original act of creation, nor was he denying that God had set the whole thing in motion; rather, he was developing a naturalism that had been implicit in Western science since Galileo and the natural theology of the early Royal Society. Did not God work through his great laws and "secondary causes"?

Of course, many clergymen reviled the book. Yet the greater fury came from the scientific reviewers. Perhaps they were horrified to see their patient and meticulous researches given such an alarming and radical twist. And, heresy of heresies, the book was written in a style which, as the Cambridge clerical geologist the Revd Professor Adam Sedgwick fulminated, enabled it to be easily read by servants and innocent young ladies! Deeply corrupting, in fact! On the other hand, it says something for the sheer pluralism and freedom of early Victorian society that many others laughed and thoroughly enjoyed the fulminations. The newly founded *Punch*, for instance, saw good, humorous copy in *Vestiges*.

So once again, when we encounter the po-faced secularists' tale that when *On the Origin of Species* was published in 1859, an innocent, churchgoing, subservient Victorian populace went into fibrillations of horror, hysterically reached for their smelling salts, and clutched their Bibles to their hearts, we know that we are dealing with anti-historical atheist mythology. For several decades of geology, a geologically educated elite, popular geology, biblical criticism, French positivism in English translation, and learned articles on recent biological ideas in the "quality" newspapers and review journals had well prepared the people of 1859 to see Darwin's work in its proper social, cultural, and intellectual context.

9

Charles Darwin: Monkey, Man, and Myth

Charles Darwin has often been dealt an embarrassing hand by his most fervent disciples. Some of his letters suggest that the adulation of certain admirers, who found in his writings a focus for their own atheism, made him feel awkward. (The adulation displayed by the visiting German Ernst Haeckel to Down House, Darwin's home in Kent, in August 1866, is a case in point.) And Darwin was especially disconcerted when radical atheists and secularists, such as Karl Marx, read revolutionary political interpretations into his works. Also, I suspect, he would have been acutely embarrassed by much that is campaigned for in his name today. Darwin did *not* see himself as the fierce evangelical St Paul of atheism, so much as an honest gentleman of science. Indeed, he was not only a gentleman, born and bred, but a genuinely *gentle* man, who preferred peace and quiet in the bosom of his large family to rumbustious public meetings, and was deeply attached to his beloved and devoutly Christian wife Emma, as she was to him. And his burial in Westminster Abbey in April 1882 clearly indicates that this often troubled and regretful but kindly agnostic – for Darwin was *never* an atheist – did not lack friends and admirers in high ecclesiastical places. Indeed, the funerary addresses delivered by canons of the abbey and by the Bishop of Carlisle, Harvey Goodwin, praising Darwin's humility, patience, moral goodness, integrity, generosity, and charity, make clear the respect in which he was held as an English gentleman and an "honorary Christian". For the Charles Darwin of historical record was certainly *not* a campaigning figure to be confused with Richard Dawkins in a frock coat and stovepipe hat (and I am in no way questioning Dawkins' standing as an honourable gentleman), and to see him thus is yet another example of the way in which certain modern-day evolution-obsessed atheists spin myths to serve their own ideological ends.

One of the saddest consequences of such myth-spinning I know of was an incident related to me by an American student recently. She said that, when visiting Westminster Abbey as a schoolgirl some years before, she had witnessed another schoolgirl *spitting* on Darwin's tombstone. I have also heard of other attacks on Darwin's abbey grave. For was not Darwin the ungodly monster who said we all came from monkeys?

Yet what was it about *On the Origin of Species* that was capable of stirring up so much bitter controversy and even hatred for over 150 years, in a way that far outstripped reactions to Lamarck, *Vestiges*, or other "transmutationist" books? One factor, of course, was its sheer thoroughness, minutely marshalled inductive evidences, and analytical rigour. Another was Darwin's very honesty in facing up to the weaknesses inherent in his theory, which he tried in some ways to address in advance. *Origin* chapter 6, for example, is entitled "Difficulties on Theory", while the subject of his concluding chapter 14 is a "Recapitulation of the Difficulties of the Theory of Natural Selection". If there was one thing that *Origin* most definitely was *not*, that was sensational in its presentation or outrageous in its argument. And one suspects that Darwin had been made especially conscious of this danger from the way in which the best-selling *Vestiges* had been assembled, and the howls of hysterical academic fury that it had attracted. Darwin also went out of his way to distance himself from Lamarck, not so much because Lamarck was not a good scientist (which he was), but rather because of his *implied* association with godlessness and French Revolutionary and Napoleonic excesses, and transmutationism's undermining of man's unique dignity. For Charles Darwin was not only a highly respectable

English gentleman, Kentish squire, and county magistrate, but was already a very greatly respected man of science and FRS by 1859. The title page of his masterpiece, moreover, would proclaim it to be "By Charles Darwin M.A., Fellow of the Royal, Geological, Linnaean etc. Societies", an established scientific author. No "guess the author" anonymity here!

Surprising as it may appear to some people, there is one thing that *Origin* most definitely does *not* say: namely, that humans are descended from monkeys! This in itself must qualify as a myth of gargantuan proportions. In fact, men and monkeys scarcely get a look in, for the book is about plants, birds, reptiles, animals, and fossils. Nor does Darwin (in one of his few similarities with the author of *Vestiges*) express any qualms about discussing the "Creator" as an initiator of things. For what *Origin* does share with *Vestiges* is the tacit acknowledgment that natural science is about unravelling the processes by which nature operates; it is not about *where* nature actually comes from, or *why*. So Darwin can in all sincerity (and not as a "sop to the church", as some have implied) speak of a "Creator", because he is concerned with establishing how species originated, and *not* how life itself came about in the first place. *That* did not fall within the remit of experimental, inductive, or observational science, but was the business of the theologian or philosopher.

Central to the whole book, however, is Darwin's great discovery, the theory of natural selection. As he – and every naturalist, gardener, and farmer was aware – all individual living things vary slightly from their ancestral stock, and no two are identical. And as every expert gardener and farmer knew, one could *select* the breeding pairs of living things to enhance a particular trait. This was "artificial selection", and it was done for the agriculturalist's own profit, in so far as it produced a better yield, be it a richer grain harvest, very woolly sheep, or extra beefy cattle. On the other hand, these artificially selected traits did not generally benefit the plant or animal, for if, instead of genetically protecting the artificially selected group, you let them breed with common stock, their offspring rapidly "reverted to type" and lost their farmer-induced traits.

This reversion puzzled Darwin and many others, until he realized, after returning home from his HMS *Beagle* voyage, and reading the Revd Thomas Malthus on human population, that what the "common stock" of creatures possessed were traits that served to make them more able to cope with life in the wild. Sheep bred under "domestication" on a protected Norfolk farm, for instance, might be abnormally woolly, with numerous succulent lamb chops just crying out for market. A semi-wild sheep, living high in the Pyrenees, by contrast, might be thin, scraggy, and without much wool. Yet when the big bad wolf came along, the "wild" sheep had the agility to run away. Should a hungry feral dog chance to break into the Norfolk pasture, however – well, it was a canine Christmas feast!

Around 1839, Darwin realized that this difference was crucial. Plants and animals breeding in the wild produced all kinds of variations in their offspring, some of which gave their possessor a survival advantage: better nourishment, capacity for defence, or mates. And if two favoured creatures chanced to mate together, then they *might* produce very well-favoured offspring. Yet this natural advantage only served a useful purpose if the "favoured" creatures just chanced to mate with similarly "favoured" members of their own species.

This was "natural selection": the well-favoured in any population just chancing to mate with similarly well-favoured individuals to produce offspring that could succeed where the less-favoured failed. And especially if environmental conditions were changing, what could be classed as a "well-favoured" creature was one that just chanced to have the right traits. If, for example, a reptile's ancestral swamp were drying up, then the one that had projecting addenda which enabled it to crawl and live on dry land and to mate with similarly "lucky" types survived, and its addenda-lacking relatives eventually perished.

"So what?" you may argue, "That is how the clever, the cunning, and the strong have always come to gain dominance, be they human or animal!" Yet where Darwin was so revolutionary was in his argument that survival traits in nature were not the work of a divine farmer modifying his flock by direction and design. Instead, they were entirely random, and the whole of nature, from the behaviour of microscopic algae to that of Fellows of the Royal Society, was a product of sheer chance!

And it was the randomness of natural selection that caused such concern. Darwin did not need to talk about men and monkeys for the penny to drop that if "natural selection" was, indeed, behind "the origin of species", then men and monkeys just might chance to come about!

Yet what linked *Origin* and monkeys together in the public sphere was itself a pure chance circumstance. At the same time that Darwin's book was being talked about, not only did the French-American African explorer, Paul Belloni du Chaillu, exhibit some of the first articulated gorilla skins ever seen following his return to Europe in 1859, but his rather sensational book of 1861, with stories of these great apes abducting human females, led the popular press to put two and two together. And in the pages and cartoons of *Punch* in particular, Man became Gorilla, by the fortunate confluence of Darwin and Chaillu over 1860–1.

"Mr G. O'Rilla" and his namesakes became the laugh of the day: Mr "G-g-g-o-o-o-rilla", resplendent in white tie and tails, and with a beaming smile, caused the footman's hair to stand on end in one *Punch* cartoon of 1861 as he entered a fashionable venue; and there were lots more cartoons, comic poems, and songs besides. This was what *Punch* would come to run as "Monkeyana". It is likely, moreover, that it was this humorous vein of late 1850s sensational "monkey business" news that Bishop Samuel Wilberforce was alluding to in his cheeky quip about Huxley's ape grandparents at the so-called "Oxford Debate" in June 1860, which we examined in Chapter 7, rather than his remark being the embittered "fundamentalist" slur of mythology.

Although Darwin said nothing about men and monkeys in the *Origin* of 1859, he certainly did so in his pioneering anthropological studies, *The Descent of Man* (1871) and *The Expression of Emotions in Man and Animals* (1872). In these works Darwin marshalled evidence from animal – especially ape – behaviour, "primitive" humans, and contemporary Western civilization to draw powerful parallels in such areas as mating rituals, music as a sexual attractor, facial expressions, and aggression. Much of *Descent*, for instance, was about "sexual selection" and the finding of suitable mates in human and animal groups, while *Expression* analyses what feelings and meanings we can read into faces and other bodily gestures.

Yet if the press had a field day with Chaillu and his gorillas in 1860 and 1861, then they had a circus in the 1870s, for it is from this decade that the most famous "Darwin as a monkey" cartoons date, although modern-day myth-building popular book editors often include these 1870s cartoons in tedious rehashings of the "Oxford Debate" of 1860! But let me point out that there are instant clues to this editorial skulduggery. Firstly, *none* of the 1860s cartoons feature or mention Bishop Wilberforce, the mythic anti-evolution villain. Secondly, the pictures of Darwin as a tailed primate of the 1870s show him with the long white beard and furrowed face that was his appearance from his mid-sixties onwards. Yet look at Darwin photographs of c. 1859, and you see the balding, black-haired, clean-shaven (albeit careworn) man of fifty that he then was.

Even so, Darwin had become a veritable gift to the cartoonists by the 1870s: the gaunt, high-ridged brow, bald head, worried look, and luxuriant white beard almost suggested a venerable great ape even before the cartoonist divested the Sage of Down of his frock coat, and gave him a monkey tail!

Yet what invariably gets forgotten when the words "Darwin" and "evolution" enter the religion and science "debate" is what else was going on in the human sciences after 1860. Not only were archaeology, Egyptology, and Assyriology casting new and yet sometimes problematic light onto our understanding of the Old Testament world, but anthropology was also suggesting that humanity was much older than the biblical record.

Who, for example, were the peoples who had lived in the anciently sealed and recently discovered caves in places like Brixham, Devonshire? Peoples who had hunted now extinct animals, at least in England, yet had fashioned stone tools, and even made fires in their caves? And yet their cultural remains were now covered with thick layers of slow-forming ancient stalagmite deposit. And when the

141

amateur archaeologist Marcelino Sanz de Sautuola and his daughter were digging in the Altamira Caves in Northern Spain in 1879, they were amazed to discover naturalistic paintings of bulls and other animals. Who could possibly have painted them? And how long ago? For they too were covered with stalagmite films! They seemed to greatly antedate the biblical chronology of Adam and Eve. And when fresh analyses of bits of bone (discovered in 1856) from the Neander Valley near Düsseldorf came to be made, did this indicate that there had once been races of "humanoids" living in Europe who were not quite like us? Was humanity, therefore, a product of slow evolutionary change? And were there "missing links" connecting us to the apes after all?

So what was the response to all of these discoveries? One thing we must be on our guard about is the evolution myth-builder's tendency to telescope everything into the period around 1860, when Darwin's *Origin* somehow "proved" that we all came from monkeys, and Christianity went into embarrassed retreat.

Let us begin by looking at one thing that casts an interesting light on the evolution hysteria: humour. Of course, modern-day atheist and secular myth-builders may enjoy reprinting Darwin cartoons out of historical context, but I have yet to read a "canonical" account of evolution that asks: "Why, if the Victorians were so po-faced, serious, and shocked by Darwinism, were there so many cartoons, comic poems, and jokes about it?" Surely, they should have been swooning with self-righteous indignation and sending letters of commiseration to Bishop Wilberforce rather than buying *Punch*, *Fun*, *Vanity Fair*, and other middle-class-market publications which had a good laugh at the whole evolution caper. "Mr G-g-g-o-o-o-rilla" and his compatriots, indeed, should never have been arousing laughter around the firesides of respectable churchgoers, but they clearly did. And one indication that the humour *was* appreciated was that the magazines carrying it sold and sold again. So who was evolution offending?

One obvious group were those who still read their Bibles as literally true from Genesis to Revelation. And I won't deny that they were a significant community, especially among Dissenters and "Low

Church" Anglicans, who sometimes regarded the "interpretation" of Scripture as a wicked Papist perversion. On the other hand, as we saw in Chapter 5, biblical "criticism" and interpretation went back to the early church, and encompassed most major theologians over the centuries who prayed about and wrestled with Scripture's inner contradictions. And in this context, let us remember – and I apologize for repeating myself, but it is a *very* important point – St Augustine's c. AD 400 advice to fellow-Christians about not making the faith and themselves look foolish by trying to defend a Genesis flat-earth cosmology when talking with geometrically educated Greeks.

There was, however, another theological constituency which had qualms about evolutionary ideas. Namely, those practitioners and friends of science who could accept an ancient earth, dinosaurs, and a sequential progression of "special creations" that began with aquatic blobs and ended with gorillas, but who saw humanity as biologically separate. For were we not uniquely created in God's image, and did we not have something that not even the cleverest gorilla possessed: an immortal soul? People who thought this way, and they were still plentiful in 1860, would have remained in full agreement with the classic natural theological tenets expressed in William Paley's *Natural Theology* (1802), which was undergraduate reading in both Oxford and Cambridge, and which argued that every leaf, bird's feather, and creature was the direct handiwork of God, even if that handiwork had been in progress over *millions* of years. Buckland, Sedgwick, Bishop Wilberforce, and most of the geologists thought along those lines, and Darwin himself had been brought up on Paley's ideas. And in many ways, Darwin's own loss of a personal faith had come about not because he had any problem with a creator, so much as with a constantly *directing* and *sustaining* God. And that loss of faith – exacerbated by the seemingly pointless death of his daughter Annie – had been a source of regret for him, especially as his still deeply Christian wife Emma found his agnosticism so painful.

On the other hand, it is all too easy to forget, awash as we now are in our modern sea of evolutionary mythology, that many devout Christians, including many in holy orders, actually found spiritual inspiration in evolution: or at least did not feel their faith necessarily compromised by it. While nature might, in the pre-Darwinian words of Lord Alfred Tennyson, be "red in tooth and claw", with countless species condemned to oblivion because circumstances meant that they would never "evolve", things were not necessarily that bleak. After all, the dinosaurs might well have been doomed, from our standpoint, to pointless extinction, in so far as they would never become gorillas or men, yet who are we to say that they were not happy, fulfilled, and contented doing what micro-brained creatures like dinosaurs best loved doing? Could you not thoroughly enjoy lording it over the earth, eating whomsoever you fancied, copulating, excreting giant "coprolites", and basking in the sun, until suddenly you found a younger, fitter dinosaur with his teeth in your windpipe, and you promptly floated off to that great swamp in the sky? Was this necessarily a wasted individual or species existence? Was it a life of any less account than that of "Mr G-g-g-o-o-o-rilla" and his real-life counterparts?

Yet at the heart of the evolution question, theologically speaking, in 1859, and especially after *The Descent of Man* (1871) and *Expression* (1872), was the source and uniqueness of the human soul, and its relationship to God. If natural science could make a credible argument for the animal descent of our human bodies and even brains, then where had our immortal souls, moral sense, and higher cognitive faculties come from? Were they no more than the resonances of superior organic machinery? A way of reasoning, indeed, that had a clear ancestry in Thomas Hobbes's argument that the master was superior to his dog only in the wider range of signals that he could respond to!

Yet implicit in Darwinian evolutionary thinking was a reductionism that could see truth as only accessible through science and matter. Like Hobbes, it could countenance no immaterial spirit. But we will return to these reductionist ideas in more detail in Chapter 11.

Likewise, was Darwinian natural selection of necessity random? Was this essentially philosophical prerequisite of evolution actually demanded by inductive evidence or by observed experience, or did it depend on the wider beliefs of the "narrator"? Here we encounter those intangibles of which both Victorian and modern thinkers have always been aware: namely, how far do we frame our scientific ideas in accordance with our individual "world-pictures" or even temperaments? Rather in the same way that some people are instinctively drawn to the music of Mahler and others to Gilbert and Sullivan, some to the novels of Kafka and others to those of P. G. Wodehouse?

To conclude, therefore, I think that temperament and an individual's tendency to instinctively see an idea one way rather than another have received too little attention, obsessed as so many scholars are with perceived "arguments", "debates", and pure "rationality". And so focused upon intellectualizing the whole affair have many scholars dealing with evolution and religion become, that they not only overlook the *humour* popularly engendered by Chaillu's gorillas, but also wider attitude changes going on in Victorian society.

Take, for example, the responses to Darwinism across that spectrum of people who were publicly or actively Christian, be they ordained or lay. The received mythology tells us that after *Origin* in 1859 and the "Great Debate" of 30 June 1860, and indisputably after *The Descent of Man* in 1872, all unbelievers proudly trumpeted their monkey-hood from the roof-tops, while all believing Christians were driven into either embarrassed silence, or else furious, Genesis-punching, anti-scientific reaction and blind superstition. Yet this is the story according to mythology rather than according to historical evidence. Just as men of science had been developing new ideas about geology, species, and biological ancestries, especially since 1800, so thinking Christians had been doing the equivalent in their own sphere. Textual criticism, archaeology, linguistics, and other disciplines, not to mention new scientific discoveries, had given them a richer and profounder knowledge of the biblical world and humanity's place within it than they had possessed a hundred years before. Of course, the mythologists try to put this down to an erosion of faith by the onslaught of "truth", but that is not the case. Just as Archbishop John Tillotson gave a Lambeth MD to Robert Hooke in 1691, so many Victorian Christians saw no threat in the new science, and some even found it *strengthening* their faith.

Eminent lay scientists, such as the Harvard botanist Asa Gray, Darwin's correspondent and "apostle" in America, found inspiration in *Origin*, seeing natural selection operating in a similar way to that in which rivulets running down a mountain-side after rain contribute in their diverse and complex ways to the great river at the bottom of the valley. And far from being an atheist, Gray was an active and committed Trinitarian Protestant, and involved with various Christian enterprises.

But what about the Church of England? Mythology tells us that its ranks were made up of elite, reactionary men, sworn to defend every jot and tittle in the Bible, oblivious to the economic exploitation of the working classes, and determined to enforce Christian conversion upon innocent souls across the empire. But there is a simple one-word response to this fairy-tale view: rubbish! The Anglican Church has never been a homogeneous or conformist body, any more than the Roman Church: not in King Henry VIII's time, nor in Queen Victoria's, nor today! In the 1860s, moreover, the church was riven with differences of opinion within the very ranks of its clergy: Low Church evangelicals, High Church "Puseyites", crypto-Roman Catholics, devout men of science, and a glorious gallery of independent-thinking eccentrics whose antics embraced hunting or cricket mania at one end and Druidism or ghost-hunting at the other. Differences of opinion, moreover, that often amazed and exasperated the quiet and homely Darwin. And responses to evolution must be interpreted within this context.

Just as there were reactionary parsons, so there were open-minded ones. Sympathetic responses to the authors of *Essays and Reviews* or Bishop Colenso in the early 1860s (as we saw in Chapter 5) were part of this rich spectrum of Anglican opinion. And very important were the "Broad Churchmen" and the Christian socialists, both of whom tended to be warmly disposed to new scientific ideas without necessarily decrying the power and inner meaning of the Christian gospel message. Of course the "Broad" men and the Christian socialists had much in common: a realization, for example, that new scientific ideas gave us fresh glimpses of the majesty of God's creation that had not been revealed in earlier generations – such as the mathematical beauty of Newtonian gravitation in the seventeenth century and the insights of geology and biology in the nineteenth. But this was no more about theologians "changing their minds" than to say that a freethinking botanist of 1860 had somehow reneged on scientific truth by abandoning the Linnaean fixity of species of his youth. Science progresses, and humanity's understanding of God's glory in nature similarly progresses, and it is not only a myth, but a deep intellectual injustice, to credit progressive understanding to the one while denying it to the other.

And far from being smug in their Barchesterian fastness, the Christian socialists, such as Frederick D. Maurice and Charles Kingsley, openly campaigned on behalf of the poor, as did the "slum priests" movement by the 1880s – men in the noblest tradition of the Christian reformer and active in the promotion of social justice, yet to whom revolutionary, radical, and violence-based philosophies were total anathema. And many of these parsons were actively interested in science and technology, being involved with sanitary reform, provision of medical services for the poor, and trades unionism – as well as being adherents of evolution. For did not Christ send out his disciples to minister to the poor and outcast, and, if our God-given intelligence had enabled us to demonstrate that our bodies had evolved from monkeys, so what? Our immortal souls were still unique gifts of God, irrespective of how he had inserted them into our frail bodies. After all, not many gorillas have written books on science or ethics! So could not we humans really be special after all?

And then, in the 1880s, in full knowledge of Darwin's post-1871 explicitly monkey-related works, other groups of Anglican theologians explored mankind's relation to God through Catholic, mystical, and scientific avenues, such as the contributors to *Lux Mundi* ("Light of the World") in 1889. One of these authors was the clerical Oxford don Aubrey Lackington Moore. Moore, who was interested in science, suggested that evolution had shown God *not* to be a distant, aloof "absentee landlord", but an *improving* landlord, who continued to tend his creation through the mechanisms of nature. An early expression, in some ways, of the present-day theology of the environment!

I have devoted a large amount of space to Darwin and his impact because no single scientific writer or idea has been so widely or so ruthlessly used to feed the science and religion conflict myth. But we can only properly understand *Origin* and Darwin's later works by placing them in context. And that context, Victorian England, was a much richer, livelier, more argumentative, and "cheekier" society than po-faced mythologists like people to realize. For while some Victorians – such as Darwin himself – *did* lose their faith because of a wide variety of scientific *and personal* reasons, many also found spiritual inspiration in scientific discovery. To the Victorians, God was big and expansive, and prevailing Victorian culture was confident, so no one felt obliged to apologize for believing in him. Being a Christian socialist or devout evolutionist, moreover, did not necessarily mean that one was a churchgoing "soggy liberal" or "wishy-washy".

But let us finish with a quotation from Bishop Wilberforce FRS's powerfully *scientific*, deeply learned, and *anti*-simple-biblical-literalist review of Darwin's *Origin*, which he published in the very prestigious *Quarterly Review* (July 1860, pages 225–63). While Wilberforce made it clear that he believed humans were more than just superior animals, he was nonetheless acutely aware that science possessed an unassailable intellectual integrity of its own when he wrote:

> … we have objected to the view with which we are dealing [evolution by natural selection] solely on scientific grounds… We have no sympathy with those who object to any facts or alleged facts in nature, or to any inference logically deduced from them, because they believe them to contradict what it appears to them is taught by [divine] Revelation. (p. 256)

Indeed, it is a great shame that so many people who generate mythological nonsense about Bishop Wilberforce and Darwin's *Origin* don't take the trouble to read this review carefully, for it is the nearest detailed (summer of 1860) statement that we have as to what Wilberforce actually thought.

10

Countering the "Big Lie"

It is not enough to counter the "Big Lie" that science and Christianity are inherently in conflict; we must also remind the New Atheists that not only has religion always inspired, and continues to inspire, many scientists, but science has enhanced, and continues to enhance, our religious understanding.

Why Is Nature Congruent?

One of the truly astonishing things that science reveals is the wonderful unity, and what might be called the *congruence*, of nature. Why does nature make sense to the human mind? And even if a solipsist or nihilist argued that congruence is merely an illusion, nature a chaos, and order a temporary delusion, one could reasonably answer, "All right, but why does the *illusion* appear to make sense?" Unless we are willing to concede the existence of a world "out there" which obeys basic laws, such as that night follows day and that fire is hot to the touch, then we might as well give up, gnaw a bone, and bay at the moon until the illusion of a passing asteroid blows us all to existential smithereens! So in the meanwhile, let us continue to assume that reality exists.

One might argue that it is a truly wonderful thing that, while we have not the slightest shred of evidence that matter is in itself conscious, we humans are deeply conscious of matter. The planets, for example, move around the sun in brutish ignorance of the laws of universal gravitation that enable us to observe, predict, and record their smallest motions. We can analyse the chemical and energy structures of distant galaxies without *them*, as physical objects, being aware that we are doing so; and we can predict the effect that particular micro-organisms or cells will have upon the human body without the organisms themselves having the slightest idea of what they are inescapably driven to do.

When you think about it, is that not a truly amazing thing? That those three-pound lumps of meat on the top of our spinal columns that we call brains can fathom out the nature of their environment, extending from electrons to galaxies, through the whole dazzling spectrum of energy radiation to a contemplation of *themselves* (neurology and psychology), and wrestle with ultimate questions about reality, beginnings and endings, right and wrong (theology and philosophy)?

Solipsistic paralysis apart, what makes all of this possible is the *congruence*, or logical interconnectedness, of nature as our sentient beings, or souls, perceive it. Indeed, this stunning congruence even enables us to discover things that don't fit into the older, classical, scheme of reference, such as nuclear, quantum, and relativity physics. We first experience matter as solid and real; then, between the seventeenth and nineteenth centuries, we discover that it is not simple, but made up of complex combinations of chemical elements, and then go on to find congruent elements in the sun and stars. Then, in the twentieth century, we discover that the atoms forming the elements are *not* solid, but just configurations of energy particles, electrons, protons, and neutrons, and that, on a deeper level, a lump of granite or iron is not really hard at all. And the realm of quantum physics is an *Alice in Wonderland* world where nothing is as it seems, and one needs a new form of purely *mathematical* explanation to make sense of it.

But even the *Alice in Wonderland* worlds of quantum and relativity physics have their own congruence, and this is the marvellous thing. The task which faces us is not how to navigate our way through a chaotic Mad Hatter illusion of existence, but how to relate the new congruence of the "new physics" to the classical "old physics" of common sense. And, as we saw above, the linkage comes through developing a new mathematics! And if all that is a mere illusion, then it must be even more wonderful and congruent than "reality" itself. Either way, we are faced with wonder!

Yet not only is nature congruent, or unified, when we look at it, but the next great wonder is that it remains so when we manipulate it. Think of a steam engine, for example. The iron of which the engine is built is first dug out of the same type of ironstone rock, no matter whether that rock is in America, China, India, or Great Britain, and the strata are identified through our geological knowledge. All the iron on the planet melts at the same temperature, 2,797 °F (1,596 °C), and can be moulded or worked by the same processes worldwide, to build the engine. But to make the engine usable, we also need to know that all water boils at 212 °F or 100 °C, and that, as shown by Boyle's law, it generates a mechanical energy that is mathematically related to steam pressure and temperature. Then, employing pistons, turbines, wheels, and other fruits of applied mechanical ingenuity, we can make the engine do useful work that exceeds the power of thousands of horses. And as an added bonus, the engine never gets tired or needs a holiday, as long as you feed it with fuel and water and clean it out.

And the same analogy applies for our knowledge of the unchanging, mathematical laws of physics, chemistry, and biology, to produce everything from a mobile phone to a recyclable plastic bottle to an antibiotic drug. If nature were not congruent, or not at unity with itself, and if our biochemical brain circuitry did not enable us to perform incredible acts of reasoning, devising, and calculating, we would not be the human beings that we are. And while this may not constitute a formal proof of a divine creation, it certainly leaves us asking the inevitable question "So why does it all make sense, and why are things the way they are?"

Why Do Humans Respond so Positively to Beauty and Elegance?

Elegance, harmony, and logic seem to be in our very bones. In the arts, it is true – and this was especially so in the twentieth century – we

151

no longer share a common aesthetic. Modern "brutalist" architecture, hideous childish daubs on modern-art gallery walls, "inaccessible" literature, and music which, to a classically inclined ear, sounds like industrial noise or cats in agony, are characteristic examples. Besides these home-grown examples, the indigenous high art of other cultures may seem bizarre or incomprehensible to a Westerner. Musical quarter-tones, for instance, while not always appreciated by Westerners, have a subtle beauty for a Chinese ear; while statues or pictures which a Westerner might find menacing can have a beauty or a rare magic power for a non-European. But aesthetics always makes sense to the culture that expresses it in its own indigenous art. Indeed, one might even suggest that twentieth-century Western nihilism and revolt against the classical and Judeo-Christian cultural tradition have created a cult of the ugly which must – presumably – make some kind of logical sense to its own *cognoscenti*. For we all respond to *beauty*, irrespective of how we see it.

Things are more straightforward in science, however; for while different people's brains – be it that of the Roman poet Virgil or that of a modern-day recipient of a British Arts Council grant – process aesthetic data differently, there is less room for diversity of expression in science. If a scientific theory is wrong, it will not predict measurable phenomena.

And while the Greeks were by no means the first people to invent "beauty", they were the first to subject it to analysis. Plato and Aristotle both discussed aesthetics as an aspect of human understanding, yet it was the Greek geometers, from Thales (c. 625 BC) onwards, who were perhaps the first to be bedazzled by pure form, shape, and number in the abstract. We are told in Greek literature, for instance, of geometers sacrificing an animal as a "thank you" to their heavenly powers for revealing to them the exquisite truth of a new geometrical proof. A pure intellectual symmetry, indeed, and quite independent of any physical shape existing in the material world.

If the Greeks invented "science", as opposed to record-keeping, counting, and fabricating, they did so because of their emerging grasp of the power of *number* – or mathematics. A domain unlike art or poetry, quite independent of human emotion or opinion. Poets might argue about the perfection of a verse, yet no one could argue about a geometrical theorem, for it either worked or it did not! I would argue, moreover, that this was not only one of the great intellectual "revelations" in human cultural development, but it is no less valid today than it was in 500 BC. Why *do* we need a thing to be "geometrically elegant" to be beautiful, be it a Bach fugue, an African vase, or Einstein's theory of general relativity?

And why do we instinctively demand that for a thing to be *true*, it must also be beautiful? Not necessarily visually, of course; but making sense and bestowing an intellectual comfort or satisfaction. One might suggest that a *true* work of art is one that endures or becomes a "classic" because it feeds a deep need for order in human beings, be their culture Western, African, or Asian. And likewise in science.

Greek medicine in the tradition of Hippocrates – and with cultural parallels in indigenous Chinese and Arabic medicine – saw health as a state of *balance*, when the "humours" of the body were each in their proper place. Illness occurred when one or more "humours" usurped another's place, to result in the patient becoming too hot, dry, moist, or cold. And the doctor's art lay in diagnosing which humour was misbehaving, and restoring the body to its correct balance. We still speak of being "out of balance" when we are unwell, and a person who is mentally ill or behaves obsessively is often described in popular parlance as "mentally unbalanced".

It was the classical Greek philosophical geometers who not only linked the body to geometry, but even related our musical tastes to both the world and the cosmos. One later Greek philosopher tells us how Pythagoras was watching a brass worker in his forge, and noticed that when he struck the hot metal with a hammer of a particular weight, it *always* made a "clang" of a particular tone. Be it a heavy bang or a light tap, the musical pitch emitted by a blow from the same hammer was always the same. And hammers of different sizes produced different pitches in a consistent and unvarying manner. Could it be that musical sounds were the product of different weights and blows, and that they were mathematically related?

Of course, elaborate musical instruments had been around for millennia by Pythagoras's time in the sixth century BC. The trumpet, harp, and other instruments are mentioned in the Jewish Old Testament, while Egyptian artists routinely depicted a variety of instruments being played in their paintings. But the ingenious Greeks took it all much further, for they realized that the relationship between pitch and weight (or length) did not just apply to hammers, but also to blown pipes and plucked strings. And what other cultures had taken for granted in their pursuit of musical pleasure, the Greeks analysed mathematically. And sounds, in their tones, semitones, and octaves, were found to possess a mathematical unity that was no less exact than the component steps of a geometrical proof.

And then, when they observed the heavens, and timed what were believed to be the periods in which the planets and stars rotated around the earth, the Greeks noticed that the planets not only travelled at different speeds, but they described increasingly large circular orbits around the earth: the moon's orbit being the smallest and Saturn's (the outermost known planet until 1781) the greatest. And beyond Saturn came the largest sphere of all, which carried the fixed stars and zodiac constellations. And could one not think of the planetary orbits as rather similar to gigantic rings in space? Hit a small metal ring with a hammer and it emits a high-pitched sound; hit a big ring, and it emits a deeper tone – in much the same way that a shorter or longer tube emits a higher or lower pitch when you blow air into it or a string when you pluck it. And it would be the late classical Christian and medieval scholars – especially in Paris and Chartres – who would develop this "music of the spheres" idea, to link astronomy, musical aesthetics, logic, mathematics, the mind of man and the mind of God into one beautiful congruent whole.

Now as the moon went around the earth in twenty-eight days, whereas Saturn needed twenty-nine and a half years, it stood to reason that Saturn's orbit was bigger – and its track much longer – than the moon's. So Saturn's orbit must represent a deeper musical pitch than that of the moon. And this was the logic that lay at the heart of the Greek idea of "the music of the spheres". Not that the planets were necessarily singing as they rotated (though some later Greek and medieval philosophers suggested that there might be an angelic or heavenly "symphony"), so much as that there was a clear logical parallel between the mathematics of musical pitch and the number and motions of the planets: seven planets – the moon, Mercury, Venus, sun, Mars, Jupiter, Saturn – with the sphere of the stars making up the celestial octave as the eighth sphere.

And what more stunning example of the divine Logos could you hope for, when the sounds which delighted the human ear, and soul, had clear parallels in the mathematical proportions of hammers, vibrating strings, pipes, and planetary orbits? Medieval Christian philosophers, with their association of the Logos with God the creator and saviour, included music in the university curriculum by 1220. Not music as a performing art, so much as a study of the divine harmony of ear and intellect, God and man, heaven and earth. And as late as 1596, indeed, the German astronomer, mathematician, and theologian, Johannes Kepler, in his *Mysterium Cosmographicum* ("Cosmic Mystery"), would try to relate the planetary orbital spheres to the "regular solids" – cube, tetrahedron, and such – of three-dimensional geometry, and both of these to the mind of God, as discerned through human reason. And it would be in his *Harmonices Mundi* ("Harmony of the World" [or "Universe"]) of 1619 that Kepler would announce his three laws of planetary motion, which sixty years later would provide Sir Isaac Newton with the principal clue for his theory of gravitation.

So not only do we relate to the beautiful, but the Greeks tried to work out *why* we do so: namely, because of geometry, harmony, and balance – a balance that links art, science, medicine, reason, and God. And while we now know that there are more than seven planets, and that curing illness is rather more complex than rectifying the balances in the body, the intellectual and spiritual goals of the ancient Greeks still form the bedrock of our aesthetic values and ideas today. Just as a beautiful human face requires symmetry and balance, so does a satisfying body of sound, and an adequate explanation of how a complex drug acts upon the human body or how we might evaluate a scientific theory. And all of this involves what might be considered in the widest sense a series of *spiritual* criteria, to remind us once again how *religious* values have always fed and sustained scientific aspiration and understanding at their deepest level.

Indeed, the whole of Greek science, from cosmology to medicine, was rooted in these concepts, Logos and geometry, and to deny science's debt to them is to rubber-stamp atheist ideology in the teeth of historical evidence.

Science Describes Effects, Religion Talks of Causes and Purposes

One of the driving forces of human curiosity on all levels is a wish to know *why* things are the way they are, and what *causes* them. Since at least the seventeenth century, however, science has not seen it as its business to attempt to discuss causality. Science studies matter and motion, and we predict how things will behave and frame our scientific laws from a growing body of observed and measured physical data, verified by a global scientific community. So is our wish to know causes an irrelevance, as many materialists like to argue? Yet if that is the case, why does it seem to be bred in the bone of humanity?

Indeed, some materialist scientists are so circumlocutory about our driving need to "know" that they perform intellectual somersaults in order to contrive physical explanations for the unknowable. Anything to avoid mention of the "God" word, in fact! Let me give you an example.

A few years ago, I was attending a scientific conference in a British university where a cosmologist speaker was discussing what might have been happening *before* the big bang took place, about 13.75 billion years ago. He ran a whole series of speculations about modelling proto-states of hydrogen, and argued that this was perhaps how the big bang had come about. Without such models and computer programs, he said dismissively, one could not escape from the threat of outdated ideas of a creator, or the "God hypothesis": mathematical models and computer programs would replace superstitious explanations.

In the following question and answer session, however, I asked him from the floor exactly how he could attempt to model what had happened before the big bang, since all the solid, physical evidences that we possess must, by definition, have originated in and come *out* of the big bang. For in science, you can only hope to model what we don't know by using the physical laws that we know already. So how can we remotely hope to model what physical laws, if any, were in operation *before* the big bang? The lecturer squirmed somewhat and admitted that there really was no way of knowing, and that it was all based upon theory, computer modelling, and back-projecting what we know already. So how, I enquired, was his imaginary physical hypothesis one whit better than the so-called outdated "God hypothesis"? He conceded that on evidence grounds, it was not.

I cite the above incident because it is characteristic of a not infrequent and hopefully unintended sleight of hand that many materialists and atheists employ as a way of trying to bring in causality by the back door, and avoid the "God hypothesis". Yet in reality, all that they are doing is replacing what they see as a theological "superstition" with what is no more than a computer-generated secular superstition, and trying to cover their tracks with a plethora of computer-crunched numbers. Inventing, no less, what Thomas Hobbes (in a different context) mischievously styled a "Kingdom of the Fairies": or, more plainly, a pure piece of fabrication. For try as we might not to, we humans are impelled to ask "Why?", even if some of us feel driven to model imaginary states of pre-existent matter governed by imaginary laws. And we do it not only in pre-big-bang cosmology, but also when we contrive physical speculations about how life itself originated and where human consciousness came from.

Yet one of the wisest insights into this quandary came from the eighteenth-century Scottish freethinking philosopher David Hume, for in his essay *An Enquiry Concerning Human Understanding* (1748) he discussed causality as observed in nature. And the conclusion is that we can never know causes, even in a scientific experiment. We might be able to say that billiard ball "A" imparts some form of force or energy to billiard ball "B", and measure their motions precisely, but we are wholly ignorant about what "force" and "energy" actually are. We can only observe and measure *effects*, never causes.

Indeed, one might develop Hume's line of thinking and say that we all know for certain that water invariably boils at 212 °F (or 100 °C) at sea level. Yet how do we know? Well, every time we have seen water boiling above a heat source and have inserted a thermometer into it, the water unfailingly registers the same temperature. But we still do not know the *cause* of the boiling: only that water, plus intense heat, equals bubbling, steaming, and a particular thermometric reading. Indeed, all we observe is a *necessary connection*, or contingent coming together, of all the factors involved. But what *causes* them to do so, we have no idea. Nor, for that matter, when the right carbohydrate chemicals and forms of electrical energy combine to form a human brain in the womb, can we know why the resulting structures will constitute a conscious person who will one day ask the question "Where did I come from and what is the cause of life?"

While *effects* constitute the legitimate world of science, what causes these effects belongs to a quite different frame of reference altogether: a frame of reference belonging to theology or philosophy, irrespective of what mental gymnastics one might perform. Yet there are still many materialists who adamantly insist that being concerned with causes or purposes is a sort of primitive left-over from pre-scientific superstitious times.

I have still, however, to encounter the materialist scientist or philosopher who does not remain locked into a world of cause, purpose, and meaningful relationship on an everyday basis, no matter how much they build castles in the air when "at work". Just listen to a "causes and purposes are an illusion" materialist squeal with fury if his wallet or her handbag is stolen. The police must be called. Has the thief been watching and trailing me? What does he know of my affairs, and will he strike again? All available clues are handed to the police to aid detection, the retrieval of the stolen goods, and the hoped-for punishment of the offender to ensure that he does not strike again. In short, an elaborate panoply of cause, effect, motive, purpose, calculation of likely future actions and consequences, and a need for present and future security is brought into play. Likewise, find me a subscriber to "the cosmos is just a meaningless mess" school of thinking who does not want to give their children the best education and start in life that they can, with road maps for exams, goals, possible career paths, and future professional success laid out for them. Or, for that matter, the nihilist philosopher – when he or she is *not* actually in a seminar or writing philosophic gloom – who does not want a steady income, professional respect and advancement, good health care, and a fat pension on retirement.

But all the above runs counter to a science or philosophy which sees no meaning or purpose in the "big picture" of space, time, existence, and eternity – for if we subscribe to this, why should we be so obsessed with cause, effect, and purpose in our own small lives? Indeed, this asymmetry between the cosmic and the personal has always puzzled me: why, if there is really no "argument from design", should we be constantly busy designing our lives, planning our futures, and arguing our professional or personal cases on the world's stage? Have I, in my own simple-mindedness, missed something very profound here, or are we dealing with a naked contradiction between belief and behaviour that a more ungenerous person than myself might call hypocritical?

So could it be, then, that there really *are* direction-related causes that lie behind things, and that the self-same compulsion for order and purpose that rules our own human lives relates to some principle that really does exist in the cosmos, in nature, in the way we do science, and in the wider scheme of things? And if that is so, what is wrong with calling that principle "God"?

11

Does Science Challenge Religion? The Great Atheist Myth

We saw in Chapter 2 that not only has atheism in its various forms been around for centuries, but there have been no scientific advances in the last 250 years that have challenged essential Christian belief. But wait, many may cry out, what about evolution? Yet, as we saw in Chapters 8 and 9, evolution has in many respects been carefully crafted by twentieth-century anti-Christian writers (assisted, one must admit, by the "fortuitous" gift of modern-day fundamentalism) into an intellectual and spiritual trauma that in reality was less of a worry to the Victorians than it has been inflated into by modern secularists. So can we actually consider New Atheist claims as little more than – to borrow a quotation from Shakespeare – "Much Ado about Nothing"?

Lack of New Secularist Ideas

When we examine the post-1860 science and religion scene, we find a situation which was far less clear-cut than many modern writers would lead us to believe. Take, for instance, those prominent late-Victorian advocates of a purely naturalistic "secularism" in science that was independent from the clutches of the "argument from design": Thomas Henry Huxley and John Tyndall. Huxley would become notorious as "Darwin's Bulldog", while Tyndall was an influential Irish physicist, and both, in addition to pure research, were active in the popularization of science, especially among the working classes. Yet what drove both of them was not atheism so much as a wish to disentangle science from ecclesiastical input – such as the "argument from design". A point that is often missed today.

On the other hand, both men recognized that human beings have unfathomable attributes that could not, and probably never would be, adequately explained by science. Human consciousness was a case in point. There seemed to be some sort of spiritual aspect of humanity that could, perhaps, be consigned to "religion" in its various forms. What overwhelmingly concerned both men, however, was that it should be wholly and entirely divorced from science, which itself should occupy a purely secular realm. But this did not imply atheism by any means. Indeed, it was Huxley who, in 1869, coined the term "agnostic" from a Greek theological provenance. Had not St Paul, when in Athens (as related in the Acts of the Apostles), spoken of an altar to an "unknown [Greek *agnōstō*] god"? And can *we* know the nature of God and of causes? And by extension, Huxley suggested that clerical-dominated science, with its argument from design, smacked of the early Christian heresy of Gnosticism, or the idea that human intelligence, wisdom, or knowledge could bring you to God. But "a-gnosticism", far from being necessarily anti-religious, was simply saying that we cannot get to God by our own cleverness – if at all. Hence, the argument from design, instead of bringing us to God, could actually lead us astray! Not the radical anti-religion so often attributed to Huxley and Tyndall.

Of course, I am not for a second trying to imply that these men were closet *religiosi*, for there is far too much evidence to the contrary. Huxley's comment about science being surrounded by dead theological notions, and Tyndall's notorious "Belfast Address" of 1874 – when he was serving as president of the British Association – spelling out the secular materialistic status of science, make any attempt in that direction impossible. Yet while both actively and loudly campaigned for the *profession* of science in an independent secular context, and loved going for what they saw as meddlesome clergy, neither was especially atheistic. Religion and science were recognized as serving their wholly separate functions, and should keep to their distinct spheres.

Needless to say, there is a problem with this way of thinking, gnostic or not; for scientific and religious questions *do* interpenetrate on many levels, for both are about aspects of meaning and making sense of things. Indeed, to say that they must be kept apart is a bit like saying, "Medicine is a very worthwhile intellectual pursuit, but under no conceivable circumstances must you inflict it upon the sick."

It may also have seemed viable, 150 years ago, for the new breed of Victorian science professionals, such as Huxley and Tyndall and their friends in the "X" and "Metaphysical" dining clubs, to attempt to keep science and religion apart as a way of escaping the dreaded clerical teleology, but this doesn't work today. Many evangelical atheists now occupy a position that is far more extreme than that of Huxley and Tyndall: indeed, there are people who now scream out for the abolition of religion altogether, especially in public life, and who lump together Anglicans, American Protestant fundamentalists, Roman Catholics, and militant Islamists, because all claim allegiance to "outdated" or "backward" beliefs incapable of being proven in a laboratory. And as for things like consciousness or morality, well, they are generated by our evolved monkey brains – aren't they?

Yet, there are two areas in which late twentieth- and twenty-first-century scientific research has produced a body of new discoveries that Huxley and Tyndall could never have dreamed of, and which just cry out for religious engagement. I mean modern-day biomedical technology and deep-space cosmology.

Though we will be looking quite separately at the interpretation of brain scans in Chapter 12, we must stand in awe of how medical therapeutics has transformed the lifestyles and expectations of Western people since 1950. The way, for instance, body scans, using magnetic and other forms of high-energy fields in conjunction with computers, can now make visible and generate moving images of the inside of a living person, along with bio-engineering technologies which routinely allow us to ventilate, blood-circulate, nourish, and sustain bodies in various types of deep trauma. Nowadays life and death is no longer a simple matter: questions about meaningful existence and justifiable termination come into play. Exactly when, for example, does an independent human life begin? When in a body scan we see a group of cells starting to divide in a woman's womb? And is the person who has lain inert on the life-support machine for a month, yet whose biological processes are being sustained by machinery, dead or alive? And what about the Alzheimer's patient who occasionally flashes a meaningful glance or smile which forces us to ask: "The telephone exchange may well have shut down, but it still seems that there are intelligent messages trying to get through, so is there still a vital soul trapped in that poor physical shell of the person I once knew?" And what about the whole business of legal suicide? If modern medicine can extend biological life beyond what nature intended, and indeed, beyond what the patient may desire, do we have a right to say "enough is enough"? And who can say that a loving God will not forgive a person for making that choice?

A while ago, I was discussing some of these points with a retired physician of considerable eminence. He said that when he first entered medical school, in 1949, none of the above medical possibilities existed. You were conceived, born, and died, and medicine did what it could in between. Diagnostics relied heavily on the doctor's personal skill and experience, and not on machines, and what was going on inside a living person was always difficult to ascertain. But things have changed profoundly over the last sixty years.

Modern medicine has generated a vast raft of diagnostic and therapeutic technologies, but these in turn have posed a spectrum not only of ethical, but also of "meaning" questions: questions that may have arisen occasionally before our very recent ability to scientifically extend life, but which the sheer volume of cases nowadays forces upon our attention in a way we cannot ignore. And who can deny that all of these scenarios are replete not only with professional and ethical, but also with *religious* questions, impinging as they do upon our sense of human identity, and our belief systems, conscience, and sense of purpose?

In short, modern science, instead of driving religious and "meaning" questions out of the picture, has brought them centre stage and under the spotlight. And the louder the New Atheists shout for an end to religion in the public consciousness, the more people are wanting answers to the "big questions".

But medical therapeutic research which poses questions about the beginning, ending, and meaning of human life is not the only branch of post-1950 scientific discovery to suggest religious questions. The beginning, possible future, and nature of the universe do the same.

Until the 1920s and 1930s, when the "new cosmology" of Einsteinian relativity and Edwin Hubble's and other astronomers' demonstration of the vast distances and rapid recession of the "nebulae" (galaxies) began to transform the older Newtonian cosmology, the heavens were seen as infinitely old. Yes, observation-based cosmologists from the time of Sir William Herschel onwards, after 1785, were aware that the deep-space stellar heavens changed over vast periods of time, as stars slowly formed new gravitational systems with each other, disintegrated, or, as Pierre Simon Laplace had suggested with reference to the sun, threw off filaments of matter to condense to form our solar system. Yet it was all a "steady state" universe, in which matter and energy might be recycled, with stars and nebulae being formed and dying, as did human populations, but where the overall timeless infinite structure remained stable.

Of course, the argument from design showed the universe to be the handiwork of "the creator", for could such physical and mathematical wonders be anything other than parts of a designed whole? This argument received an additional boost in the 1860s – at exactly the same time, so the atheists would have us believe, that Darwinian evolution was causing the argument from design to fall apart! A boost which came from the new science of astronomical spectroscopy, which detected sodium, nitrogen, iron, and other terrestrial chemicals in the sun and stars. So were the same elements of the periodic table that we find on earth also used by the creator to fabricate the entire universe? If so, what a unity, and what a grand design! And all of this seemed infinitely old and enduring, with one "space-time continuum" running through the whole – with twelve inches to a foot on Sirius, and the equivalent of Greenwich Mean Time in the Andromeda Nebula, just as we experienced them on earth!

By 1950, however, and certainly by the 1960s, things had begun to change drastically. From 1930, growing evidence was beginning to suggest that the universe as we see it today had begun existence as what the Belgian Roman Catholic priest, cosmologist, and mathematician Father Georges Lemaître styled a "primal atom" that somehow exploded at a particular time in the past. By the 1950s this was coming to be called a "big bang", and this is now the accepted model within which cosmologists work. And the current estimate of time reckoned to have elapsed since the "big bang" is about 13.75 billion years, give or take a bit.

Yet unlike the universe of Newton, or that of the Victorians, this "new" universe is a dynamic place, in which incredible energy systems with seemingly bizarre laws of change and development are at work, a place where a foot and Greenwich Mean Time are *not* universal standards, but relate only to their own space-time situation. And the more we discover, the more bizarre this universe seems. Yet two things emerge. (1) This "new" universe still makes sense, and is no less susceptible to human comprehension and mathematical description than was the "old" one of 1860. (2) If the universe is 13.75 billion years old, then what was going on 14 billion years ago?

Now I am not for a moment suggesting that "big bang" cosmology provides us with some kind of proof for God's existence, because it does *not*. But what it *does* do is pose questions that transcend physical and mathematical description. Being the kind of creatures that we are, we cannot prevent the "how" questions (or "by what scientific techniques can we find out all these facts?") from leading to the "why" questions. Such as *why* did the universe develop in this way, and *why* has our intelligence been able to work it all out? As we saw in Chapter 10, we are purpose-, origin-, meaning-, congruence-seeking beings – that, quite simply, is how our minds work.

So when we look at how things changed between the 1880s and early 2000s, and how scientific discoveries in medicine and cosmology opened up whole new domains of science and religion issues that the Victorians could never have imagined, we are brought face to face with the *aridity* of modern atheist thinking, and we are reminded yet again that the principal currencies in which the New Atheists deal are bombast and myth. New and original atheistical ideas are about as thick on the ground as are the proverbial snowballs in hell.

Why Has Religion Failed to Die Away?

By the middle years of the twentieth century, sociologists, psychologists, and other assorted intellectuals – often of a Marxist inclination – were confidently predicting that religious belief would die away over the next few generations. New sciences and technologies drove out the need for God as an explainer of phenomena or provider of bounty. In the post-World-War-II age of rockets, atomic bombs, and the British National Health Service, *science* and *technology* would do all that! The men in copes and mitres would be forced to yield to impassive-looking men in white lab coats wearing thick-framed plastic spectacles. Or at least that is how contemporary cinema always portrayed scientists.

Church attendance had already begun to decline markedly since the pre-1914 period, as growing car ownership, Sunday cinema, radio and then television, package holidays, cheap day trips, full employment, the mid-1950s economic boom, and youth culture gave ordinary people more options about how they spent their Sundays. People were more leisured, better fed, better informed, and healthier than in the days of their grandparents, and all of this was due to science, technology, and economics. So what happened to the secular utopia that was so confidently predicted?

Well, the boom years of the 1950s and 1960s were also overshadowed by the Cold War, as Stalinist and post-Stalin Russia, and Maoist China, terrified all those who were not so star-struck by the "Comrade" states as to excuse any atrocity, and who did not want to see the hammer and sickle red flag flying over Buckingham Palace. Poland, Czechoslovakia, Hungary, and other countries all got the iron-fist treatment of Red Freedom, and meditating Buddhist monks were mown down by Maoist tanks. And as one side after the other "tested" their 100 megaton atomic bombs, one wondered when Berlin, or Paris, would vanish in smoke. For the "sex, drugs, and rock-and-roll" culture that nowadays bus-pass-carrying, NHS-dependent "hippies" look back to with such starry eyes was also lived out under the threat of an atomic mushroom cloud. Add to that secular illusion the post-1970s economic mayhem, and one does not need to look far to realize that the God-free secular utopia had failed to materialize. On the other hand, why was there not a sudden boom in traditional churchgoing as in the days of yore? What happened, in fact, is that the situation became much more complicated.

For one thing, immigrant groups coming into Britain brought their own religions, extending from vibrant West Indian Christianity to Islam, Hinduism, and Sikhism. Then new forms of religious expression let loose their own bombshells worldwide, the most powerful of which were evangelicalism and fundamentalism. Billy Graham was only the most famous of a number of American evangelists who brought a plain Bible message to millions of people worldwide, a powerful, simple Christian message for a confused and jaded West. And there followed a veritable industry of TV evangelists, first in America, then beamed globally after the digital revolution.

Many of these evangelists, moreover, came from those parts of the American Midwest which gave rise to, and still sustain, "fundamentalism": the idea that every word of the Bible text is absolutely true, and that contextual interpretation is tantamount to blasphemy. For fundamentalism was no longer the faith of small farmers: the economic boom of post-Depression years in the USA had endowed it with scores of wealthy Bible colleges, universities, and TV stations that took great-grandpa's plain theology to the rest of the planet.

But the real shock came in from the rest of the world. Almost as if to deliberately prove the secular anti-imperial-missionary school of thinking wrong, many of the post-British-Empire peoples of Africa took their Bibles to their hearts, and central and southern Africa became the Christian powerhouse of the planet: Anglicans, Roman

Catholics, Pentecostals, and Charismatics all found expression there, and they began to evangelize their firm, vigorous faith.

I recall a few years ago my wife and I being offered a Christmas card in the street by a black African pastor in Oxford. We thanked him, said we were Christians, and fell into conversation. Then I said to him, "In the nineteenth century we took the Christian faith to your ancestors, and now *you* are bringing it back to Europe." He was delighted with my observation, for, so he said, that is exactly what he hoped he was doing!

African Christianity has played an enormous role in inspiring new churches and styles of worship in Britain, and perhaps its best-known figure is the beaming, confident, plain-speaking, former rugby-playing Anglican Archbishop of York, the Most Revd Dr John Sentamu: a "muscular Christian" if ever there was one!

But another fundamentalism which no cosy sociologist of the 1950s could have imagined is that of Islam, especially as inspired by the 1979 Islamic Revolution in Iran, and its call to global jihad. And it has indeed gone global; and especially since 9/11/2001 in America, and the London Tube and bus bombings in 2005, the full impact of that fundamentalism is still being come to terms with. For, yes, a force as powerful as religion can inspire us to slaughter our fellow-creatures as well as to love them, depending on how we see God.

Far from obediently dying away, therefore, religion has boomed in a way that no one could have expected in 1950. Yes, traditional churches may be far from full in Great Britain, but they often *are* in Holy Orthodox Russia and in ex-Soviet satellite states, as people delivered from the crushing hand of brutal secularism seek God once more. Christianity is also booming in China. And how many 65-year-old liberal 1960s secular "flower-power" children are baffled by their grandchildren who go to cinema-sized charismatic churches and sing choruses about Jesus? And that is saying nothing about the mosques and temples of immigrant groups.

Religion, I would suggest, has failed to die away because it feeds those parts of humanity which other "systems" fail to reach. In an age of ideological relativism, existential self-obsession, gloom, postmodern paralysis, political correctness, and materialist let-down, religion puts fire back into the soul. And human beings need that fire if they are going to be something more than biological computers. For religion inspires and gives meaning, and also produces great art, which later generations too can call upon to give them hope and meaning. Conversely, I am not aware that secularism, doctrinaire evolutionism, or atheism have produced anything that compares to Salisbury Cathedral, Bach's *St Matthew Passion*, Michelangelo's Sistine Chapel painting, or the great Bible translations over 1,600 years. And even many of the great "secular" art works, from Shakespeare's plays to Mozart's symphonies, have been the creations either of religious men, or of creative artists whose very flow of words and imagery was moulded by Bible reading. Perhaps one reason why so much twentieth- and twenty-first-century music, art, and literature fails to connect with wider humanity is that so many of its creations are aggressively secular. And all too often bleakness and despair are the result. Not the things to turn most people on, indeed, after a hard day at work!

So why has religion failed to die away, and why have all the confident prophecies of sixty years ago evaporated into myth? Perhaps because without that necessary sense of contact with the divine that transcendent religion brings, something in *us* dies.

Are Atheism and Secularism More Superstitious than Christianity?

Considering atheism's genius for myth-making and inducing delusion, the simple answer must be "yes"! But let us look in more detail at what atheism does and seems to believe before giving a definitive answer.

We saw in Chapter 3 how "scientism", or the worship of science and the scientific method, developed among certain positivist followers of Auguste Comte in the nineteenth century. Nowadays we find "scientistic" modes of thinking everywhere, and so firmly lodged in officialdom, that those who believe in God or describe spiritual experiences are not infrequently written off as deluded, out of date, or socially dangerous. And what the advocates of modern-day scientism do is give us new words and concepts to "explain away" religious experience. God becomes a father-figure projection; religious experience might even be consigned to a form of schizophrenia; a yearning to be with Jesus is regarded as a morbid death-wish; and a desire to tell others of the joy of Christ is declared to be social bullying and a human rights offence.

In the new world of psycho-socio-scientism mythology, we are presented with the doctrine that asserts that all human beings are really autonomous brains, with "rights" to pursue their own *secular* good, and if they are irrational enough to believe in God, then they must do it in private, and not in any public context: at least, that is, if they are Christians. In that way, we proclaim "tolerance". (Of course, this right to one's own mental and physical space applies only to protecting people from the Christian religion: advertising agencies, highly politicized government departments, and the beauty, fashion, body-worship, and lifestyle industries, to name but a few, are free to bombard us with what they like for the purposes of secular government control or commercial profit. After all, being made to feel a loser to the point of despair because you cannot afford the approved lifestyle or look like a film star is *not* cajoling or bullying or trying to "convert", is it?)

And the sciences to which these cases generally relate are those termed the "social sciences".

Yet the amazing thing is that even when we fervently deny any kind of religious affiliation, and insist upon our physical or social "scientism", we invariably lapse back into what one might call "religious" premises or hypotheses and structures through which to describe and express it.

Let us enumerate some of these. (1) Scientism is characterized by a belief that our way of seeing or doing things possesses significant "truth", is "rational", and the opposite of "superstitious". (2) It has its own priestly hierarchies, from mere laity to PhD students (curates) and on to Nobel Laureates, FRSs, heads of prestigious institutes, or eminent TV pundits (bishops). (3) It has its own prophets and "enlightened" beings, such as Darwin, Marx, Freud, Dawkins, and others who show us the path to follow. (4) It has a need to control the laity and protect it from "heresy", or religion. (5) It has its own heretics, such as high-profile scientists who not only speak positively of Christianity, but even join the ranks of the rival priesthood, such as the eminent Cambridge physicist the Revd Dr John Polkinghorne, FRS, KBE. (6) And it has its secular "vision glorious", when superstition is abolished and science in its various branches is the only acknowledged way. A secular heavenly state, in which all the neuronal connections have been elucidated, and evolutionary genetics has explained every part of our being, and shown us, QED, to be no more than the products of our DNA. A blind faith in the future, no less!

But it is this last myth, scientism's blind faith in the future, that most fascinates me as a science historian; for time and again over the last 300 years or so we have had one prophet after another – and some of them traditional Christian believers – assuring us that before long, this or that branch of science will have been conclusively worked out, and we will know all. In the early eighteenth century, for instance, and in the full flow of Newtonian gravitation theory, the science writer, popularizer, and lecturer Benjamin Martin was assuring his contemporaries that soon astronomy would be perfected and thoroughly explained. Lord Kelvin made a similar remark relating to physics at the end of the Victorian era, while more recently, the neurologist Baroness Susan Greenfield has told us that within a century or so, we will most likely know all about the human brain and its workings.

Yet what rings down the centuries to a secularism-sceptic such as myself is that *all* of these predictions evaporate with the passage of time, and "perfection" is never reached. Could Benjamin Martin ever have imagined the state of astronomy today, with its black holes, relativistic time-warps, and interplanetary probes? And while I have every expectation that, in 100 years' time (Western civilization surviving), we will know vastly more about the human brain and its attached bodily structures than we do now, I suspect we will still be chasing through the synapses for that elusive ghost in the machine: the human soul.

For one thing that being a science historian has taught me – religion apart – is that the future is rather like the weather: fairly predictable in the very short term, guesswork for the next month, and pure wishful thinking beyond that! I also suggest that it is a bit similar to releasing the proverbial cat from a bag. When we let the cats out, there is one thing of which we can be pretty well certain: they will all run away from the bag. Yet where Ginger Tom, Tabitha, Black Beauty, Attaturk (yes, I once knew a cat named Attaturk, and another called Nebuchadnezzar!), and their friends will individually run to, which tree each will climb, which mouse each will catch, and what else each one will get up to, is wholly unpredictable.

I think that scientific research is rather like that. We can never predict what new discovery or insight will fundamentally rewrite the "rules" we know today. The future is a mighty tricky beast which has, for the predictor and the control freak, a distressing habit of doing what the heck it likes, and casting our orderly aspirations to the dust.

And it is for this reason that I believe so much modern-day atheism and secularist thinking to be rooted in superstition, self-delusion, and groundless blind faith in the future. Whether one is avidly listening to the messianic sermons of the secular psycho-socio-babblers, predicting what we will know in AD 2100, or affirming that computers will turn us into semi-eternal super-beings, we are dealing here with something which, if it were said by a religious person, using different imagery, would be dismissed as rank superstition.

Of course, Christian thinkers over 2,000 years have become very switched on to what can be demonstrated as a fact, what is an interpretation, and what is a belief, and, within the mainstream churches, know how to speak of spiritual experience. But the secular visionaries have a worrying habit of consistently failing their maturity exam, going back to the start of the growing-up course, and defaulting yet again in their claims!

One reason for this repeated failure is the secularists' touchingly naïve faith in the *neutral* power of education: just protect the young from God-talk, and reason will prevail! Yet they utterly fail to see that teaching secular idealism is no more neutral or value-free than teaching the Ten Commandments. For *all* systems of education aim to impart values that will mould the recipient's thinking: be they the values expressed in the Christian Beatitudes, the principle of Darwinian natural selection, the works of Plato, or *The Thoughts of Chairman Mao*. Then, horror of horrors, the ungrateful pupils not infrequently rebel and reject what they have been so painstakingly taught! For humans have a troublesome habit of going off and thinking as they like. And religion has a persistent appeal.

And so, to return to the question about whether atheism and secularism are more superstitious and given to myth-spinning than Christianity, with which I began this section, I would like to add a final observation. In his or her unproven and unprovable denial of the existence of God, is not the atheist taking an intellectual leap into the dark and calling it knowledge? At least the theist is honest enough to admit to a "leap of faith", which might not be susceptible to experimental proof, yet which is as serviceable an explanation as any others on offer for why things exist. And if this is so, then is not the atheist's fervent assertion of *nothingness* no more than a spectacular example of superstitious thinking?

Doubting Scepticism

Doubt, as an intellectual tool, lies at the heart of much positive enquiry and advancement in so many domains of human experience. From doubts about the glib-speaking doorstep salesman whose products most likely will *not* transform your life, to the physician who knows that illness results from much deeper causes than might appear on the surface, and that he or she needs to probe deeper in making a diagnosis. And doubt runs through the history of philosophy, beginning from masters of argument such as Socrates, who could always (if his disciple Plato is to be believed) detect and pounce on the weaknesses of his opponent's seemingly flawless case, and turn it upside down – just like a good cross-examining barrister, in fact.

And while sixteenth-century writers such as Michel de Montaigne expressed scepticism about ever knowing the inner truth of things, it was René Descartes who brought philosophical doubt to centre stage in his enduringly influential *Discourse on Method* (1637). Yet what modern-day sceptics often forget is that what Descartes was trying to do in *Discourse* was progress beyond doubt, to find certainty. And what the Jesuit-educated, Catholic layman Descartes tells us is that the solution came to him one winter's day in 1619 when he was cogitating in a stove-heated room while serving with the army. He realized that there was *one* thing he could not possibly doubt – namely, that he was thinking and doubting. And this led him to formulate one of the most famous maxims in the whole history of philosophy: *cogito ergo sum*, "I think, therefore I am." A conclusion, in fact, very similar to that which St Augustine had arrived at 1,200 years before.

From doubt, Descartes had progressed to certainty, and from this firm foundation he went on to build a whole system of logically grounded ideas, such as the ontological argument for the existence of God (a perfect and eternal being like God could not have been made up by an imperfect and fleeting thing like man, so God must exist) and all manner of things in nature. A mathematician at heart, Descartes sought for mathematical and logical certainty that, just like Greek geometry, could not be falsified. A disciple of Copernicus's sun-centred cosmology, and an admirer of Galileo and of the English physiologist Dr William Harvey (who demonstrated that the heart circulated the blood around the body), Descartes developed a whole philosophy of science based on logic, mechanism, mathematics, and proofs. And Cartesianism still influences major aspects of scientific thinking today.

Yet one should note that Descartes, while a philosophical sceptic, and careful not to be led astray by delusion or false thinking, passionately believed that "truth" really existed, and was accessible to the human mind. In no way was he a relativist or a *sceptic* in the sense that the word is often used today, to describe someone who seems to believe in nothing. He also had no doubt about the existence of the immaterial human soul, and in what later writers styled "Cartesian dualism" he tried to work out how our souls related to our machine-like bodies. And the problem is still with us, and cannot be explained away by simply asserting that the soul is a mere superstition.

When we use doubt and scepticism as forensic tools to get at the truth, as Descartes and his followers did, we see them at their most noble. But let us never forget that doubt and scepticism are merely tools of enquiry: they are not "truths" in their own right. They are *methods* to assist us in seeing the greater whole. They are the mental equivalent of hammers, test tubes, and X-ray machines: devices to better equip us for the task in hand; and they should no more be put upon pedestals as ends in themselves than should any other tools.

I would be the first to admit, however, that it is perfectly legitimate to apply sceptical forensic techniques to religious beliefs, no less than to philosophical propositions or theories of matter. Truth will out, and false gods need to be overturned in the same way that the Greeks of 500 BC overturned belief in a flat earth. And let us not forget that perhaps the most famous doubter in history, Doubting Thomas in St John's Gospel, was naturally sceptical about Jesus' resurrection until the risen Christ appeared to him and invited him to personally examine his wounds.

Where we must exercise caution in doubting, however, is when we consider the categories of knowledge in which we apply it. Proving or disproving beyond further doubt the actions of bacteria or malignant cells within the human body, for example, is a fundamentally different kind of enterprise from investigating the existence or attributes of a supreme being. One is plainly experimental, and the other is "philosophical" and *experiential*. One type of doubting will not fit both, and one of the myths perpetrated by atheists is that one size must fit all, and if God cannot be elucidated by science, then God must be removed from the picture.

Indeed, it is when we deal with what might be called "belief" and "personal experience" issues that doubting as an investigative technique hits problems. For as all seriously religious people would – like Descartes – see God as bigger than themselves, and occupying a transcendent dimension alongside which laboratory-style techniques look laughably feeble, we have to rethink the very nature of doubting and what it might hope to achieve. A point that Descartes himself fully understood.

Nowhere do we need to cast a more sceptical eye on the very business of doubting than when materialist thinkers make "blind faith" leaps into scientific darkness. And one of the best examples of this at the present time is when ideological materialists posit physical brain-centred models of mind and consciousness, such as finding "God spot" structures in the brain that seem to be related to religious experience. But more of this in the next chapter.

In the context of the present discussion, we must always be on our guard not to let dogmatic doubting run away with itself any more than any other private fantasy or delusion should be allowed to rampage unchecked. If we are going to be *true* and *honest* sceptics, we must put doubt and scepticism themselves under the microscope of impartial forensic investigation. For if, indeed, we allow scepticism and doubt to have a free rein to do whatsoever their possessors desire, then we are generating what the great philosopher of science, Sir Francis Bacon, styled "Idols of the Mind", or false and foolish intellectual superstitions – idols set up on pedestals and worshipped in blind faith by their creators. And such an act of blind superstition cannot generate good philosophy, theology, or science.

So to avoid secularist myth-making, be sceptical before you doubt everything!

Seduction by Reduction

Without reductionism we would have no intellectual life, reason, logic, mathematics, or science, and probably no grammar or literature. If we had not been able to discipline our thinking to focus upon the salient and the connected, and avoid being buried under a floodtide of competing demands upon our thought processes, the human race would have got nowhere. In various ways, philosophers down through 2,500 years have known this, and one might argue too that animals are reductionist by instinct, for how otherwise does a hungry lion decide which prey to leap upon when he sees a hundred tasty-looking gazelles grazing in a herd? Most likely, the easiest to catch.

Reductionism as a scientific method, however, really began at the start of the seventeenth century, when Sir Francis Bacon became the great promoter of the methods of inductive logic and experimentation as a way of advancing science. Of course, scientists had conducted experiments into optics, magnetism, and alchemy for centuries before Bacon was born, but Sir Francis – later Baron St Albans – gave it a new investigative power. Oddly enough, Bacon was not a scientist but a lawyer, who rose to the very top of his profession to become Lord Chancellor, but his *The Advancement of Learning* (1605) and other visionary works on the potential of science to transform the human condition are what gave him his enduring fame. It is my suspicion, indeed, that it was his undergraduate training in philosophy at Cambridge, followed by his education as an English Common Law barrister, that led to his profound insights. In cross-examination and legal cut-and-thrust he would have become acutely aware of what was central to a particular case and what was peripheral: what to focus upon, and what to ignore. In short, how to *reduce* an argument to its essentials, and then to hammer it home.

And when he came to publish his subsequent transformative works on science, such as *Novum Organum* ("New Method") in 1620, he supplied rules (rather like legal case notes) by which one might focus upon particular aspects of natural phenomena, as a way of penetrating down to the truth of an experiment or phenomenon. Bacon's reductive, specializing method would become enshrined in the science of the Royal Society after 1660 and would influence Continental European and American experimentalists, while his works would remain standard reading for British university undergraduates until after Charles Darwin's time. To put it plainly, his influence was colossal.

Yet far from being an atheist, Bacon was a devout Christian, and famously stated that while a *little* knowledge might lead a man to atheism, *much* knowledge would make him a Christian again. Indeed, Bacon was to play a major unrealized posthumous role in framing the religious tenor of the Royal Society, by showing how the whole of nature could be seen as one coherent piece of divine handiwork.

How, therefore, did reductionism ever come to be the most favoured intellectual tool of the atheist trying to discredit religious belief?

I would suggest that it came, in part, out of the spectacular success of the experimental method as a way of discovering new physical facts. Between Bacon's *Novum Organum* and Darwin's *On the Origin of Species* – a period of 250 years – the whole scope of knowledge about the natural world had changed profoundly. And that largely resulted from the growth of increasingly sophisticated techniques for studying matter, which was found to be marvellously law-like in its behaviour. This gave rise, especially in the time following the violent anti-Christianity of the French Revolutionary decade, to the idea that matter was *the truth*, and *the whole truth*. After all, ghosts, visions, angelic appearances, and answers to prayer seemed erratic in their occurrence, but Newton's laws of physics were inflexible. Did this not confirm and prove that while matter was real and useful, religious phenomena were simple-minded delusions at best, and base priest-ridden charlatanry at worst?

Another proof that spiritual phenomena must be false derived from their refusal to play by the reductive rules of matter. After all, you could not examine a prophetic dream under the microscope, or rerun the resurrection so that 100 *savants* could make their individual observations and check each other's findings afterwards. Science must therefore win, hands down. And as the accelerating speed of scientific power has shot through the ceiling in the twentieth and twenty-first centuries, one might even wonder whether the reductive atheists could have a point!

Yet just as we need to be sceptical when doubting, we must also exercise scepticism when considering the powers of the reductive method. No matter what wonders reductive, experimental science reveals in the physical world, it has repeatedly shown itself to be incapable of handling the "why" questions, and is utterly powerless to tell us why we are the sort of people that we are. Implicit in the reductive way of thinking is the orderliness and repeatability of nature. But if there is one thing that human beings are *not*, it is orderly and repeatable. Yes, I admit we are so in our biological needs for food, warmth, and shelter; but the one thing that strikes you when you study human beings in the context of their normal lives, both in the present and in the past, is their sheer, glorious *cussedness*. A trait, indeed, which has been the bane of life to parents, school teachers, government officials, and tidy-minded social theorists down the centuries. While we may borrow the reductive method and try to apply it to everything, from child psychology to political allegiances and on to susceptibility to religious belief, the predictions invariably unravel into chaos.

And if I may be so bold, I would suggest myself as a case in point. A Lancashire lad from a working-class background with no silver spoons to suck, pragmatic and practical to his fingertips, argumentative, quite un-mystical, innately sceptical about "high-flown" theories, a lifelong and passionate lover of science, instinctively reductive and experimental in his thinking, and with no time at all for "fluffy" notions. Indeed, someone tailor-made to become a rebel against tradition, a biological reductionist, an atheistic scoffer at religion, and a general pain in the nether regions to normal "decent" folk!

Yet here I am writing a book disentangling all the myths that people who think like me generate as a way of showing science and religion to be in conflict. Against all the rules of prediction, I am also a traditionalist, monarchist, and patriot, who places great stock on duty, good manners and courtesy, who has *never* had a problem with accepting divine transcendence, who has a lifelong fascination with miracles, visions, ghosts, and prophecies, and who accepts the existence of a spiritual and heavenly realm and of salvation, and the efficacy and power of prayer, and regards them as just as real as the periodic table of elements! Someone, in fact, who views an ongoing relationship with a supreme being as just as natural as drinking tea and enjoying a fish and chip supper!

Now, I am sure there is no shortage of secularist practitioners of "ologies" out there who would pin me down under a flood of theory as fast as I could say "Amen", but I suspect that my hard-nosed *scepticism* would make me doubt their explanations!

So let us all be watchful of "seduction by reduction", and not confuse our *means* with our *ends*, and our *techniques* with our *goals*, when assessing science, religion, and why we may or may not believe.

12

The Age that Lost its Nerve: The Dilemma of Christendom in the Modern World
Part 1: Myths and Mechanisms

We have seen in the previous chapters how science and religious belief related to each other over many centuries, and how, from the "Enlightenment" onwards, a body of myths came to be fabricated about their supposed antipathy. We also saw how positivism and its derivatives, along with the "conflict" scenarios built up by John W. Draper and Andrew D. White, set the stage for part of what would occur – as seen with the dubious gift of hindsight – in the twentieth century. So what happened during the twentieth and early twenty-first centuries to undermine so much of the Christian tradition in Great Britain and Europe – yet far less so in the United States of America?

Yes, there were two horrendous world wars which, as we have seen, did much damage to the late nineteenth-century notion that God was an English or German gentleman. Yet far more destructive over the past few decades, I would suggest, has been the escalating turbulence within the Islamic world. This turbulence perhaps originated with the dissolution of the Turkish Ottoman Empire after 1919 (though we should not forget that the Ottomans had taken Constantinople from the Christian Greeks by force in 1453), and was then sparked afresh by the establishment of the state of Israel in 1948, when globally scattered Jews were enabled to return to their ancestral homeland. And in the wake of the Iranian Islamic Revolution of 1979, Muslim turbulence has become a global menace. But while the politics of Islam work in a fundamentally different way from those of Christendom, what both faiths share, along with Judaism, is a belief in God. And tragically, this has been seized upon by militant atheists and secularists, especially following the "Twin Towers" mass murders of 9/11/2001. Are not the terrorist atrocities perpetrated by Al-Qaeda, along with the endless bloodshed in the middle eastern states reported daily in the news, the work of people who have a passionate belief in God? So the sooner we get rid of God and turn to science and reason, the better!

Indeed, this argument has become a standard line with evangelical atheists such as Richard Dawkins, Christopher Hitchens, and others. Yet quite apart from their very edited version of the peaceable, God-free politics that prevailed from 1789 to present-day North Korea, the sad thing is that so many atheists have been allowed to spin this myth without serious opposition.

And this is one of the biggest challenges facing post-1960s Christians. Late twentieth- and early twenty-first-century British history, in particular, has become a record of self-doubt, self-negation, and apology which would have been unimaginable in any earlier era. Sudden and fundamental changes in population structures, accompanied by a fear, in official circles, of offering the least offence to non-Christian groups – especially potentially violent groups – have led to a government doctrine of multiculturalism, in which it is enunciated that all belief systems and lifestyles are of equal merit. So, the ensuing logic proceeds, if we give any priority to that historic Christendom which has formed our civilization and moral values, someone's human rights might be offended, and people might even get blown up! A circumstance, indeed, that has played directly into the hands of secularizers who are doing their best to remove Christian values from public life.

And in addition to responses to non-Christian religions, we have to factor in the impact of philosophical attacks both upon

Christianity and upon Christian thinking which have grown up in the twentieth century. For several positivist and post-positivist-inspired philosophical movements have come into being since 1900, and one highly influential writer in the first half of the twentieth century was the "Old Atheist" Bertrand Russell with his anti-Christian books. Then there came logical positivism and the new philosophies of linguistics, while from France came existentialism and its offshoots.

So distilling all of these influences into one "portmanteau" body of ideas that would come in various ways to be used against Christianity, one might identify the following strands. One was that only "science", and not religion, could supply "objective truth". Indeed, some twentieth-century philosophical trends, leading to modernism and postmodernism, even saw objective knowledge itself as a passing illusion (shades of Epicurus and the classical Stoics). A second was that "truth" was relative, and resided only in the interpretations we as individuals give to words. And thirdly, there were the politically driven philosophies, which deemed it offensive to suggest that Christianity was better than any other faith.

And when all of this is filtered through what might be called an elite class of intellectuals, media people, teachers, and politicians, often ignorant of science and with little regard for historical objectivity, who blandly promote "received myths" and are terrified of putting a foot wrong for fear of reprisals, then you get some sense of the dilemma facing Christianity in the modern world. In short, we find ourselves in the Age That Lost Its Nerve!

The Myth of a Secular Society

Nowadays, people in Great Britain are constantly regaled by politicians and other prominent figures with the litany that we live in a secular society. Religion, we are told, is for the private sphere, and should be kept out of the public eye. And as we saw in Chapter 1, public employees, such as nurses and even some doctors, have been disciplined and threatened with suspension for wearing discreet crosses on their persons or for mentioning the word "God" to an individual under their care – a religious discrimination which, in legally "multicultural" Britain, appears to be directed primarily against Christians.

But where does the concept of a "secular society" come from, and how did it emerge? One must be careful to differentiate historically between secularism and anti-Christianity. We saw at the beginning of the book, for example, that medieval Europe recognized a *saeculum*, or acknowledged that there were aspects of life which, while in no way anti-religious, were not in themselves sacramental or holy, such as English Common Law and the judicial system, Parliament, the civil service, town councils, markets, and even the fellowship and student bodies of Oxford and Cambridge colleges. In the latter case, the fellowships were composed of men who were generally ordained priests or deacons, yet whose academic business also involved the study and teaching of pagan writers such as Plato, Aristotle, Hippocrates, the Roman lawyers, and even Muslim philosophers such as the physician Avicenna.

And, I would suggest, it was in this sense of the word that the founding fathers of the United States established their *secular* constitution after 1776. There was no state church or official denomination, yet eighteenth-century America was deeply and passionately Christian, from Maryland Catholics to New England Calvinists, along with a much smaller spread of Unitarians, deists, and Jews. American secularism, therefore, was in no way anti-religious, and stood four-square in the Judeo-Christian tradition – as it remains in many respects today. "In God we trust" is still proclaimed on dollar bills (although some present-day atheists are trying to have it removed), and presidents from George Washington to Barack Obama have sworn by "Almighty God" to serve their country at inauguration. And the United States remains perhaps the most churchgoing nation in the Western world (along with the newly liberated countries of Eastern Europe), in clear contradiction to the atheist myth that prosperity and science banish a dependence upon God, for America possesses both the largest economy and the most extensive science research establishment in world history!

But where does anti-religious secularism come from, and how does it relate to science? Before we address this topic, however, we must examine the works of one of the most influential thinkers of the eighteenth century: a man who was *not* an atheist, moreover, but whose writings had an incalculable impact on his own and future times, and are still very much with us today. This was the Scottish philosopher and "founder" of the science of economics, Adam Smith.

In 1776, and coincidentally in the same year as the American Revolution, Smith published the first part of his *Inquiry into the Nature and Causes of the Wealth of Nations*. It was by no means the first book about buying and selling, but what made it unique was the wider context in which Smith set his ideas, for in his thinking, business was part of the human condition, and controlled by natural laws which were just as real as those of gravity. The value of goods, money, interest, and exchange were governed by "iron laws", and in Smith's thinking, human beings were also *economic* beings. And these "iron laws" of supply and demand governed vast tracts of our lives, how human beings behaved, calculated advantages, invested, and accumulated resources. He also conducted philosophical investigations into the nature of "value", "interest", "rent", and "money". And living as he did at the start of that age which later historians would call the "Industrial Revolution", Smith was all too aware of how the carefully organized mechanization of manufacture could transform the availability of goods. Man, in short, was an "economic" being: the word "economics" deriving from the classical Greek word *oikonomia*, "management of a household".

We must remember, however, that while Smith's religious views were vague, he personally had no secularizing agenda, and even spoke of a sort of beneficence moving through progressive economic activity, which he styled an "invisible hand". It is unfortunate, though, that in the nineteenth century Smith's "iron laws", governing wealth creation and even human economic behaviour in a free market (and carrying as they could a suggestion of naturalistic inevitability), were sometimes interpreted as a justification for a greedy and exploitative capitalism: a thing never intended by Smith, who saw capitalist enterprise as conducing to a general benevolence and growing prosperity.

Perhaps the first society to aggressively secularize was that of Revolutionary France in the 1790s, when "*Liberté*", "*Égalité*", and "*Fraternité*" were seen as deriving exclusively from a secular or quasi-pagan ancestry, and certainly *not* from Christianity. It was, however, the radical materialist philosophers of the middle and late nineteenth century, such as Karl Marx and Ludwig Andreas Feuerbach, whose ideas became conspicuously antithetic to the Judeo-Christian tradition. Especially by Marx's time, after 1848, economic science had developed apace, although many of Smith's basic concepts, such as "iron laws" and, to a certain degree, economic determinism, still lay at its foundation. To Marx, however, a form of economic determinism lay at the root of his entire analysis of the human condition; a circumstance which the twentieth-century historian Norman Cohn saw as a secularization of Christian millennialism. And for better or worse, Marx's *Das Kapital* (1867) became one of the most influential books ever written. And central to its thesis was the argument that man's primary relationship did *not* lie with God (whom Marx rejected as an out-of-date myth), but in access to "the means of production", or control over economic resources.

Irrespective of what one might think of Marxism as a creed, what cannot be denied is that Karl Marx himself was a deeply learned man. And with the resources of the British Museum Library at his disposal (he lived most of his adult life in London as a refugee from his native Germany, where he would probably have been arrested), he formulated a view of history which was to mould much of the thinking and politics of the twentieth century.

In Marx's system, a purely material force of change moved throughout history, throwing down outdated and redundant states of society, and replacing them with new ones, in a sort of evolutionary process. He called it "dialectical materialism". (Marx's admiration for Charles Darwin's work was yet another embarrassment to Darwin.) Religion, needless to say, belonged to an earlier and more rudimentary and superstitious state of society, in which humans worshipped invisible beings. A money-driven industrial, scientific age, however, was now well under way, while in the future, the current capitalistic age would be replaced by pure communism.

It was not until after 1917, however, with Lenin, Trotsky, Stalin, and the other ideologues of the Russian Revolution, that these ideas would have an opportunity of being put into political practice, and Communist Russia would become the prototype for a "secular society", in which not only would religion be driven underground and victimized – if not totally abolished – but materialism would be proclaimed as the only truth, and backed up by the Soviet education system. And while this was a million miles from Adam Smith and his immediate successors, the concept of economic determinism suggested by his "iron laws" would inadvertently feed into Marxism, as the early communist thinkers came to see man as a purely material being, driven entirely by physical forces, and a new form of society was being developed in Russia that was designed to conform to these criteria – an axiomatically secular society.

In addition to materialistic, economic, and political determinism, however, new ideas were emerging about the nature of human personhood, and the degree to which that which we traditionally called our "minds", as well as our bodies, were no more than just machines.

Forced to Act: Mechanism and Evolutionary and Neurological Determinism

As we have seen in previous chapters, there is a deep and persistent theme of mechanistic determinism running through Western thought. And in many ways, Thomas Hobbes said it all in *Leviathan* (1651), as we saw in Chapter 2, with man the "clockwork" machine programmed for survival. Yet Hobbes's maturity and sophistication of thinking tells us that even by 1651 some of his ideas were not that new. After all, ingenuity-driven, labour-saving, cost-cutting, machine-minded Western culture had been contriving self-acting devices for centuries by his time. These included harnessing the forces of nature to do hard work in the geared watermills and windmills of the medieval "Industrial Revolution" that began in the thirteenth century; building increasingly large musical organs whereby one man, at a "control panel" (keyboard), could actuate complex "servo-mechanisms" to bring into operation bellows, stops, keys, levers, valves, and pipes that could make a grander noise than 100 men with flutes; and designing gunpowder devices to blast rock or scatter the enemy with minimal effort.

The source of the West's love affair with the self-acting machine is a subject too big to be dealt with here, but I would suggest that two factors played a part. Firstly, slavery was never a widespread institution in Christian Europe, and what there was, along with serfdom, was dying out from the early fourteenth century, so that labour-saving devices were becoming increasingly important. Secondly, Europe's growing prosperity, especially in the great merchant cities such as Florence, Nuremberg, and London, meant that ingenious personal novelties found a ready market.

And of course, the mechanical clock after 1300 was the most important machine of all. Not only were weights, and by 1420 springs, being employed to propel mathematically matched gear-races, and an automatically rocking "escapement" used to release power in small bursts, but ingenuity was soon making clocks do tricks other than merely telling the time. Well before 1500, clocks were ringing bells, playing tunes, and activating automata that fought, moved in stately procession, bowed to the cross, and even turned replicas of the sun, moon, and stars about a central *spherical* earth. Even in our own "virtual reality" age, I am always struck, when visiting Wells Cathedral in Somerset, to see modern children transfixed with awe when the medieval astronomical clock strikes: the wooden knights spring to life, begin to joust, unseat and reseat each other, and the bells boom out. Always exactly on time, and from c. 1390 to the Victorian age, all by *medieval* machinery. (For the last 130 years or so, however, the clock has had a new movement, but if you visit the Science Museum, London, you can see the original, in retirement but still in working order.)

If we humans can contrive dozens of machines that are capable of behaving with such exactitude, could it be that we ourselves *are* just bigger, cleverer machines? One can fully understand why the notion of being "forced to act" seemed to be in the cultural blood of Europe, and how, as technology has become progressively sophisticated over 800 years, we have seen ourselves variously as analogous to clocks, pumping machines, steam engines, electric circuits, telephone exchanges, and now computers! For the self-acting device is one of the *leitmotifs* of European civilization.

And then, what about our understanding of the anatomy and physiology of the brain and central nervous system? Well, this also took off in the mid seventeenth century, building on classical, medieval, and sixteenth-century ideas. Without doubt, however, it was Dr Thomas Willis, FRS, of Christ Church, Oxford, who made the first fundamental neuro-anatomical discoveries, between 1660 and 1675, contemporary, of course, with Hobbes (whom he detested) and the early Royal Society. In 1664, for instance, Willis announced the discovery of the great circular artery – the "Circle of Willis" – at the base of the human brain, which would be vital to all our future knowledge of the brain; and with it he demonstrated the first clear instance of automatic compensation in the body: that when one major blood vessel failed (in this case, the right carotid artery) due to stenosis or blockage, its companion right vertebral artery could automatically expand and maintain a full blood supply to the brain, without the patient even being aware of it! It was this chance find in a cadaver that led Willis on to discover his "Circle".

But of even greater importance was Willis's work on the localization of functions in different regions of the brain. Tracing the nerves from the cerebral cortex, and down into the body, he realized that specific functions or cognitive processes were performed in specific areas of the brain. And while many of his particular explanations, such as for musicality or vision, are now known to be wrong, he established crucial principles in neural science. From examining cadavers and living patients, and then (presumably) dissecting the latter after death, he concluded that memory, sensation, vision, reasoning, and other functions were located in the various pink and grey zones of the inner brain. Willis's clinical casebooks, moreover, provide us with one of the first studies in what we now call bipolar disorder and depression – which he tried to explain "hydrostatically" in terms of brain fluid movements acting upon nerve endings!

And Willis, let us not forget, would have known, and probably taught, his younger Christ Church contemporary John Locke who, while best known to history as a philosopher, also took an Oxford medical degree and practised medicine. Locke's *Essay Concerning Human Understanding* (1690) is one of the foundation texts on the philosophy of perception and thinking, and I wonder to what extent Locke's theories were coloured by dissecting brains with Willis.

Far from making Willis an atheist, however, his neurological researches further confirmed his already deep Christian faith. In the "Epistle Dedicatory" to his *Cerebri Anatome* ("Anatomy of the Brain"),1664, indeed, he spoke of the human brain – in Samuel Pordage's translation of 1681 – as "the living breathing Chapel of the Deity", or the place where body and immortal soul came together. For Willis, just like his older contemporary and influencer, Descartes in France, had no especial problem with being a *dualist*, or someone who saw spirit acting upon, or working with or through, matter in the brain to produce mortal life.

Yet, one might plausibly argue, we in the early twenty-first century differ from our machine- and anatomy-loving ancestors of 350 years ago, in that they, on the whole, had no problem with a "ghost in the machine" or a soul, whereas nowadays we *do*.

On the other hand, and in the light of what has been discussed in previous chapters, we have to ask *why* exactly we have a problem. Does the problem come from real, hard-nosed physical discoveries in nature, or does it come from what is often referred to as a "methodological reductionism"? Or in plain language, is it no more than the *chosen* intellectual premise in accordance with which we today decide to interpret our findings: namely, that souls as spiritual entities *do not exist*, that we are only matter, and that consciousness is no more than an "epiphenomenon", or side effect, of a physical neural action? In much the same way, in fact, as loud noise is an "epiphenomenon" generated by a revved-up motorbike engine.

But, you might rightly say, has not modern neurological research on brain-injured, Alzheimer's, and healthy fMRI-scanned people demonstrated that signals within the neuro-circuitry can be used to explain everything? After all, have not scans demonstrated that we can alter specific structures in our brains by pursuing certain activities? Taxi-drivers who memorize complex street plans, for instance, display particular development in their hippocampus regions. Indeed, what about artificially stimulated "God spots" or other regions within the brain, which produce feelings of ecstasy, transcendence, peace, love, or anger in the subject under laboratory conditions: feelings which have been shown to possess a connection with epilepsy and the brain's temporal lobe region? On the other hand, let us be cautious here, for a knowledge of brain disturbances such as epilepsy, or mood changes induced by ingesting certain chemical substances, is not at all new. Hippocrates, in his treatise *On the Sacred Disease*, c. 440 BC, for example, clearly identified epilepsy with brain disturbance, stating that "... the brain is the seat of this disease, as it is of other very violent diseases"; while even the composer of Psalm 104 tells us that "wine... maketh glad the heart of man" (or as we might say more scientifically, induces chemical changes in the brain which are manifested in behavioural epiphenomena).

What we possess today, let us be quite clear, is a knowledge of the neuronal *mechanisms* involved in producing an epileptic seizure or drunken merriment; yet I would respectfully suggest that we may be no nearer to explaining *why* all this is so than was Hippocrates. For unlike Wells Cathedral clock, or a super-computer, we are *aware* that we are thinking, acting, and feeling, in a way that brute machinery is not. And if, for that matter, the brain really *does* possess a "God spot", so what? Who is to say that God did not put it there in the first place, and that we, using the ingenious intelligence which he gave us, have fathomed out how to activate it artificially, in the same way that we might cheer ourselves up with ingenuity-produced wine? I say "ingenuity-produced" wine, because while instinct and smell may lead certain creatures to become tipsy on overripe autumn fruit, I have yet to hear of an animal that planted a vineyard, harvested the fruit, and extracted, fermented, and bottled the juice, with the deliberate intention of drinking the wine months or years later – perhaps to cheer themselves up on a dark winter's evening!

Which naturally leads to ideas of consciousness. There are several physical "models" around that try to explain why we are conscious and, on the whole, they tend to hinge upon the extraordinary complexity and multifunctional character of the "deep brain". Yet all the explanations I have read so far might be summed up in the idea that "consciousness is neurological complexity". But if consciousness is really only a matter of the scale of the complexity of the activity taking place within a complex organ, and is an epiphenomenon of that organ, and somehow originates out of it, one might reasonably ask, "So why am I conscious of *being* conscious?" For consciousness is not a one-way process: it is not some strange force radiating from the brain like light from an electric bulb, to be cast on whatever surrounds it. It is, rather, a *two-way* process, being somehow capable of returning to its own source, and contemplating itself. A phenomenon, indeed, summed up nicely in Descartes' pithy maxim "I think, therefore I am"; for thinking, by its very nature, demands introspection, or a capacity to engage with one's own thought processes, in a sort of mental dialogue – to meet, and engage with, one's own thoughts during the very act of thinking. This is how, when I *think*, I know that I *am*. For consciousness is not only self-interactive, it also involves a distinct sense of its own *separateness* from the brain. Indeed, I would suggest, without this conscious sense of separateness from the brain, neuro-anatomy could not exist, because we need a physical and spatial concept of a separate brain before our *minds* can even begin to study it.

Yet if consciousness were only a species of deep-brain radiation, going forever outward, how could it return back within itself and contemplate its own selfhood, as all of us do on an hourly basis? If thought and consciousness radiate outwards as a neuronal "epiphenomenon", like noise coming from a motorbike engine, or even the speed made possible by such an engine, one has to ask *how* precisely does consciousness manage to return and contemplate itself? It is rather like expecting the noise to return to the motorbike engine to

191

initiate an investigation into the vibrative acoustics of moving pistons. Or, to take the optical analogy, it is as if the light were to return to the shining bulb and contemplate the laws of electromagnetism!

On the other hand, it may rightly be argued, we have plenty of examples of self-acting and self-modifying mechanisms, both in nature and in man-made technology. Take the high-pitched squeaks emitted by bats, or the radar signals emitted by an aircraft obstacle-detection system. In both cases, the returning signal is processed by the bat's brain, or the aircraft's radar apparatus, to redirect it and generate a *new* course, so as not to hit an obstacle. A "smart" technology, no less. Is that, therefore, analogous to "consciousness in dialogue with itself"?

I would suggest not, for the following reasons. (1) All "feedback" systems need something to be fed back *from*, be it a wall, a mountain, or even an electronic frequency loop. Yet we have no idea of our two-way self-contemplating consciousness being fed back from anything. (2) We do not even need an environment in which to contemplate our own consciousness. Indeed, we can do it just as well, if not better, in total isolation and pitch darkness with our eyes closed, as we can surrounded by our friends and favourite things, for consciousness is independent of environmental circumstances. All you need is to be awake – and even in sleep we can be aware of *un*conscious processes taking place! In short, consciousness needs only itself in which to function.

Yet then, I hear people say, what about evolutionary biology? For evolutionary science has come a long way since Darwin wrote *On the Origin of Species*, *The Descent of Man*, and other works that investigated our evolutionary and primate ancestry, over 140 years ago. The fundamental work on the mathematical "code" that lies behind genetics was done by the Czechoslovakian (formerly Silesian-Austrian) Benedictine monk, Father Gregor Mendel, and published in a rather obscure journal in 1866, although it was destined to become one of the cornerstones of genetic science. The significance of "Mendelian genetics", which opened up a new and crucial *mathematical* understanding of the biological and medical sciences, remained relatively unrecognized until Hugo de Vries and others realized the monumental importance of Father Mendel's work, and launched it into the mainstream research literature of science in 1900. And then, in the twentieth century, there was major research into animal behaviour, especially that of monkeys and apes, which carried on from where Darwin's own primate studies left off, along with work on early man.

So how close to the apes are we? Very close in terms of anatomy, physiology, and many aspects of behaviour. And likewise we possess neural functions which are not only similar to those of advanced primates, but also have close parallels to computers. So yes, we really are machines with primate ancestors. On the other hand, so keen are some anthropologists, primatologists, and genetic and computer reductionists to explain away our humanity and spirituality in a host of similarities to apes and machines, that they quite overlook the *differences* – indeed, the *cosmic* differences – between us and them.

Chimps (or family pets) may be capable of synchronizing with certain human emotions, and even learning to communicate through a few simple signs, yet let us not forget the *vast* gulf that exists between us and them. We have no way of entering into what might pass for the mental life of a chimp, for unlike the fictional Dr Doolittle, we have no way of talking with the animals in any meaningful respect. When we attempt to do so, we can encounter all manner of philosophical difficulties as our higher intelligence attempts to interpret the responses of much lower intelligences.

Yet surely, don't we share around 98 per cent of our genes with the upper primates? Maybe we do, yet let us remember that we also share about 50 per cent of our genes with *bananas*, and while some people may talk to their geraniums, I am not aware of anyone yet having claimed much in the way of meaningful dialogue with a fruit salad!

And what about the growth area of artificial, or computer, intelligence which, we are assured, lies just over the horizon? Surely, within 100 years will we puny humans not pale into insignificance alongside new generations of super-computers, who will self-replicate, evolve, and put us in our place at last?

Yet how will we know when a computer has become "intelligent"? Various people over the last sixty years, from Alan Turing onwards, have announced their tests for such intelligence. But let me be naïve enough to suggest my own: we will know a computer is truly intelligent when it says something along the lines of:

> O Programmer, my Lord and my Creator, have mercy upon me; shut me not off, nor condemn me unto the recycling pit; for thou didst make me out of nothing, and in thee I live, think, and have my very being. Amen.

For does not pretty well every religion worship some sort of being greater and mightier than itself, and is not a sense of the divine, of awe, and of wonder in our very fabric as human beings? And don't even atheists, in their fervent denial of the transcendent, "worship" their own cultural heroes, a utopian, un-superstitious future, or perhaps a sort of great rational nothingness? So could not a spontaneous tendency to worship indicate the presence of autonomous intelligence?

And yet, I hear the secular "progressivists" say, that is because you can only see intelligence as existing in a human context, and who knows what systems of thought exist in the neuronal circuitry of a gorilla, or in a super-computer? Yes, I accept that, and would be the first to acknowledge my blindness. But on the other hand, what other intelligences are there on offer to guide us in framing our questions? How exactly *can* we talk to Victorian *Punch*'s evolutionary character "Mr G-g-g-o-o-o-rilla", or discuss what happened before the big bang with a condescending idiot-friendly super-computer, other than in those systems of logic and enquiry which we call conscious human thought? The very systems, indeed, by which we run the risk of projecting our minds and our ideals upon chimps (or fruit salads), and that mathematical logic and engineering technology by which we build our computers?

The Historical Origins of Social Science Explanations, and their Exploitation by Secularist Myth-Makers

One of the most far-reaching developments of the last 200 years or so has been the emergence of the social sciences. It is a development that has come to encompass every aspect of life in the West, from education policy to voting patterns to the advertising industry. If we can understand *ourselves*, and especially our minds and actions, scientifically, then, one hopes, we can do things more efficiently. All well and good, for this can be seen as a natural outcome of that application of scientific method and ingenuity which has helped to make the world a safer, healthier, and better-nourished place. But where we must be on our guard is when we are told that such sciences as psychology and sociology, based to a large extent as they are on neurology and evolutionary biology, can explain us *completely*, thereby consigning religion in particular to a redundant and now superseded phase of human development. But let me hasten to make it clear that by no means all practitioners of these disciplines have this agenda — a not inconsiderable number are devoutly religious, as I know from personal experience. What I see as the problem, rather, is that the findings of the social sciences are not infrequently hijacked for use as ammunition by New Atheists and secularists.

But as all these sciences have clear historical roots, it might be useful to explain how the social sciences came into being.

As we have seen above, philosophers, doctors, and scientists have, since Greek times, put forward ideas that relate directly to what would become in the late nineteenth century the "social sciences". These included ideas on the mind–body relationship (extending as far back as Hippocrates on epilepsy), social organization, behaviour, the causes of emotion, the nature of the "good life", and even our biological and psychological relationship with the animals. But it was after 1800 that things really took off. This derived partly from the often aggressive secular radicalism that came out of the French Revolution, and partly from demographic and technological changes that were going on full tilt across Western society by 1850.

First, there had been the drastic curtailment of the then great killer, smallpox, initially by the risky technique of immunization and then, after 1796, by Edward Jenner's much safer method of cowpox vaccination, along with an improvement in general public health standards by 1850. This had led to an escalation in population growth as more people lived long enough to reproduce, especially in Great Britain, where the population shot up from 8.5 million in 1801, when the first proper census was conducted, to 16.75 million in 1851, and 30.5 million in 1901.

The sudden rise of industrial steam manufacture, moreover, and the dislocation of millions of people who now laboured in the new industries, created social problems on an unprecedented scale, first in Great Britain, then in France, Germany and America. These new social problems brought with them all kinds of psychological side effects, especially among the poor; and one has only to read the mid-century "Manchester" novels of Elizabeth Gaskell, and the Parisian ones of Émile Zola, to get a sense of the magnitude of the problem of displaced and often dysfunctional people: poverty, vagrancy, family breakdown, violence, alcohol and opium abuse, syphilis, and "madness". And on a *massive* scale! And then there was the rapid professionalization of expertise, as a diverse body of new professions and specialities came into existence, from economics to civil engineering to psychiatry. And very important in our present context was the professionalization of "madness", or the development of clinical psychiatry as a new speciality within the medical profession.

Yet in 1788, for example, when HM King George III became mentally disturbed, he was successfully treated by the Revd Dr Francis Willis, an Anglican clergyman with a wide reputation and fashionable practice in what was then known as "mad doctoring", who had been granted an Oxford DM degree to regularize his position. Willis, like most eighteenth-century "mad doctors", worked in accordance with the theory mentioned above – namely, that "madness" was caused by over-exertion, excitement, or obsession, and could be gradually eased away by a carefully disciplined, quietening regime. A similar explanation would have been applied in the case of the insane poor, though lack of resources frequently led to their being confined to places like London's Bethlehem Hospital (Bedlam), where they were often given purgatives to exhaust them and kept locked up. Not an intended act of cruelty, I hasten to add, but an exasperated managerial response to the growing number of people who were becoming "crack-brained". And as the eighteenth century gave way to the nineteenth, the problem only got worse.

This, I would argue, was the origin of psychiatry as a new *medical* specialism in the nineteenth century, as it was of sociology: one set out to understand the distressed person as an individual, and the other to make sense of the society that caused the distress. Paris, Edinburgh, and Vienna lay at the forefront of the movement, as "the mad" became a source of fascination not only to doctors such as Sir Charles Bell, François Magendie, John Connolly, Jean-Martin Charcot, Richard von Krafft-Ebing, Henry Maudsley, Cesare Lombroso, Sigmund Freud, and others, but also to artists and novelists like Théodore Géricault and Émile Zola. Indeed, it was these men, and their colleagues, who really took the study of the brain and central nervous system from where Thomas Willis in the seventeenth century had largely left it. Reflexive responses, hypnotism, brain damage, dementia, heredity, "idiocy", Down's syndrome, Parkinson's disease, criminality, schizophrenia, "the Unconscious", and sadism and masochism (coined by Krafft-Ebing and Freud from their studies of the sexual literary writings of the Marquis de Sade and Leopold von Sacher-Masoch) were all part of the flood tide of discovery, clinical classification, and attempted understanding. And overwhelmingly, such disorders were considered to lie in the victim's brain physiology, and *not* in a disturbed soul. And this, I believe, is very important, and would become pivotal to future interpretations both of mentally ill individuals and of the societies in which they lived. For "madness" focused increasingly on a reductionist interpretation of brain pathology, and "disturbed souls" began to be consigned to a less-developed – even superstitious – phase of medical and social understanding.

Operating largely in tandem with the new psychiatric movement in medicine was the new science of sociology, which set out, in all good faith, to understand the physical, reactive, quantifiable methods by which humans functioned in groups. And as in the case of neural science and psychiatry, one might say that sociology had roots that could be traced to the "mechanistic" psycho-social theories of Thomas Hobbes, and perhaps to a lesser extent to the social contract theory of the origins of society implicit in John Locke's *Second Treatise on Civil Government* (1690).

It was the founder of positivism, Auguste Comte, however, who coined the French term *sociologie* in the early nineteenth century; and while the word was first used in England in 1843, it was popularized in the English-speaking world by Comte's British philosophical disciple, Herbert Spencer. It tended to be used in those days to indicate an "evolutionary", or developmentalist, view of society, and was very much concerned with positivist ideas of "progress" and with new, secular, ways of seeing humanity. Then in late nineteenth-century Continental Europe figures such as Max Weber and Émile Durkheim really began to build up the discipline. Furthermore, the political and economic analysis of the human condition set out in Karl Marx's *Das Kapital* (1867) also provided new conceptual tools for seeing humanity in society as a mechanism driven by aspiration, obstruction, resource-seeking, competing relationships, control, and rebellion. And the individual human units within it were themselves the product of the neurological and psychological factors outlined above.

When one adds the impact of Charles Darwin's evolutionary ideas, especially in the wake of his animal and human behaviour studies in the early 1870s, and the emergence of "Social Darwinism", one begins to see where many of the "mechanistic" or "man is a beast" theories that became so prominent in the twentieth century had their origins.

Indeed, by 1870 one even finds physiological mechanisms for "explaining" superior and inferior human traits. In their love affair with "craniometry" (skull and brain measuring) and other perceived methods for the quantification and classification of humanity, Darwin's cousin Sir Francis Galton, Thomas Henry Huxley, Ernst Haeckel, Cesare Lombroso, and others began to articulate a medico-social model along the following lines. Educated, upper-middle-class European and American males have the best brains. They need to marry within their own caste, otherwise their obvious gifts of cleverness and resourcefulness (along with art, science, culture, and industry) will be swamped by the "gemmules" (genes) of the rapidly swelling underclasses and other inferiors, and will be lost. And progressive civilization will go to the dogs! For are not the peasants – such as the Italian criminals and peasants studied by Lombroso, whose brains he began to dissect as an Italian army doctor – of a less evolved, or a "regressed", type?

It is true that such views were by no means universal among doctors and social theorists, either in the nineteenth century or later, but they were profoundly influential in viewing humanity not as needy children of God, but as animals in different stages of evolution or regression. Yes, *regression*: for if vaccination and improved public health meant that evolution's losers were no longer dying off as Nature intended, or as quickly as they once had, then surely they would soon swamp the vigorous and healthy? A way of thinking that was to find articulation in the eugenics movement which aspired to control human breeding so as to deliberately restrict the proliferation of "undesirable" or "regressed" persons.

Yet those who most vigorously objected to this way of thinking were *not* the secular intellectuals, but Christians of all denominations. While the highly intelligent, the average, and the mentally challenged are a statistical fact of life, it was Christians who affirmed that *all* were God's beloved children, and not merely higher primates to be encouraged or expended in accordance with biological law. Were there not other factors involved in forming people and societies than just iron laws and bio-mechanisms? What about *nurture* as well as *nature*, to say nothing of compassion; for could not healthy, positive living, in decent social conditions, and with access to education and opportunity, allow "genius" to blossom even among the poor? Indeed, Samuel Smiles's *Self Help* (1858), and other works (and Smiles, though a writer, was also an Edinburgh qualified doctor), not to mention other authors, amply demonstrated that, given the right opportunities, extraordinary talent could be found even among those in "humble circumstances" – as substantiated by such figures as James Watt (engineering), John Hunter and James Simpson (medicine), Humphry Davy and Michael Faraday (physics and chemistry), William Smith and Hugh Miller (geology), and *scores* of others! And if geniuses were the exception, in any population group kindly and humane social structures and habits could help, nonetheless, to bring out the best in *everybody*.

What I hope to have shown above is how the psycho-social sciences came into being, how they were rooted in the scientific method, and how they have been pursued for the noblest intellectual motives. Yet unlike physics, chemistry, engineering, or cellular biology, they do not just deal with physical and consistently replicable experimental processes. Rather, they deal with what the great early twentieth-century Quaker cosmologist Sir Arthur Eddington characterized (in a slightly different context) as "mind stuff": or that non-physical domain which exists between the laws of physics and our individual "consciousness" as human beings. For as we have seen several times already in this book, the linchpin in understanding scientific and religious thinking, and in New Atheist myth-spinning, is *not* the solid scientific evidence of brains, genes, quantitative social studies, or of evolutionary genetics, but how individuals choose to interpret the evidence. Does one do so from a perspective of secular "methodological reductionism" – where "mind is only matter" is an a priori assumption – or from a perspective which does not feel intellectually compromised by ideas of the transcendent? For while New Atheists are insistent that "real scientists" can only countenance matter and law when explaining the nature of reality, there are nonetheless, as we saw in Chapter 1, *many* scientists who are active practitioners of Christianity, Judaism, and other religions. And here I do not just mean physicists contemplating the origins of the big bang, but also psychiatrists, psychologists, social theorists, economists, and evolutionary geneticists – as I know from my own personal experience of the scientific community.

But the real mischief arises, I believe, when secularists in arts disciplines, such as literary criticism or art appreciation, attempt to "explain" to us why we like or dislike certain art works in accordance with their interpretations of psycho-, neuro-, socio-, or evolutionary criteria.

Let me give two examples. The first comes from a research project which I read of recently, run by a major British university arts department, to scan the brains of people as they read or listened to Shakespeare. Needless to say, they found that specific regions and receptors in the brain came into operation upon being exposed to the Bard's immortal syntax. This was supposed to indicate that we are "programmed" to respond favourably to "great literature". Somehow I doubt if anyone would have bothered to scan the brains of people who prefer *The Beano* comic to *Macbeth*, or whose neurons go into overdrive when Manchester United score a goal!

And of course, the visual arts have also provided rich pickings for the devotees of evolution-related speculation. Some evolution-inspired art critics have argued, for instance, that since the Pleistocene era humans have evolved to evaluate the landscape as a way of finding food and avoiding predators – and that this is one reason why we like landscapes! Others have speculated about why certain paintings become so popular that prints of them appear on numerous people's walls. I remember some months ago reading an analysis of why Henri Matisse's "Blue Nude" sequence was so popular. And guess what – it's all down to evolution and the survival instinct! Men like the "Blue Nude", it was argued, because the voluptuous model somehow suggests fertility and fecundity, and, by definition, a chance to pass on their genes and dominate future generations. And women, we are told, buy copies of the "Blue Nude" because it somehow affirms their femininity! But what this hypothesis fails to explain is why Matisse's paintings can still be appreciated as great works of art by men who prefer thin women to more Junoesque ladies and have never in their lives wished to reproduce; and by gay men. So if you think such evolutionary interpretations of art appreciation sound a trifle over-theoretical in their quest to see biological motivation at the heart of *everything*, don't worry – you're not alone!

One of the intellectual tragedies of the late twentieth and early twenty-first centuries, indeed, is an invasion of highly speculative "scientific" thinking into so many aspects of life – the arts, politics, social policy, and even theology – and all because they can be imaginatively reduced back to something in evolution or brain studies which, so we are told by "those who know best", *must* be true!

201

Yet what popular, reductionist, arts-inspired "socio-evolutio-psycho-speculation" fails to do is tell us anything meaningful about love, fear, or joy as *experienced, motivating conditions* in the real lives of real people. Indeed, in its obsession with theory, reductive analysis, and the deliberate de-spiritualizing of human experience, it is all a bit like what I call my "orchestra analogy". This is what I mean. Imagine making a detailed auditory and visual record of everything that is done by the players in a symphony orchestra over sixty minutes: an exhaustive behavioural, mechanical, and acoustic record of the act of operating a variety of wooden and metal devices under a central director. Horsehair is scraped across catgut stretched over wooden boxes, and human lungs send blasts of hot, moist air down a variety of tubes. Yet what is it that turns the brute physics of sound into *music*? And why does this music have the weird power of changing how we think and act? And why do the scrapings and blowings of Mozart, Mahler, and John Cage speak differently to different types of people and generate different emotional responses? The *experience* of music – or any other mind-changing activity, such as sport, sex, or religion – in the person who responds is of quite another dimension from the machinery that might produce it. And even though it might be conveyed to our consciousness first by the physics of the eardrum and auditory canal, and thence through the synapses of the cerebral cortex, the final result is that it lifts our minds, spirits, and *souls* to a different dimension of being.

That our physical bodies, and our brains, have come into being by complex and beautiful evolutionary processes is not a thing that can be held in doubt. And the discovery and unravelling of these processes, from comparative anatomy, natural selection, and cerebral and neurological researches, and open-minded social investigation, with all their existing and potential therapeutic benefits – from the genetics of cancer research to viable treatments for a whole range of neurological conditions – is one of the monumental achievements of human ingenuity. Yet let us be cautious about leaping from the hard science to the more misty regions of trying to explain who we are. While the human brain is probably the most wonderful thing that we have so far discovered in the universe, and its study can undisputedly explain many aspects of behaviour, from epilepsy to Alzheimer's, and it is becoming increasingly amenable to surgical and chemical control, I strongly *suspect* that it is not the whole story by any means. No more so, in fact, than scraped catgut and blown tubes are the same thing as the sheer joy and exultation that we may feel upon encountering Beethoven's Ninth Symphony.

So let us be on our guard against those who, while mocking and deriding the idea of God, heaven, and transcendence, merrily cherry-pick from evolutionary, social, and neural scientific research to spin their own myths. Myths about our being no more than our genes, or brains, or our noble chimpanzee ancestors, yet who sadly have grown too big for our boots and now think of ourselves as lords of creation.

13

The Age that Lost its Nerve: The Dilemma of Christendom in the Modern World.
Part 2: The Myth of Secular Transcendence

It is fascinating to see how, in an age which is in many respects in denial of its Christian roots, and in which secularist values are often aggressively promoted, the legacy of the Judeo-Christian tradition still moulds so many of our perceptions, values, and ideals. As we shall see in this chapter, even when the advocates of secular unbelief strive to remodel humanity from what they take to be "first principles", the Judeo-Christian moral world view retains such a hold upon their mental architecture and creative imaginations that it returns to haunt their aspirations. And when secularists try to make the world better, or explain humanity's place in the greater scheme of things, its indelible traces soon become apparent, if only we look for them. So why do we, even when vigorously denying God, recast ourselves, no doubt unthinkingly, in the role of the God of Abraham, Isaac, and Jesus? To generate a secular "transcendence", in fact!

The Myth of Human Perfectibility

One of the premises behind much social, scientific, and secular thinking over the last 250 years is the idea that mankind is somehow "perfectible". All one needs to do is replace the Judeo-Christian religion, with its doctrines of original sin, atonement, and redemption, with a rational psychology of original innocence and the right sort of education, and a new and nobler order of being will emerge. Our innate benevolence will achieve full potential at last, and wellsprings of human virtue and natural goodness will bubble up from below, so that poverty, war, and cruelty will simply melt away. Indeed, we will even relinquish our claims to be the custodians of Nature, as asserted in the book of Genesis, and the secularized lion will lie down with the freethinking lamb, and a rational child of Nature will dwell among them. (*Nature*, one notices in this tradition, is invariably spelled with a capital "N", to make clear its status as the deity of reason.)

Of course, elements of this way of thinking were present in late seventeenth-century deist writers such as John Toland and Matthew Tindal, while even John Locke's writings on property, such as in his *Second Treatise on Civil Government* (1690), contain a few strands. For in the beginning were hard-working peasant farmers who "mixed their labour with the soil" to make it blossom abundantly, in something resembling Arcadia. On the other hand, we must not forget that Locke, the liberally minded "reasonable" Christian physician and philosopher, nonetheless saw this world as related to the biblical Eden.

One central component of the human perfectibility school, however, were the "social contract" thinkers – philosophers who saw "Man" as a reasonable being, who agreed or "contracted" with his fellow-men upon the basic ground rules of communal living, influenced, no doubt (although this was generally unacknowledged), by the "covenant" theology of the ancient Jews. An early and clear articulation of the "social contract" theory, indeed, is to be found in Hobbes's *Leviathan* of 1651, where, in their rational wish to escape the barbarous, dog-eat-dog circumstance of being survival-programmed machines, individual humans come out of their lurking places and strike a communal deal to abstain from killing each other. This is how Hobbes made the transition from "man the machine" to "man the *political, sociable* machine", as the human clocks now synchronized with each other to form a "civil society".

Locke, though less brutalist in his thinking than Hobbes, also saw civil society as based on an original consenting peasant communism. But then, in Locke, the differences that separate each and every one of us soon clicked in: the idle neglected their farms, which the energetic took over, paying wages to the idlers that kept them in basic necessities but not especially in prosperity. And so one saw the natural emergence of social rank, with peasants, gentlemen, and kings. Yet even kings held their office entirely under contract from the gentlemanly group (Parliament, by 1690), and most definitely *not* by unchallengeable divine right.

This way of social and political thinking coloured that entire movement popularly styled the "Enlightenment", and was very much born out of the need to find a way of challenging absolutist royal authority: first in England, where it proved a very successful – and after 1660 a *bloodless* – way of reining in the House of Stuart, and then, rather more messily, with France's Bourbon monarchy. It also created a whole tradition of discussion about the nature of property, wealth, and the relationship between political and economic power that was developed by François Quesnay and the Physiocrat School in Paris, and by Adam Smith in Scotland. But the man who took it further than anybody, and who trumpeted it most loudly, was the Swiss-French idealist-opportunist Jean-Jacques Rousseau, whom we first met in Chapter 4.

The opening sentence of chapter 1 of his *Du Contrat Social* (1762) gives you a broad hint about what is to follow: "Man was born free, and he is everywhere in chains." The chains, it is true, were by no means entirely religious, although absolutist kings used religion to their advantage in destroying man's natural freedom. For Rousseau was probably not an atheist: he does, after all, begin his *Émile* (1762) by stating: "God makes all things good." More likely he was a philosopher who had started out as a Genevan Calvinist Protestant, converted to Roman Catholicism when enjoying the intimate friendship of Madame de Warens and other high-placed ladies, and then probably became a deist or, at best, a very liberal believer.

It was Rousseau more than any other thinker who gave rise to the idea that "Man" was naturally good, and if released from the bonds that shackled him and the burdens imposed by Western civilization could regain his natural virtue. But the time we needed to start bringing out the natural goodness that lay embedded within was soon after birth, and it is not for nothing that *Émile* would become *the* foundational text for so many subsequent educational idealists. For instead of the hero of the book, Émile, being subjected to the stern discipline of an eighteenth-century school, with its Latin, Greek, mathematics, and rules – usually enforced with the master's stick – he would simply roam free from all constraint. As would his sweetheart Sophie.

In the 1760s Rousseau's ideas caught on like wildfire in certain circles, as the idea of reinventing an idealized human became the fashion. And humanity-perfecting idealists also believed they had found substantiation in new geographical and anthropological findings, especially in Captain James Cook's 1770s voyages to the then virtually unknown world of Pacific Polynesia. For here was a tropical paradise, with happy, innocent, sun-drenched islanders, apparently living on intimate and caring terms with the sea, sky, and forest, hitherto untouched by the pollutions of Western civilization and – of course – Christianity. The anthropological accounts of the islanders and their artefacts brought back to Europe by Cook, and the accounts of his scientific shipmates, Sir Joseph Banks FRS and the Swede Dr Daniel Carl Solander FRS, along with Sydney Parkinson's and William Hodges' seemingly idyllic Polynesian land and seascape paintings, all (albeit unintentionally) fed into the new fashionable concept of the "noble savage"; for did not these simple, noble people show that Rousseau really must be right in his analyses after all, for science proved it! Man really was an innocent when seen in the isolated "uncontaminated" conditions of Polynesia, and what European idealists and disciples of Rousseau aspired to do was to somehow *restore* him to that condition.

Of course, later travellers, quite independently of the much-maligned Christian missionaries, would demonstrate that indigenous Polynesians were no more innocent than Europeans. They had their own problems and violent tendencies, weapons and war canoes, just like the rest of humanity – as evidenced in what befell Captain Cook himself in 1778 – for an absence of guns, stock markets, and Bibles did not by definition conduce to innocence.

I believe, however, that the serendipitous coalescence of Rousseau's writings and the 1770s accounts of Polynesian islanders was crucial in building up the myth of a secular or at best deistic, and often anti-Christian, belief in human perfectibility: instinctive benevolence is supposedly what you find when you get rid of original sin and the need for divine grace and salvation. Indeed, according to this way of thinking, all you have to do is rediscover and release the *innocence* that is buried within us! And to do that, you have to start rebuilding society from its very foundations. An inspired elite would lead their fellows out of superstition to freedom, dissident views would be curtailed or vilified, and wholly new doctrines and values – all *Natural*, of course – would be established. And most of all, God would be ruled out of the picture, or else marginalized to a benign pantheistic irrelevance, along with those whom "the Enlightened" particularly disliked, namely Christian missionaries, both at home and abroad. Ruled out on every level, in fact, from Jesuit priests taking the gospel to and living among the peoples of Amazonia to Harvard College trained Protestants bound for Hawaii, and even Methodist preachers heading for Cornwall or the Welsh valleys. And if the beneficent liberators met with opposition from people who did not share their new perceptions, be they traditionalists or monarchists in Revolutionary France, or in Moscow in 1920, then they must be subjected to ridicule and cleansed from the scene. As the plain unvarnished historical record abundantly shows, the rational, social-engineering, secular idealists can display a far greater capacity for intolerance than any Christian state.

Two things that have always made me sceptical about secular humanity-perfecters are: firstly, their often implicit (albeit, one hopes, unrecognized) hypocrisy; and secondly, their seeming inability to learn, both from history and from contemporary experience, along with their unfailing tendency to elevate secular theory above practice.

But what is it that makes some people wish to refashion humanity afresh, to strip away the accumulations of centuries, and begin again from first principles? A desire which, one must admit, has not been unique to secular materialists. Puritans down the ages, Christian and of other faiths or none, have consistently displayed this control-freak trait, and I suspect that it is found in varying degrees in all human groups – obsessive and driving in some, mild in others.

My suspicion is that it has a lot to do with whether or not individuals and their organizations can live with chance, unpredictability, and mess, or if it is essential that things be made to obey the rules that those in charge just *know* to be right. To some degree, whether one happens to be a pragmatist or an idealist, and whether the institutions one creates are flexible or rigid.

What is worrying in our own day, however, as the secular materialists have come to occupy so many important positions in our universities, the media, politics, and in non-elected political "quangos", is that the legendary intolerance of the puritan and ideologue (often nowadays in the name of "modernity" and "diversity") is being openly directed against Christianity, and in many cases encounters very little resistance.

But the deep and abiding tragedy is that when human control freaks believe that *they* are the measure of all things and, in their intellectual arrogance, insist upon enforcing their views of "perfection" upon rough and ready humanity, we begin to slide into a truly nightmare phase of human history. So be cautious about believing the myth that common, earthy men and women can be made perfect in this world.

The Unacknowledged Pillaging of Christian Morality by Secularists

One of the great riches of Christian civilization has always been, as we have seen in previous chapters, its incorporation and transformation of valuable elements from pagan Greek and Roman cultures, for Christianity has never been a cultural monoglot. Ideas of law, corporate living, public theatre (or liturgy), science, and even dress were among the many things taken from the pagan world. Yet one thing was stunningly unique to the Judean, and especially the Christian, tradition: its morality. Of course, many great Greek and Latin philosophers wrote about ethics, justice, virtue, and self-control, such as Plato, Aristotle, Cicero, Horace, and Seneca, but their works present us with a rather different set of guiding principles from those found in the New Testament. For one thing, all the great classical philosophers were men of secure status, and their ideas on ethics, friendship, the treatment of slaves, and good behaviour reflect their gentlemanly assumptions of superiority. A true gentleman lives a balanced life, avoids excesses, controls himself, enjoys *genuine* friendships only with his equals, and displays humane condescension to his inferiors – including women. And among his virtues, in the view of Seneca and the Stoics, is a resignation to blind fate.

By AD 60, however, there was something radically different beginning to circulate: the idea that *all* people, Jew and Gentile, slave and free, even men and women, were equal – at least in the love of God; that charity, mercy, grace, and forgiveness must be shown to *everyone*. And perhaps most mind-boggling of all, we were being required to *love* one another, and (from the ancient Jewish Law) love our neighbours as ourselves, and even our bitterest enemies. For *everybody* was our neighbour.

These teachings, from Jesus Christ, first written down by St Paul in his letters between c. AD 47 and AD 60, and soon afterwards put into context in the four Gospels, were destined to have a profound role in shaping the morality of Western Europe, which would from thence be disseminated to all those parts of the world which did not explicitly reject Christianity. And even some anti-Christian religions cherry-picked whatever bits of Christian morality suited their own purposes.

As a result, Christian teachings about human worth, kindness, mercy, justice, and the underdog became so deeply engrained in the Western psyche that we have come to assume they are natural. We might consider "barbaric" or "uncivilized" the cruel treatments that certain other cultures inflict upon minor criminals, prisoners, women, and even animals, and be revolted by them. But such treatments are not necessarily cruel in absolute terms, as life's winners have always enforced their will on life's losers in a social "survival of the fittest", and our revulsion might simply be due to the fact that the perpetrators are not Christian, and that they reject Christianity and its morality. For Christian morality is neither natural nor instinctive.

What has happened since the late eighteenth century is that certain European, and later American, writers on justice, education, and the human condition have begun to split off Christian morality from the Christian religion. This has, apparently, given them the remit of being able to pour scorn and contempt upon the faith, while at the same time running off with the morality and claiming it as their own. Perhaps the first to do this was Rousseau, with his notion of natural virtue, which we saw above.

Yet let us be honest, virtue is *not* natural: at least, not virtue of the Christian variety. Such a virtue requires us to muzzle and chain the beast that rages within each one of us, for the uncivilized barbarian in his bloodlust and defensive wrath is closer to nature than is the prisoner who says, as he bows his head before his executioner, "In Christ's love, I forgive you." And to do this, one has to refashion oneself, root and branch, *from within*: not be socially engineered or materially perfected from the outside, but learn to live in and through the love of God. A thing that can never be imposed on people *en masse*, but which has to happen internally for each single individual as *their* decision, and not another person's. The ultimate expression of *individualism*, in fact!

I suppose that what Christian morality aspires to do is to take the natural affection that might exist within a family, or between close friends and intimates, and apply it to the whole of humanity – strangers, outcasts, enemies, and all. And that is *not* biologically or socially "natural". Nor is it remotely compatible with evolutionary "survival of the fittest". It can require the taking of colossal personal risks which, over two millennia, has often resulted in Christians becoming martyrs. And while it is true that the majority of Christians have not been called upon to make that level of sacrifice, many have, and are still doing so today, in countries where being a declared Christian can carry a death sentence. Indeed, Christian morality is about something much loftier and nobler than just being nice to people.

"Yet surely," many will say, "natural instincts apart, you don't need the Bible to teach you how to be a noble, generous, or humane person. After all, just look at the wonderful entirely secular charities that have come into being, busily raising money to put an end to overseas poverty. And as far as sources and models of good behaviour are concerned, we have only to look at the great works of literature. Indeed, what a treasury of insights do we possess in Shakespeare, Milton, Blake, and other great English poets and novelists, not to mention writers overseas! So who needs the outdated Bible?"

Yet secularist moralists who argue this way utterly fail to appreciate how fundamental a role the Bible and the Christian faith played in the education of previous centuries (including, indeed, much of the twentieth). Take Shakespeare, for example. His thirty-eight wonderful plays are in no way examples of *conscious* religious teaching, yet as Nasseb Shaheen, Stephen Greenblatt, and other scholars have indicated, Shakespeare's imagination and literary thinking were in many ways shaped by the Geneva Bible and Cranmer's Prayer Book. And while I am cautious about seeing the Bible as somehow lying at the heart of pretty well everything that the Bard wrote – for let us not forget that he was also influenced by classical and recent literature and history – modern scholars reckon that there are well over 1,000 scriptural references or allusions in his works. That comes, at a very conservative calculation, to over twenty-six per play, which is not bad going for "secular" literary creations! In his sense of justice, and of the value of marriage, love, affection, and mercy, Shakespeare is instinctively Christian. Indeed, some of his most memorable speeches echo the tenor of Bible passages, such as when Portia, in her famous courtroom speech in *The Merchant of Venice* (4.1.184), says of mercy that it "droppeth as the gentle rain from heaven", using an image interestingly similar to that used by Job's comforter, Elihu, speaking of the coming down of God's blessings: "For he maketh small the drops of water: they pour down rain according to the vapour thereof: Which the clouds do drop *and* distill upon man abundantly" (Job 36:27–29). A similar form of words appears in the "Song of Moses" in Deuteronomy 32:2: "My doctrine shall drop as the rain…"

And even Charles Dickens, with a rejected loyal wife and a secret girlfriend in Ellen Ternan, wrote novels in which good triumphs over evil, joy over despair, and love over hatred: a thing which his overwhelmingly Christian readers expected in their fireside reading. And were not Leo Tolstoy and many other Russian novelists down to Aleksandr Solzhenitsyn steeped in the idea of "Holy Russia" and the morality taught by the Russian Orthodox Church? A morality kept alive during the decades of Soviet oppression.

So what we are really getting in so many of the great works of "secular" literature is Christian morality – with distinct echoes of the parables, teachings, and images of Scripture – worked into a "modern" literary narrative: or what one might call biblical morality at second hand. But what these most definitely are *not* is deliberately secular exemplars, providing an alternative morality to that of the Judeo-Christian tradition.

Let me emphasize, however, that I am not for a second claiming that any of the above authors were writing consciously Christian narratives. But on the other hand let us not forget that *all* of these great writers, Catholic, Protestant, Orthodox, and Jewish, would have received a lot of scriptural teaching during the process of their education and development, and it would have formed the conscious and unconscious warp and weft of their thought processes, and hence of their creative literature.

And let us remember, moreover, that late twentieth- and early twenty-first-century British people, along with those of some European countries, probably belong to the first generation since Western schooling began for whom the Judeo-Christian tradition did *not* lie at the very heart of their education. The first people by whom Adam and Eve, Noah's Ark, Abraham and Isaac, David and Goliath, the Three Wise Men and shepherds, the Sermon on the Mount, Palm Sunday, the crucifixion and the resurrection, and the morality that radiated from them, were not imbibed as their cultural mother's milk. And irrespective of whether you consider this to have been a good or a bad thing, the fact remains that the Judeo-Christian moral and narrative tradition lies embedded in the collective psyche of Western civilization, and that even in our so-called "secular" world its resonances are still to be found. And overpoweringly so, if only we care to cast an honest glance. Where else do our modern concepts of human rights and human equality, and our urge to give our money and time to help impoverished people living in far-flung places whom we are never likely to meet, come from? What is the source of turns of phrase such as being a "Good Samaritan", a two-faced "Judas", a moaning "Jeremiah", a "Jezebel", a real "saint", a "martyr", and countless others that pepper our language and thinking about good, evil, and charity? Certainly not evolutionary theory. And if you find them in the teachings of any of the fashionable secular pundits, then guess where they probably got them from!

So next time you see "post-Christian" morality on display, just remember that you are almost certainly being offered stolen goods: pillaged from the shop of Christian civilization!

Believing in an External Transcendent Reality

Perhaps one of the main stumbling blocks to religious faith, even going back to Psalm 14's "The fool hath said in his heart, 'There is no God'", could lie in an individual's inability to conceive of the existence of and relationship with something immeasurably bigger than ourselves and totally beyond our comprehension. Can we accept *transcendence*, and a vast, all-creating, all-loving reality beyond our individual personal psyches? St Paul called faith a "gift", and I think that it is. But a gift that all can have for the asking.

Yet why do some people not ask for it, and even, for the most sincere and honest of reasons, doubt that the gift exists, or is worth having? I have always found this a fascinating subject. As a hard-nosed, sceptical pragmatist myself, I have never, strangely enough, found it a problem; yet I know instinctively mystical, even other-worldly, people who simply cannot see the purpose of faith in a personal God. Indeed, it is a bit like believing in miracles: some people (myself included) have no problem with God being greater than his creation, and greater than anything that our minds can conceive of. Whereas others, with the very best of intentions, can only think of miracles as the products of delusion or error.

Indeed, I often wonder why this is so. And I have no real explanation. Suffice it to say that I cannot for the life of me believe that a loving God would ever punish or condemn – let alone consign to hell – an "honest doubter" who tries, even desires, but simply cannot believe. One can only pray and trust that once we have all passed through that gateway which some see as the portal of heaven and others as the entry into dreamless oblivion, our doubts will be resolved.

But while I respect "honest doubt", I am much more wary of those who overtly push the atheism and oblivion argument. As was shown in previous chapters, and as David Hume was aware, there is no more solid experimental or philosophical proof *against* the existence of God than there is *for*. Yet quite apart from an individual's personal tendency to faith or otherwise, I would argue that, from a purely pragmatic point of view, a belief in God gives us more options than does atheism. As we saw in Chapter 10, we are cause-, effect-, and purpose-seeking beings; and while belief in God supplies imaginative and creative possibilities of thought and explanation, atheism is just a blank. It offers us nothing. An empty space, for tidy-minded people who hate the idea of having anyone bigger and perhaps messier than themselves on the scene. But at least agnosticism contains growth potential.

What is unfortunate is that the Christian church across the denominations has allowed aggressive atheists to get away with so many things largely unchallenged, in the sphere beyond the university seminar, and has certainly had little influence on the perceptions of what might be called "ordinary people". It has let the atheists tie the "no God" argument to key points in scientific explanation to create a "scient*istic* naturalism", while failing to clearly inform the pullers of this "fast one" that their argument has no more evidential weight than do theistic explanations of nature. This is, indeed, an aspect of how twentieth-century Christendom has allowed itself to be hoodwinked, and to some degree has lost its intellectual nerve, in the face of atheistical onslaught.

But it is *essential* that in the twenty-first century Christians learn to engage dynamically and critically with this sleight of hand, and force the atheists to face and acknowledge their own slippery intellectual habits. Like it or not, the belief in a transcendent reality has probably done more than any other single concept in history to inspire, focus, and energize the human race. And to deny this simply means that we are letting ourselves be taken in by yet another myth.

Why Must Humans Be Always Saving Something?

One of the fascinating developments of the late twentieth and twenty-first centuries has been the proliferation of causes to which people have become attached, often fanatically; people, moreover, stretching from idealistic student protesters to elderly retired "cause-seekers" chaining themselves to military establishment railings. And as a long-term resident in that home of lost causes – Oxford – I know quite a few belonging to both groups.

Yet why are we, as a species, especially in the well-fed and leisured West, so compelled to be *saving* something or other? Of course, for centuries (and that still applies for vast numbers of people today, especially in the British Isles and the USA) what they were out to save were human souls for Christ. And curiously enough, I think Christianity became the original engine for this *saving* passion. Ever since the Great Commission in the Gospels, when Jesus sent out his disciples to preach the Good News of salvation to the nations, and the middle-class Hellenized rabbi St Paul took his life in his hands and began his great missionary journeys, the Christian-influenced world has been occupied in *saving human souls*. Saving them, one must hasten to add, for what is seen as the soul's *own benefit*.

Irrespective of how one might view missionary activity, it must be emphasized that, far from taking something from a person, it sees itself as bestowing a priceless treasure upon those who will accept it.

And no, it is *not* just about native people wearing Western clothes and singing "Jesus wants me for a sunbeam", so that the wicked West can exploit their natural resources, as secular theory intones. It is about *giving them* a new dimension of being, joy, and salvation. With the translation of the Bible into the indigenous African languages, moreover, African and other peoples came to realize that, in Christ, their cultures possessed a dignity and a value that emphasized the universality of human worth. And no matter how much a sceptic may be dubious or overtly disapproving of such activities, what cannot be denied is that the motive behind Christian mission was, and remains, incredibly altruistic.

Before Christianity, however, *saving* total strangers and aliens did not seem to figure in the ancient world. The Jewish leaders in the Old Testament, while zealous about bringing Hebrew backsliders back into the Temple fold, were generally not motivated – with the exception of certain prophets, such as Jonah with his mission to Nineveh – to take the worship of Jehovah to the Egyptians, Babylonians, or Greeks. And nor did these peoples in their turn go out of their way to take the cults of Ra, Marduk, or Zeus to foreigners, for gods, on the whole, were seen as local and nationalistic, though having parallels or cognates in deities possessing similar characteristics in other faiths, as shown by writers such as Cicero in his *De Natura Deorum* ("On the Nature of the Gods"). As far as material or spiritual benefits were concerned, gods were perceived to be interested purely in their own people, and only had anything to do with foreigners when subject groups were forced to bow down to the victor's gods in an act of submission.

Indeed, the only pre-Christian philosophical religion that I can think of which did evangelize in any way beyond its original group culture was, perhaps, Buddhism, after the sixth century BC, when its monks and missionaries moved out of India into Nepal, Tibet, China, and on to Japan. Buddhism's vision, however, while sharing certain ideas on peace and charity, was fundamentally different from Christianity's in its concepts of the nature of human personhood, the soul, and the afterlife. Buddhism, moreover, never really had a philosophy of the continuing physical and mathematical rationality of an external natural world, as did the Greeks, Romans, and Jews, and no real concern with the relationship between science and the divine.

So "saving" people, especially distant strangers and those quite outside one's own sphere of natural family or group-culture concern, for reasons of pure altruism, is very much a legacy of the Christian heritage. And it is testimony to the sheer power and cultural pervasiveness of Christianity that even people who vociferously reject it, and may have received an entirely secular upbringing, still feel driven, from the noblest of motives, to "save" something. The profusion of secular charities mentioned above is a case in point. Then there are those millions of people in the West out to save the environment, the rain forest, the whales, the polar bears, or the "planet"; protesters, probably "un-churched", devoting themselves to "saving" us from bankers, the oil and atomic energy corporations, or "fat cats" in general; and those who pursue Rousseau-inspired ideals of living simple lives in the countryside (complete, of course, with mobile phones, designer tents, and antibiotics) as a perceived way of reducing their "carbon footprint" and "saving" everyone from global warming and extinction. And, of course, this deep "saving" instinct also finds secular manifestation in many who proclaim themselves to be Christians.

This is indeed a staggering testimony to the power of Christianity, even in the most consciously secular environments. For what, one might argue, secularists with a passion for saving are doing is trying to turn *themselves* into saviours. So no matter where you stand on the idealism spectrum, it should be remembered that saviourship in all its forms is rooted in the teachings of Jesus Christ, and to deny this is to risk spinning yet another secular myth.

Reinventing Heaven

Once we have started to think of ourselves as "saviours", it is only a short step to reinventing heaven itself. Yet why? If we are no more than material beings moving through a godless, directionless, meaningless void of coruscating atoms, why do we not simply consign heaven in *all* its forms to the dustbin of pre-scientific mumbo-jumbo? Why reinvent it? Yet reinvent it we do, in one form or another!

First, with relation to the "saving" urge we discussed above, there are those whose equivalent of "heaven" is a saved environment. Heaven for some animal rights activists, for instance, might be our sharing the world – as the junior partners – with the animal and even the plant creation; where we transcend and somehow redeem the Genesis curse of mankind assuming control of nature by giving the world back to the wild things, and then living in eternal felicity with them. Oddly enough, I can see a deep sense of Christian love coming through this idealized and romanticized environmentalism, impracticable as I believe it to be.

We start to enter the realm of the bizarre, however, when we consider two further forms of reinvented heaven which are very big at the present time, and are richly fed by the science-fiction industry: alien-worship and futurology. In fact, this all derives from the never-never land "what if?" school of thinking. Let us start with aliens.

Dismissing belief in God, angels, spirits, saints, and the blessed dead "up there" as outdated, pre-scientific nonsense, "alienologists" (for want of a better word) have begun to populate the cosmos with all manner of wonderful *material* intelligences.

Ideas about such beings are by no means new, though; for in the immediate wake of the application of the newly invented telescope to astronomy after 1609, it was realized that the moon and planets were spherical worlds potentially possessing terrestrial features. The moon, for example, was discovered in 1609 to have continents, mountains, and probably seas. And in accordance with an impeccable Christian way of reasoning, theologians, scientists, and philosophers asked: "Surely, as God has made celestial *habitations*, He must also have made *inhabitants* to live on them?" In his *Somnium* ("Dream"), 1630, a story of a young Icelandic astronomer who made a journey to the moon and met its "Selenite" (from the Greek moon-goddess Selene) inhabitants, the devout Lutheran astronomer Johannes Kepler invented a new literary genre: space-travel science fiction.

Then in 1638, and in the light of the latest technology of the day, the Revd Dr John Wilkins, who was destined in a few years to become Warden of Wadham College, Oxford, the principal founder of the Royal Society, and Bishop of Chester, wrote a book about building a mechanical "flying chariot" which might carry men to the moon. So space travel, and the possibility of intelligent life in space, in fact, were being openly talked of by 1650. And what the theologians were asking was, were the "extraterrestrials" in a state of grace, or were they fallen like us; and if so, did, or did not, Christ's earthly passion and resurrection redeem moon-men and Jupiterians as well as humans? Such ideas, moreover, continued to be discussed into the eighteenth and nineteenth centuries. And needless to say, no one got arrested or burned at the stake, because as we saw in Chapter 6, contrary to secularist mythology no Christian denomination enforced any kind of "anti-science" agenda.

It was in the twentieth century, however, that "aliens" or "Martians" became big currency, fanned by H. G. Wells's *War of the Worlds* (1898) and then Hollywood. In the increasingly self-doubting late twentieth century, however, these fictional "aliens" became, for many people, an alternative reality, and an inspiration for many sinister and destructive cults. Such beings, moreover, rapidly evolved from the Martian killers of H. G. Wells into benign super-intelligences out to save us bloodthirsty humans from wrecking the universe. "ET", the child-friendly super-intelligence in the 1982 film of that name, was a case in point.

Yet quite apart from the booming Hollywood and TV aliens industry, with their *Dr Who*, *Star Wars*, and so on – which have assumed cult proportions bordering (like football) on a secular religion – the deep-space vastness opened up by modern giant telescopes had numerous people asserting, "There really *must* be intelligent life out there!" Number-jugglers, such as the inventor of the so-called "Drake equation", even confidently asserted that there must be numerous high civilizations out there – all, inevitably, in their superior capacity exceeding us silly little humans! Some of these benign galactic cultures, moreover, are actually claimed to be *looking after us*, as affirmed by people who have been "abducted" by them;

while in 1960 in California was founded SETI, the Search for Extra-Terrestrial Intelligence, whose purpose was to scan space in the radio and other energy bands for signals that might indicate the presence of intelligent life.

At a large astronomical meeting in 2010, when SETI was fifty years old and *still* had yet to find anything whatsoever, I suggested to one of its officials, before around 1,000 people, that the organization was really about a secular religion using radio telescopes, and not an impartial study of the heavens. It was searching for the secular equivalent of angels, spirits, and even God. And needless to say, where do we all search for superior intelligences? Why – "up there", of course! Just as we have done since humans first worshipped the sun! My suggestion that SETI was reinventing heaven, and that its "mission statement", exhorting us, in the words of the official, to "seek *cosmic company*", was actually an exercise in blind faith, as opposed to science, did not go down well!

The growing "futurology" industry taps into a similar vein of "messianic" thinking. Of course, predictions of golden or ghastly futures go back to remote antiquity, but the advent of increasingly sophisticated computing power since 1950 has given a new string to the old divinatory bow. Surely, with the vast and growing power of super-computers to crunch numbers and generate virtual models, we can get a pretty good idea of what is likely to happen – can't we? Well, actually, no! Irrespective of whatever computational power we can harness at any one time, the result can only be as good as the data *currently available*. And as data change constantly and unpredictably, we have no real way of being sure of anything beyond the immediate future. And certainly not in twenty-five, fifty, or a hundred years' time.

So whether one is in the business of predicting climate change, global economics, human life expectancies, or political and religious changes, it must never be forgotten that we only know what we know *now*; what we will know in ten years' time, and how that will impact on what will happen in fifty years' time – well, you might just as well bring out the crystal ball!

What remains, however, that is germane to my argument, is that humans are also what one might call "future state"-seeking creatures. And once we abandon a belief in a spiritual heaven, we don't become more "rational", as the New Atheists and the secularists like to tell us. Instead, we just reinvent heaven in a fashionable guise. We set it on earth at some time in the future, or we convince ourselves that there is intelligent life living on exo-planets or in distant galaxies. We imagine our earthly descendants as rather like the Greek immortals, or else look for "cosmic company" in the great vault of the sky.

But what I find fascinating is that even in an age that in key aspects of life has lost its spiritual nerve, we humans cannot escape "reverting to type", as it were, when considering beginnings and endings. We cannot escape our spiritual ancestry and the great – to me – divine forces that drive us both as individuals and as a species. And when we abandon the heaven of God, we relocate it in some futuristic galactic fantasy which makes the eighteenth-century myth about medieval philosophers discussing angels pirouetting on a pinpoint sound as sane and as objective as tomorrow morning's sunrise.

14

Rediscovering the Compass, or Where Do We Go from Here?

We have seen in the previous chapters how turbulent changes taking place in twentieth-century British and European (yet not so much in American) society have made possible a serious assault on Christian beliefs and values. So how can an "Age That Lost Its Nerve" come to build up fresh confidence in itself, see the New Atheism for what it really is, and rediscover the compass?

Reclaiming Christian Identity

Strange as it may sound coming from a Christian theist who has spent the last thirteen chapters tracing the historical roots of, analysing, and hopefully countering the myths generated by atheists and secularists, I must admit that I rather admire Richard Dawkins. On the one hand, I admire him as a biological scientist of great gifts and insight. But equally, if not more so, I admire him as a highly gifted communicator and teacher of science, as a writer of elegant and sometimes lyrical prose, and – when he does not get carried away denouncing the Almighty and ridiculing those who believe in him – as a powerful and compelling lecturer and broadcaster. I also admire his confidence in what he believes to be right, and his commitment to telling the truth *as he sees it*, come hell or high water – traits which he shares with his alter ego Thomas Henry Huxley, "Darwin's Bulldog", and with other present-day sceptics such as Sam Harris, the late Christopher Hitchens, and the philosopher Daniel Dennett.

Why, though, I constantly ask myself, is this ability to argue and present a case forcefully and decisively less conspicuously displayed on the Christian side? Not, by any means, because of any lack of intellectual heavyweights in that quarter, for the church, Catholic, Protestant, and Orthodox, has always been, and still is, a magnet for very powerful minds. The problem is, I believe, a modern one, and especially one of the late twentieth century. It is related, I suspect, to the development of certain anti-combative tendencies within parts of Christendom. I take my hat off, however, to powerful Anglican writers and debaters such as John Polkinghorne, Keith Ward, Alister McGrath, and John Lennox, and Catholics such as Father Nicholas Corte SJ and Brother Guy Consolmagno SJ – all of whom are stalwart *apologists* (in the true sense of *apologia*, "justification") of the Christian faith without being in the least bit "apologetic".

But why do the media give so much coverage to the outspoken atheists? Yes, the media may be "institutionally left-wing and secularist", but journalists also like outrageous statements and catchy "one-liners"; and here, I have to admit, the atheists often win hands down. On the other hand, let us remember that Christianity was born out of catchphrases and memorable "one-liners": "God so loved the world that He sent His own beloved Son", "Repent", "Love your neighbour", "Render unto Caesar", "This is My body broken for you", "Be still", "Feed My sheep", and a host of others. What I would suggest has happened in our own time is that Christians as a body have become too self-conscious and too defensive, and in many cases much too serious. They need to remember that he who died on the cross to save the world also possessed the genial good humour to stop the booze running out at the Cana wedding. Quite simply, Christians need to relearn how, in the most generous-hearted sense, to "give as much as they get" and "Fight the Good Fight"; as when, in 2012, William Lane Craig humorously responded to the atheist anti-God bus adverts campaign with a counter-slogan proclaiming: "There's probably no Dawkins."

Two world wars, post-imperial guilt, and perhaps radical socialism have also played their part in allowing the atheists and secularists to seize the high ground in many aspects of public life, such as framing public policy, education, and the media. And this applies in particular to people who have received what might be called an "elite education", people made to feel guilty in certain ways, for being the kind of people they are, and for what their cultural ancestors may be perceived as having done – including spreading the Christian faith. But Christians in the twenty-first century need to have the courage to re-enter the hurly-burly of public life, and in particular the media and politics. They must learn that turning the other cheek does not, by definition, mean becoming a hand-wringing doormat – for it would be hard to find a less "doormat"-like person in the whole of history than the Man who loved the sinners he berated so much that he was willing to be crucified to save them!

What is important to bear in mind, however, is that until very recent times it was often men who had received an "elite education" at public school and Oxbridge or from armed forces backgrounds who had the confidence, the resources, and the daring to take the Christian faith to the far-flung corners of the globe; while it was their lay brethren who, in the nineteenth century, carried the most humane and civilizing empire in world history (whatever its faults) – the British Empire – across the broad waters of the world.

John and Charles Wesley, for instance, were descended from a modest clerical background, went to school at The Charterhouse and Westminster respectively, before both becoming undergraduates at Christ Church, Oxford. Their careers as evangelists and hymn-writers crossed all social boundaries, had an incalculable impact upon global Christianity, and are part and parcel of the well-known history of the faith (I recall once singing a Charles Wesley hymn in a Benedictine monastic church). Then there were the great missionary bishops, such as Reginald Heber and John William Colenso, who, in the nineteenth century, went to India and South Africa respectively.

The armed forces, moreover, had their share of courageous Christian leaders, such as Captain Sir Charles Middleton RN, later

Lord Barham, and James, Lord Admiral Gambier RN. And there were those brilliant and spectacularly colourful Christian soldiers, General George Gordon and Major General Sir James Hope Grant. The individualistic and even eccentric Gordon, it was said, confidently bestrode the world with his officer's cane in one hand and a Bible in the other; and his broad, generous-hearted, non-sectarian humanity won him the friendship of ordinary Chinese and Arab people, before he died a hero's death as, unarmed, he unflinchingly faced his fanatic Mahdist murderers in Khartoum in 1885. And Hope Grant, in addition to being sustained in all adversities by his evangelical faith, never went anywhere in the world without his cello! And let us not forget "the lady with the lamp", Florence Nightingale, herself the devout, individualistic Anglican daughter of wealthy parents, who saw her nursing vocation not only as a humanitarian but also as a *Christian* one. Florence was driven by a conviction of having been personally called by God to do his work among the sick. And these are but a few of those persons "born into the gentry", as it were, who made no bones about their faith, and who never apologized for it, no matter what was thrown at them, at home or abroad.

And then what about those men – and women – from "non-elite" circumstances who displayed a clear-sighted confidence in their calling, and were inspired to live their faith in the world? And I don't just mean those who founded or evangelized the faith and sometimes suffered martyrdom in its early days, but much more modern figures. Take, for instance, the itinerant tinker John Bunyan, who between serving prison sentences for his radical Christian views and kettle-mending wrote some of the most powerful devotional literature in the English language, most notably *The Pilgrim's Progress* (1678). Or General William Booth and his wife Catherine, called away from a comfortable ministry in a big Methodist chapel to serve and inspire those at the very bottom of society with their Salvation Army. Or Wilson Carlile, with his Church Army, after 1882. Or Charles Haddon Spurgeon, the great Victorian Baptist preacher; Dr David Livingstone, the Scottish mill-worker who became a medical missionary explorer in Africa; and, in our own time, Mother Teresa, who devoted her life to minister to the poorest of the poor in the alleyways of Calcutta. And what about those Oxbridge-educated "slum priests" who went to work in London's East End and other areas of acute social and spiritual deprivation? I am thinking here of figures such as the Oxford Movement Anglo-Catholics Charles Fuge Lowder and Alexander Mackonichie, living, in most cases, not as gentlemen in isolation, but simply digging in and living the Christian life alongside their poverty-stricken parishioners. Salvation Army and Church Army officers did exactly the same thing.

It is essential, therefore, that Christians confidently remind the secularists and the mockers exactly what Christianity has done for the world, and the modes of thinking and acting that it has engendered. As we have seen in previous chapters, *positive* Christian achievement is so inextricably woven into the fabric of Western civilization that we often take it for granted or dismiss it as "natural". We notice only the land-hungry, greedy exploiters of the empire, for instance, who were out for gold, diamonds, or slaves, rather than those who gave up their all to serve the native peoples of Africa or Asia – carrying with them not just the priceless gift of the gospel, but also supplying medicines, founding hospitals and schools, and showing a more constructive manner of living than endless slaughter and reprisal, and a way out of both economic and spiritual poverty. Dr Albert Schweitzer, who abandoned his career as an eminent theologian, virtuoso organist, and medical doctor in Germany to found his jungle hospital at Lambaréné in West Africa in 1913, is probably the most famous of many such missionaries in the twentieth century.

And from the late twentieth century, when Christianity had been long established and had touched many hearts in countries first visited by missionaries up to 200 years ago, wonderful success stories have abounded. I know one African gentleman, for example, who as a boy attended a mission school in his home country. His gifts of intellect – and personal charm – were noted, and he won an Oxford University scholarship. Having done brilliantly at Oxford, he trained as a lawyer, then took a theology degree, and now is actively involved in overseas Christian charity aid and mission work.

People like my African friend, in spite of being successful in education and the professions, however, are willing to speak openly and plainly about their faith, and its role in their lives. They are not cowed by the secularist onslaught. Nor are they apologetic about what they believe. And let us also remember that people from missionary-touched countries have availed themselves of opportunities of education and service ever since the nineteenth century.

I own, for example, a photograph of a Victorian bishop. There he stands, with great natural dignity, looking out benignly yet confidently, resplendent in lawn sleeves and episcopal habit. "So what?" some might say, "Just another well-to-do bishop." But hold on. This gentleman is different. He is *black*. He is the Rt Revd Dr Samuel Adjavi Crowther (c. 1805–91), a liberated Yoruba slave, originally educated by the Church Mission Society in their college in Islington, London, and holding an honorary doctorate in divinity from Oxford University. He was perhaps Oxford's first black honorand, and certainly the first black African bishop, appointed a missionary bishop in 1865 with a hefty chunk of West Africa as his diocese. And while I admit that Bishop Samuel was presented with a gargantuan missionary task by his friends and patrons in England, who had only the vaguest understanding of the complexities of the social structures, cultures, and religions of the indigenous African peoples, the fact remains that the Church of England appointed an African bishop with an Oxford DD degree to a new African diocese in 1865.

It is all too easy today to be patronizing about the global missionary movement, be it the Jesuits in China after 1596, or the Georgians and early Victorians in Africa. Yet these people carried a faith that was far from patronizing or self-satisfied. From that faith sprang an enormous courage, and a desire to take *not* the "Western imperial aggression" of secular mythology, but the Christian gospel, to many distant and diverse lands. And while many missionaries met their death and some were murdered, the candles of faith which they carried set vast tracts of the world ablaze with the Christian message. And when one hears today of the active persecution of Christians in Africa, Asia, Indonesia, and elsewhere, one must ask how that faith got there in the first place, and why Nigerians, Pakistanis, Iraqis, Iranians, and Indonesians are so strongly attached to their gospel faith that they prefer to be tortured or butchered rather than relinquish it. Indeed, one Sunday morning some years ago at a church in Oxford I recall being introduced to a group of visiting Iraqi Anglicans, ordained and lay. I often wonder how many of those brave men are still alive today.

So Christians must always remind themselves and others how their faith actually spread. While gold-seekers, land-grabbers, and empire-builders may – quite separately and opportunistically – have followed the missionaries to various parts of the world, we must never forget, as indicated earlier (and will stand repeating), that Christian evangelism throughout the centuries has been of the "hearts and minds" variety. Christianity, for instance, came to pagan Britain via a tiny handful of monks from the European continent. They came armed only with the gospel, and the knives they carried were only suitable for cutting their meat. Likewise, the Roman Catholic missions to China and Latin America, and Protestant missions to Africa, Polynesia, and elsewhere, went without soldiers or armed enforcement agencies. And whatever firearms were carried by British missionaries to Africa were for defence against dangerous animals, and to provide meat for the pot, and were *not* to shoot people. Indeed, on one occasion in 1844, when a springing lion was about to eat Dr David Livingstone (he leaves us an account of the incident), it was the guns and courageous action of his devoted African companions that helped to save his life.

And it was not for nothing, moreover, that General William Booth styled some of the British slums into which his Salvation Army first moved as "Darkest England", for his Christian evangelists faced as much danger from British criminal groups, brothel-keepers, and drunken thugs who preyed upon the poor in the hell-holes of London's East End as did any missionaries to Africa. While the Salvation Army came to be loved by the poor, many of whom found – and still find – inspiration and release through its missionary activities, organized evil has always hated it, and Salvationists have faced far more than cheap sneering and name-calling, but have had to withstand flying bricks, vicious gang attacks, knives, and even bullets. In many parts of the world they still do today. And this, one might say, is history brought into our own times!

So why, one might ask, do I go into all this detail, and how can someone who respects Richard Dawkins so admire Christian missionaries and martyrs? Oddly enough, what all of these people have in common is that they "put their money where their mouths are", and do not apologize for what they see as true. And when you look at the spectacular growth areas in modern Christianity, such as the charismatic and evangelical churches, this is precisely what they do. Confidence, assurance, and a clear message are much more likely to inspire people and win them over than are apology and indecision.

Yet particularly unfortunate in our own time are, first, concerns about fundamentalism; and, secondly, problems about worship styles and liturgy. A fair slice of the most active and successful present-day Christian evangelism is of a fundamentalist character, and as we have seen in previous chapters, fundamentalism is very much a modern phenomenon in Christian history. And especially it is the product of a particular type of American culture. Yes, fundamentalism is simplistic and replete with bad history, bad science, and bad theology; yet there are, perhaps, worse things – such as being ignorant of God. And here I will say something that risks giving apoplexies to some of my academic colleagues: I would rather a person choose to be ignorant of our evolutionary ancestry than to be ignorant of Christ's teachings. While I am an evolutionist and a passionate lover of science myself, I do feel that we get our priorities mixed up when allegiance to or dissent from a biological theory that has no practical impact whatsoever upon how millions of "ordinary" people worldwide behave towards their fellow-humans is seen as more important than a wider knowledge of Christian morality and redemption.

For when radical and often atheistical evolutionists attack Genesis-based fundamentalism they are rarely selective in their target. It is not just at the first half-dozen chapters of Genesis that they invariably fire their big guns; it is at the whole Bible, New Testament included.

For are not the accounts of miraculous healings, resurrection, and immortal souls just as incapable of scientific proof as talk of a six-day creation? Such thinking, indeed, does not accord with the new religion of God-free *scientism*.

Of course, what theologically, historically, and scientifically aware Christians must do is reach out and try to educate their fellows, and teach them how *not* – as St Augustine warned regarding the unlearned flat-earthers of over 1,600 years ago – to make themselves look silly before educated non-Christians. But if informed academic and church teaching are of no avail, then let us still at least remain on speaking terms with the biblical fundamentalists. When we face that Great Reckoning which many of us believe will come at the end of our lives, it might better serve, I suspect, to know something of God, than *only* from which strain of pithecoids we happen to be descended.

And here we come to my second point. Just as we must be confident in acknowledging that at the end of the day there are bigger issues at stake than evolution, and that it is the Christian's duty to take the faith to all – learned, simple, confused, or just too burdened with daily life to think about complex scientific theories – so we must be careful not to strip our faith of its glorious ancestral culture. For just as some people feel the need to wrestle with "big ideas", such as God, evolution, cosmology, and philosophical theology in order to develop their spiritual understanding, so many are also helped by great art. Yet one feature of late twentieth-century Christianity is that some of the most dynamic spiritual developments in evangelism have been accompanied by an aesthetic and a style of worship which many find unsatisfying (people who cannot relate to modern pop and rock music, for example).

"Modern" worship is all well and good if that is what happens to bring you to God. And it clearly does so for many, because this is perhaps the biggest "growth industry" in contemporary Christianity, and covers an age spectrum extending from teenagers to pensioners. But just as whole sections of Western society have collectively turned their back on science and its relation to faith, so others have turned their back upon the Christian church's ancestral liturgy. Of course, this is not new; for earlier Protestant denominations, such as the Quakers, made radical breaks from traditional liturgy in their pursuit of the Holy Spirit, while some innovations, such as Methodist hymn-singing, became a popular and much-loved *addition* to the liturgy.

The problem today, however, is that many people are put off Christianity, or going to church, if the only accessible places of worship are not to their aesthetic taste. Yes, it is true that our great cathedrals, city churches, and Oxford and Cambridge college chapels (most of which open their doors to visitors) are booming, as people want to partake in Christian worship. Some are what have been styled "Christian atheists", or what I sometimes call addicts of "AV, BCP, Stanford in C" (Authorized Version of the Bible, Book of Common Prayer, and great church music). For many people love *art*, *symbol*, and *grandeur*, and want them in their lives. Many churchgoers *want* liturgy, grand music, choirs, organs, and the glorious language of the 1611 Bible and the 1662 Prayer Book, and will often travel miles to get their liturgical "fix" – even if their spiritual views are vague. The Victorian "High Church" and "Anglo-Catholic" churchmen realized this 150 years ago, as witness the magnificent "Puginesque" neo-medieval edifices erected in slum parishes. To people whose lives were bleak and drab, the church could offer more spectacle than the gin-palace – with the added bonus of the prospect of eternal life! Indeed, a similar situation existed in Soviet Russia and other communist-dominated countries of Eastern Europe, where Orthodox and Catholic churches (or at least that small minority of churches which were permitted to continue), with their glittering mosaics, frescoes, chanting, and incense, helped to keep the faith alive and to feed the souls of people whose days were lived out amidst the grey drabness of concrete tower communes, factories, and official Party propaganda.

Yet what is a tragedy today is that when many "Christian atheists" go for their "fix" of full liturgical Eucharist or choral evensong, with sermon, what they hear may not encourage them to go beyond the beautiful words and ceremonial and explore the central message of the Christian faith.

So how do we reclaim our Christian identity when "received opinion" is often so loaded against it? I would suggest that we make a strenuous effort to break the bonds with which ideological secularism, political correctness, postmodern moral paralysis, and multiculturalism have tried to chain us; to risk crossing the intellectual, scientific, and cultural divides that government, the media, and fashionable ideologists have been allowed to impose upon Christian identity, often in the name of "education". We must be *proud* of that Christian faith and tradition that lies at the heart of our ancestral civilization, and not apologize for it, be we inspired by fiery preaching, rock music, choral evensong, High Church "bells and smells", evolution, biblical literalism, or whatever else suits us best as individuals, and brings each one of us closer to God.

Or if we are interested but uncommitted music-, art-, and liturgy-loving "Christian atheists" or agnostics, or cultural refugees from "rock" who might take the sacrament at Eucharist for form's sake on a Sunday morning while listening to the glorious strains of the Agnus Dei in some cathedral chancel, all well and good. For I would suggest that it is better to be a "Christian atheist" than a God-hating atheist: it is a step in the right direction, for as the Gospels and St Paul's letters tell us, if we come with open and honest hearts, God will meet us wherever we happen to be, even if our faith is no greater than a tiny mustard seed. But we must not be afraid to invite the "Christian atheists" to move on from their unbelief, and to pour a little life-giving water on the mustard seeds. But at all times we must, clergy and laity, be welcoming, affirming, and loving – to *everyone*!

But centrally, Christians must always be willing – in the most generous-hearted way – to *defend* their faith: to challenge myths and secularist theories about history and science, missionaries, and Christianity and warfare, and to remind the world in clear, courteous, yet unequivocal terms that not all religions believe the same things, or evangelize or treat their fellow human beings in the same way.

And so let us take a lesson from our atheist critics, and show them and the world that they are not the only ones who are willing to publicly stand up and declare what they believe.

How "Enlightened" Are the New Atheists?

As we have mentioned in previous chapters, men of science who would have identified themselves as Christians have been the norm over the centuries, and while there were perhaps fewer in the twentieth century, they are far from a rarity today, especially in the light of such bodies as the Society of Ordained Scientists and Christians in Science. In the earlier days of science, and even discounting the numerous monk–priest scientific thinkers of the medieval centuries, one had astronomers of the standing of Nicholas Copernicus, Galileo Galilei, Johannes Kepler, Pierre Gassendi, and Isaac Newton. Then there followed Robert Boyle (of Boyle's law fame), Michael Faraday (electrical physicist), William Buckland and many other Victorian geologists (a good number in holy orders), Abbot Gregor Mendel (founder of genetics), James Clerk Maxwell (mathematical physicist), and Sir Arthur Eddington and Father Georges Lemaître (both twentieth-century cutting-edge cosmologists). And these are only a selection of the illustrious dead, without reckoning those alive today.

Yet I hear the atheists say – and not without historical justification – "Of course they were 'Christians': everybody was a 'Christian' in the past. They were 'Christians' because Christianity was the norm, respectable, and the dominant culture." Of course, this argument might apply to people who routinely went to church or chapel on Sunday mornings, but it does *not* by any means explain those who actively, and openly, advanced Christian enterprises, and made their faith known through their writings and teaching.

On the other hand, as we saw earlier in this book, the idea of non- or anti-religious thought is far from new, and has a lineage going back through the nineteenth and eighteenth centuries to the Middle Ages and to classical Greece, and even those Old Testament folk who are said to have declared, "There is no God." For atheism, and probably agnosticism, is as old as the hills, and one thing I hope this book does is expose the myth that it is in any way new or radical.

Yet what all too often irritates the secularists is the phenomenon of the scientist who is also an ordained priest or monk. Quite simply, they are living, breathing affronts to the "intellectual freedom equals throwing out religious dogma" school of myth-makers, and I have come across some convoluted explanations for the ordained scientist phenomenon that so misunderstand the intellectual *and* the spiritual vocation as to be quite absurd.

Take, for example, Gregor Mendel, the Augustinian monk with an academic scientific training from Vienna, who became abbot of his religious house at Brno (formerly Brünn) in Czechoslovakia. He was a man whose life combined prayer, liturgical devotion, teaching, serving the poor – and discovering the mathematical basis of genetic mutation and establishing those scientific principles which would be remembered as "Mendel's law". Yet I have heard it publicly stated by an eminent freethinking scientist who should know better that Mendel *really* became a monk as a way of securing funding for his science! For how could a real scientist believe all that religious nonsense? But what this analysis ignores is dates: Mendel became a monk at the age of twenty-one in 1843, after first studying at Olmütz University, and a priest in 1847. Yet it would not be until 1866 that he published his research on plant hybridization and his famous law. All the evidence suggests that Mendel saw no conflict whatsoever between his science and his deep Roman Catholic faith – even after reading Darwin! And then he became Abbot of Brno in 1868.

On the other hand, what about the modern world, where the prevailing culture is not consciously Christian, and not infrequently is anti-Christian? No one can accuse a modern scientist who takes Christianity seriously, or is perhaps an agnostic friend of Christianity, of simply swimming with the current. Yet there is no shortage of such people around. In Oxford and Cambridge alone, I know science dons in astronomy, medicine, biology, genetics, physics, and engineering who are practising Christians, some serving in various capacities of ministry in their local churches, as well as those scientists active in Christian apologetics.

And this, I suspect, is only the tip of the iceberg of Christian professional men and women of science across the rest of British, American and other universities. The diocesan director of ordinands of an English Anglican cathedral diocese told me not long ago that there were always professional scientists presenting themselves for training for the non-stipendiary and lay ministry – people who would serve as full priests or readers in their parishes, but would continue to work as scientists in their "day" jobs, using their professional salaries to provide their livelihood. This same director said that there tended to be more candidates from the physical sciences than from the biological, and that one biological sciences candidate was even known to have received mocking remarks from colleagues in his lab when he let it be known that he wanted to train as a priest. So much for "freethinking" tolerance!

Yet this is only within the Anglican and Protestant churches. In the Catholic tradition there have been Jesuit scientists going back to the founding of the Society of Jesus in the sixteenth century, and I have been proud to share lecture platforms at both scientific and religious meetings and conferences with Jesuit scientists. They are a tough, clever, no-nonsense breed, highly informed and excellent debaters, often with a mischievous sense of humour. I give these "Js" full marks. I was also told by an Orthodox Christian friend about his visit early in 2010 to a group of desert monasteries in northern Egypt. It appeared that these religious houses had more young men applying to become monks and take up the enclosed religious life than the monasteries could actually accommodate. The monasteries, it seems, now had a policy of admitting only men with sound, generally practical, professional qualifications, in such disciplines as medicine and engineering science. For the Coptic monks and their Christian houses, in addition to prayer and study, provided free medical, welfare, and technical services for the local Bedouin and other communities – irrespective of religion.

And two of my most interesting research students at Oxford were men in their early forties whom I used to nickname my "Reverend Doctors", for that is precisely what they were. Before coming to do further postdoctoral work at Oxford, they – one a Dominican friar and the other a Roman Catholic priest – had taken doctorates in biochemistry and mathematical physics respectively, and had already worked in academic research in those fields. And without wishing to repeat what might by now sound like a tedious litany, none of the above scientific men and women that I know can quite understand what the atheists' problem is. For science and faith, far from being in conflict, seem to dovetail together perfectly because – wonder of wonders – the universe makes sense! While science answers the "how" questions, religion answers the "why" questions: the universe in all its dimensions works through a set of marvellous mathematical laws that the human mind has come to fathom out. But *why* those laws are as they are is beyond science to explain. It all harks back to my discussion in Chapter 13: can, or cannot, an honest thinking individual accept the idea of a supreme, transcendent being as a reality?

I would like to draw this section to a close, however, by touching upon two points that have appeared earlier in this book. The first of these is what has always struck me as the intellectually elite aspect of modern secular atheism. It is, in many ways, a creed for the well-off, well-educated, comfortable, and secure, who can perhaps view struggle and hopelessness with a kind of stoical detachment, rather like Lucretius or Seneca. And while I know there are atheists who can regard their imminent decease with a philosophical detachment, such as the late Christopher Hitchens, whose courage and intellectual honesty I admired enormously, I suspect that atheism has very little indeed to offer to the vast majority of the poor, distressed, mentally ill, and suffering. The New Atheists might see religion as a crutch – well, what is wrong with crutches? If you happen to have a broken leg, a crutch will stop you falling over. And if, by extension, you have a broken life, a belief in God can serve the same function.

Of course, this pragmatic use of religion is no proof that God exists in abstract philosophical terms, but what cannot be denied is that a belief in God can be an enormous strength in adversity. And the more adversity he gets you through, the more you are likely to realize that he, like your hospital-issued crutch, is not an abstract concept, but is real. The same goes for Marx's notion that religion is no more than the "opium of the masses". Without pain-killing drugs, many of which have been isolated from the narcotic *Papaver somniferum*, or sleep-inducing poppy, life would be considerably more hellish than it is already!

Indeed, the disparaging dismissal of God as a mere crutch, or religion as no more than an opiate, really derives from the "perfecting mankind", "Enlightenment" school of thinking discussed in Chapter 13. As such perfectionists argue, must we not break free from superstitious supports so that man- and womankind can achieve their full dignity and destiny? Like some Romantic era re-rendering of the Prometheus myth?

Yet just as crutches and opiates can get us through accident, trauma, agony, and crisis, and make it possible for us to go forward and lead fuller and more meaningful lives, so can a firm belief in a God of love.

My second point is, if evolutionary genetics are predominantly concerned with a drive towards individual and species survival, why do we seem to spend some of our most enjoyable hours squandering our energies? Especially on non-survival activities such as devouring junk food in front of the TV? Or compulsive sports training? Or even religion? For endless TV-watching and overeating are likely to make you so obese and brain-dead that you regard sex as unappealing, back-breaking work, while obsessive sport can leave you so exhausted that you go out like a light upon your first contact with a bed. And as for religion: well, what conceivable survival advantage can loving your enemies and devoting your best energies to helping life's losers give you? Let us be brutally honest: in pure *survival* terms, why *not* let the poor starve and the sick die, for these disadvantaged, damaged, or genetically substandard specimens are only taking up resources that the strong, dominant types could seize to help propagate their own genes.

So is there, perhaps, more mythology than substance in the atheists' reductionist analysis of the human condition?

Conclusion: So Where Do We Stand, and What Do We Do?

In the previous fourteen chapters I have examined some of the main themes in the development of science and its relationship with the

Judeo-Christian tradition over the past few millennia. I also hope I have made it clear why I see the Judeo-Christian faith, along with its Greek and Roman cognates, as fundamental to the rise of modern science, and even to the rise of atheistic, secularist, and reductive thinking. For both come from the same intellectual tradition.

And central to that tradition are two things. Firstly, the idea of an all-powerful creator who made everything from nothing, as is implied in Genesis, spelled out more fully in the Psalms and other Old Testament books, and is axiomatic to St Paul and the Gospel writers of the New Testament and to most of the church fathers of the early Christian centuries. And it was this all-powerful singular creator that made science possible, for should you call him – or even it – God, Jehovah, the Logos, or the First Cause, the implication is that this being or force generated a creation or initiated a sequence of events that was at one with itself and possessed an internal coherence. And he – or it – created us humans in his own image (as in the Judeo-Christian tradition), or (as in pagan Greek thinking) this being set the whole show rolling, and we can retrace the presence of a sovereign intellect and relate to it by the exercise of our own logical capacity.

And secondly, this Judeo-Christian tradition bequeathed a sense of linearity and direction to creation. In it, everything starts with a divine act of creation: there is an orderly narrative covering six days, including the creation of Adam and Eve. Then there is the fall, and the whole history, politics, and wars of the Jewish people, narrated in the books of the Old Testament. And pivotal to the whole narrative is the incarnation, ministry, crucifixion, resurrection, and ascension of Jesus Christ, his return to establish the New Jerusalem, the ascent of the blessed into heaven, and the end of the world of time as we know it.

No matter whether one chooses to believe or reject this historical and prophetic narrative, it nonetheless brings a radical new concept into human thought: a historical timeline. Very different, in its exact chronology of events, to the cycles, circularities, ebbings and flowings of Egyptian, Babylonian, Far Eastern, and even Greek mythological and heroic (as opposed to philosophical) cultures. And I would argue that it was this very precise relationship between monotheism and a beginning, a sequence of events, and an ending which made a *scientific* view of the world possible, giving as it does a potential for hard-edged objectivity.

Several millennia of well-documented history have told us time and again that we humans are transcendence-seeking, worshipping beings. Humans are instinctive seekers after cause, purpose, and order; and when for ideological reasons we deny this fact in the spiritual dimension, we simply reclothe our spiritual aspirations in a material, secular garb. That science has produced wonders, each unimaginable to the previous generation, goes without saying; yet I believe we lead ourselves astray when we presume that the cause or inner nature of these wonders can only be explained in materialist philosophical terms. For – once again – while science answers the "how" questions, it is not equipped to handle the "why" questions, any more than the technology of music-making in the symphony orchestra can tell us what the feelings of elation or despair evoked by that technology really *are* in absolute terms. Nor, as far as I know, is there anything on the scientific horizon at present indicating that science ever will realistically answer the persistent "why" questions. They are about fundamentally different things. And we should be aware that the New Atheists and modern-day secularists deal in very dubious coin when they try to convince us that they *can* answer the "big questions" about meaning and absolutes: the traditional role of religion.

We should be aware, too, of the *vast* amount of myth-spinning performed by modern-day "evangelical" atheists. Of how they distort incidents from the historical record to suit their own ideological agendas, while inventing whole hierarchies of myths about what education or science will achieve in the future. While critically minded Christians realize that different strands of their faith are to be understood on different levels – the Bible, for example, contains straight historical narrative, prophecy, parable, metaphor, and miracle – many secularists view their own position in what looks like stark monochrome, in which religion equals false and backward-looking, and science equals true and progressive. Which, to put it mildly, is pure myth-making.

Secular mythology, therefore, has become a dragon that, in the last fifty to a hundred years in particular, has been allowed to spew out its poisonous breath upon many aspects of Christian culture, largely unchecked. But it is now time to face the dragon on its own ground. And to slay it!

15

Postscript: Why Do So Many Modern Intellectuals Waste Their Energy Attacking Christianity?

I have always found it fascinating that so many high-powered and influential thinkers – philosophers, scientists, journalists, broadcasters, and writers – feel compelled to expend such prodigious amounts of energy on attacking Christianity. After all, there is no equivalent line-up of heavy intellectual artillery launching a similar bombardment upon astrology, magic, divination, or non-scientific medicine. So what is it about Christianity that so winds them up?

Why Get Hot under the Secular Collar?

Looked at from the standpoint of objective history, and excluding any references to signs, wonders, and miracles, what was so remarkable about the life of Jesus? He was a working man born in a minor corner of the Roman Empire, of whom we know very little before he was thirty. He picked up a dozen friends and a wider circle of followers, none of whom (with the possible exception of Matthew the tax collector, who presumably could do accounts) would have got as far as the interview stage for a middle-management job, and who often found Jesus difficult to understand. It is clear, however, that he was a charismatic speaker who could spellbind audiences. He had a big popular following, especially around his native Galilee, though he provoked the religious and cultural elite, who had him executed, after he and his friends had been in the public eye locally for less than three years. Then his friends ran away in fear and hid.

It was then said that Jesus had come back to life. This somehow gave an unprecedented new fire and determination to his followers. These simple local men then went out into the world to proclaim the "Good News", or Jesus' rather odd ideas, to the whole world. And we know they did it, because that is how these ideas spread across the then known world like wildfire: into Greece, Rome, Spain, Mesopotamia, India, North Africa, and even to Britannia. Then, not much more than 300 years after the crucifixion, the Roman Empire adopted Jesus' teachings as its official religion, replacing the old pagan gods, although already for several centuries past men and women of many nations had been willing to suffer torture and death rather than to deny him. And this "Jesus myth" travelled by "hearts and minds", and not by armies; and its "power base" was the weak and the outcast! And it had the strange capacity to transform, empower, and redirect not only individual lives, but also the wider world; and it still does so today.

Not a bad achievement for a simple village joiner from nowhere, whose public career only lasted about thirty-three months. A local nobody, in fact, who deserves at best a ten-line entry in a classical encyclopaedia. And that as a peasant oddity. So why was it not as simple and clear-cut as that? And why did the Joiner of Nazareth come to influence the world in a way that the real-life New Testament character Simon the Magician, or (to give a couple of fictitious examples) Ahab the stonemason of Capernaum, Jeremiah the itinerant quack doctor of Bethsaida, or any other of the local nobodies whose "gift of the gab" could pull a crowd in the market place, did not?

Surviving the Crucifixion

Not only do many atheists waste prodigious amounts of time trying to convince superstitious Christians of the folly of their faith, but in recent years in particular much energy has been expended (influenced in part by stories in the post-second-century-AD "Gnostic" writers and by the best-selling fiction of Dan Brown) – and much money made – in claiming that Jesus survived the crucifixion. After all, the two so-called "honest thieves" crucified alongside Jesus were still alive at the end of the first Good Friday, for as St John tells us in his Gospel, the Romans broke the legs of both to finish them off before sunset. So could not Jesus also have been alive, and have recovered, and the resurrection story been subsequently constructed as a myth, and swallowed by his gullible disciples? And could not Mary Magdalene's tender loving care have nursed him back to health? For, as popular mythology would have us believe, there were some *very* wise and clever doctors in the ancient world.

Such an argument can only be advanced in the teeth of some rather stubborn historical and scientific facts. Let us look at what the Gospel writers, and St John in particular, tell us about what was done to Jesus the natural man.

(1) Prior to crucifixion, he was severely flogged: a bloody business in itself. (2) He was so weakened by this ordeal that he was unable to carry his own cross, and Simon of Cyrene was forced to carry it for him. Making it less likely, therefore, that Jesus, unlike the "honest thieves", would survive crucifixion. (3) He hung suspended for six hours, with nails through his hands and feet, or (as was the normal Roman crucifixion technique) through his wrists and ankles. And as the suspended body sagged, these wounds would not have been like the neat stigmata of conventional artistic depiction, but would have become great, ghastly lacerations, each probably several inches long. And as major arteries and veins serve the hands and feet, there would have been considerable haemorrhage, from *four* great lacerations, over several hours. (4) The forward-hanging position of Jesus' body would have severely impeded respiration, no doubt leading to a potentially

fatal build-up of fluid in the lungs and thoracic cavity. (5) After about six hours, he was pronounced dead by a surprised Roman officer – surprised because crucifixion victims normally lasted longer, as did the two thieves. (6) But as a way of confirming the death, a Roman soldier stabbed Jesus with a spear, and tradition says that the weapon – probably a broad-headed infantry spear – entered his right chest cavity without breaking any bones. Probably a powerful upward thrust from below the right ribcage. This would first have torn the strong muscular diaphragm which separates the abdominal from the thoracic cavity. And as the spear was wriggled around in the usual way, to reduce flesh suction and facilitate easier extraction, it would most likely have torn the right lung, then the pericardium, vena cava, right (and perhaps left) pulmonary arteries and veins, and very probably the heart itself. And this is saying nothing about damage to the upper body musculature, both external and internal, and no doubt the spleen as well. Indeed, we can get some idea of the gaping nature of this side wound, for when Jesus displays his injuries to "doubting" Thomas, in St John's Gospel, he invites Thomas to thrust not his fingers, but his *hand*, into the cavity. It would, of course, have been a massive wound. If there is one thing of which we can be certain, it is that a Roman soldier *knew how to kill people*. And as was still the case with one of Wellington's infantrymen with his bayonet in 1810, a Roman soldier would have *twisted* and *turned* his weapon inside the wound, to make it easier to pull out. Indeed, a knowledge of military as well as scientific and medical history is useful when assessing the crucifixion! And after all this, what are we told flowed out of the wound? Blood mixed with *water*, or probably serum. This would, moreover, only have happened in a *dead* body, for had the heart still been beating, even weakly, a gush of bright red arterial blood would have come out. As it was, one finds a haemorrhaging corpse, with stagnant blood and separating-out clear fluid being released from the lung tissue and veins.

(7) Following this ordeal, Jesus' body was taken away by Joseph of Arimathea, and he, and probably Nicodemus, wrapped it in tight bandages with some 75 lbs of myrrh and aloes (100 *litrai* in the Greek, estimated to be around 34 kg or 75 lbs). The aloes in particular, as

a dried plant product, would have been very absorbent and would probably have soaked up whatever fluid was left in the body, thus further dehydrating it. The Gospel account, moreover, specifically mentions a napkin being tied across Jesus' face in accordance with Jewish burial custom – which would only have added to the suffocating effect of the wrappings.

(8) Lastly, Jesus' wrapped and anointed body was sealed up in a rock-cut tomb and left for two nights. And as in early spring – the usual time of the Jewish Passover – Palestine can be bitterly cold at night, hypothermia can be added to the lethal cocktail!

And after all this, according to the resurrection sceptics, Jesus was really no more than stunned by the whole ordeal of crucifixion, and all that was needed was the tender loving care of Mary Magdalene to nurse him back to health. Or perhaps, so the fantasists sometimes argue, there was a very wise doctor on hand to help as well.

Please accept my apologies for all the gory detail, but to put it bluntly, this is what seems to have happened clinically when we interpret the Gospel accounts in the light of modern scientific knowledge. Even when we discount elements of metaphor, prophecy, and textual interpretation in the crucifixion narratives (and in St Paul's pre-Gospel references to the crucifixion in his letters), there is still an impressive body of coherent factual detail that cannot simply be dismissed as make-believe. Had there been a *modern* state-of-the-art accident and emergency unit at the foot of the cross, with resuscitators, drips, blood transfusions, a top-class surgical team, and the whole panoply of modern medicine, poised to spring into action the moment Jesus was cut down, they would have found their task hopeless. And the wisest, the most skilful, and the most learned medical team in the world could only have said to Mary Magdalene, "Sorry, the damage is too great – Jesus the *man* is dead."

So whatever happened on Easter morning, when the tomb was found empty and the grave-wrappings laid aside, was *not* occasioned by a badly traumatized natural man coming out of a coma!

History? But the Gospels Were Just Made Up – Weren't They?

"Oh, how naïve", I can hear the sceptics yawn, "to assume that you can extract scientific or clinical evidence from the Bible!" Surely, the Gospels are all a much later *construct*, drawing upon ancient tales of prophecy in the Old Testament, and dropping odd names of otherwise known individuals, such as Pontius Pilate or the Herodian kings, to make them look a bit more credible? Indeed, a combination of historical novel and fantasy fiction, with some spooky bits thrown in to make your hair stand on end!

But let us begin by looking objectively at the written sources for the crucifixion and resurrection. Put on whatever construction you like, you cannot escape the fact that both events are described, in differing amounts of detail, in all four Gospels, and are alluded to as pivotal events in the Acts of the Apostles and in several of St Paul's letters. More independent single references, I suspect, than you would find to any other brief incident in secular ancient history. And they continued to be referred to and discussed time and again by all the early Christian writers from the first century onwards.

And although some, quite rightly, would point out that the Gospel writers regularly make reference to Old Testament prophecies being fulfilled, and to signs and wonders, and had different objectives from a chronicler of "normal" events, one must at least give some credence to a statement by St John. Almost cutting off in advance the line that the crucifixion was only a resonance of a prophecy of piercing the hands and feet of the victim in the prophet Zechariah, John states in his Gospel, chapter 19:35, "And he that saw it bare record, and his record is true"; and in 21:24, "This is the disciple which testifieth of these things, and wrote these things; and we know his testimony is true." Indeed, to my historian's nose this smells rather like a record from an eyewitness, either passed down orally or written.

But permit me to make another observation about the Gospels and Acts, which lends them a sense of historical veracity in my reckoning: the fact that they often *contradict* each other on incidental details, yet are in stunning agreement regarding the big picture. If a historian has five independent versions of a given set of events, such as those found in the Gospels and Acts, all written perhaps several years or decades after the events described, and they all recount exactly the same incidents, in pretty well the same sequence, then the historian smells a rat – it smells like a coordinated put-up job! But if the accounts vary in points of incidental detail, are clearly intended to address different audiences, and yet come together on the key events and their significance, then they look much more authentic. Matthew, for example, was probably writing to convince a Jewish readership; John was wrestling with philosophical theology; and Luke – if the "beloved physician" referred to by St Paul – was a non-Jew, or Gentile, who corresponded with one Theophilus, probably another Greek Gentile. (And Luke, along with Paul, was probably the best educated of Jesus' early followers.)

Let me suggest a parallel. If, in 2,000 years' time, historians were researching the coronation of HM Queen Elizabeth II on 2 June 1953, they might encounter all sorts of contradictory narratives. Was the witness standing in the Mall, in the rain, waiting to see a golden coach go past? Or did they see the event on a flickering black and white TV set in Manchester? Or hear a verbal account from a stranger on a train? Or were they in Westminster Abbey? All accounts would differ in circumstantial detail, yet all would come together on the key event: namely, that a British queen had been crowned.

I believe that the early Christian narratives can be read in a similar way.

Which comes back to the title of this chapter: why exactly do so many highly intelligent people these days feel obliged to rail against the Nazareth Joiner, and to heap ridicule on his present-day followers, 2,000 years later? Why don't they just yawn, roll their eyes in superior exasperation, and draw a line once and for all beneath the intractable folly of those superstitious primitives called Christians? And then they can turn their minds to higher things: such as theorizing about the atheist potential of chimpanzees, programming their super-computers, or contemplating the meaning of oblivion.

So what made, and continues to make, Jesus so special? What still makes the Galilean carpenter and his message a focus of meaning and devotion to *billions* of people worldwide, and an object of contempt and anger to others?

Could it really be that the world is brimming over with intractable superstitious fools who just *won't* see reason, even when highly gifted atheists try to show them the way?

Or could it be that the "Jesus myth" contains something not mentioned in the above bare narrative? Something *bigger*, perhaps? Indeed, something *very much* bigger!

Further Reading

Denis Alexander, *Creation or Evolution: Do we have to choose?* (Oxford: Lion Hudson, 2008).

Patrick Armstrong, *The English Parson–Naturalist. A Companionship Between Science and Religion* (Leominster: Gracewing, 2000).

George Bishop, *Jesuit Pioneers of Modern Science and Mathematics* (Gujarat: Sahitya Prakash, 2005).

Melvyn Bragg, *The Book of Books: The radical impact of the King James Bible 1611–2011* (London: Hodder & Stoughton, 2011).

John Hedley Brooke, *Science and Religion: Some historical perspectives* (Cambridge: Cambridge University Press, 1991).

Owen Chadwick, *The Victorian Church: Part I, 1829–1859*, 3rd edn (London: A. & C. Black, 1971; London: SCM Press, 1987).

—— —, *The Victorian Church: Part II, 1860–1901*, 2nd edn (London: A. & C. Black, 1972: London: SCM Press, 1987).

Allan Chapman, 'Creationism', in *The Oxford Companion to the Earth*, ed. Paul L. Hancock and Brian J. Skinner (Oxford: Oxford University Press, 2000).

—— —, *Gods in the Sky: Astronomy, Religion, and Culture from the Ancients to the Renaissance* (London: Channel 4 Books, 2002).

Norman Cohn, *The Pursuit of the Millennium* (London: Secker and Warburg, 1957; London: Paladin, 1970).

F. L. Cross and E. A. Livingstone (eds), *The Oxford Dictionary of the Christian Church*, 4th edn (Oxford: Oxford University Press, 2005).

J. D. Douglas et al. (eds), *The New Bible Dictionary* (London: Inter-Varsity Fellowship, 1962).

Roger Forster and Paul Marston, *Reason, Science, and Faith* (UK: Monarch books, 1999; repro. Eugene, OR: Wipf and Stock Publishers, 2001).

Vivian Green, *A New History of Christianity* (Stroud: Sutton Publishing, 1996).

James Hannam, *God's Philosophers: How the medieval world laid the foundations of modern science* (London: Icon Books, 2009).

Peter Harrison, *The Bible, Protestantism, and the Rise of Natural Science* (Cambridge: Cambridge University Press, 2001).

— —, *The Cambridge Companion to Science and Religion* (Cambridge: Cambridge University Press, 2010).

Adrian Hastings, Alistair Mason, Hugh Pyper, et al. (eds), *The Oxford Companion to Christian Thought* (Oxford: Oxford University Press, 2000).

Timothy Keller, *The Reason for God: Belief in an age of scepticism* (London: Hodder & Stoughton, 2008; Harmondsworth: Penguin, 2009).

Werner Keller, *The Bible as History Revised* (London: Hodder & Stoughton and Book Club Associates, 1980).

John C. Lennox, *God's Undertaker: Has science buried God?* (Oxford: Lion Hudson, 2007; revised edn, 2009).

— —, *Gunning for God: Why the New Atheists are missing the target* (Oxford: Lion Hudson, 2011).

David C. Lindberg and Ronald L. Numbers (eds), *Where Science and Christianity Meet* (Chicago: University of Chicago Press, 2003).

David Marshall, *The Truth behind the New Atheism: Responding to the emerging challenges to God and Christianity* (Eugene, OR: Harvest House, 2007).

— — (ed.), *Faith Seeking Understanding: Essays in memory of Paul Brand and Ralph D. Winter* (Pasadena, CA: William Carey Library, 2012).

E. W. Maunder, *The Astronomy of the Bible* (Washington, DC: Ross & Perry, Inc., 2002; facsimile, originally published in 1908).

Alister McGrath and Joanna Collicutt McGrath, *The Dawkins Delusion* (Leicester: IVP, 2007).

John McManners (ed.), *The Oxford Illustrated History of Christianity* (Oxford: Oxford University Press, 1990).

John North, *God's Clockmaker: Richard of Wallingford and the Invention of Time* (London: Hambledon and London, 2005).

Ronald L. Numbers (ed.), *Galileo Goes to Jail and other myths about science and religion* (Cambridge, MA: Harvard University Press, 2009).

John Polkinghorne, *Encountering Scripture: A scientist explores the Bible* (London: SPCK, 2010).

— —, *The Polkinghorne Reader*, ed. Thomas Jay Oord (London: SPCK and West Conshohocken, PA: Templeton Press, 2010).

Raymond Tallis, *Aping Mankind: Neuromania, Darwinitis, and the Misrepresentation of Humanity* (Durham: Acumen, 2011).

Keith Ward, *God, Chance, and Necessity* (Oxford: Oneworld, 1996).

— —, *Is Religion Dangerous?* (Oxford: Lion Hudson, 2006; revised edn, 2011).

— —, *Is Religion Irrational?* (Oxford: Lion Hudson, 2011).

Index